SERVING
WITH
PRIDE

This book is dedicated to those we 'lost' from the Armed Forces communities and those 'found' in the journey of Fighting With Pride.

We are here, until justice is done.

SERVING
WITH
PRIDE

CRAIG JONES

Pen & Sword
MILITARY
AN IMPRINT OF PEN & SWORD BOOKS LTD.
YORKSHIRE – PHILADELPHIA

First published in Great Britain in 2024 by
PEN AND SWORD MILITARY
An imprint of
Pen & Sword Books Limited
Yorkshire – Philadelphia

ISBN 978 1 03612 394 9

Typeset in Times New Roman 11.5/14.5 by
SJmagic DESIGN SERVICES, India.
Printed and bound in the UK by CPI Group (UK) Ltd.

Pen & Sword Books Limited incorporates the imprints of Atlas, Archaeology,
Aviation, Discovery, Family History, Fiction, History, Maritime, Military,
Military Classics, Politics, Select, Transport, True Crime, Air World, Frontline
Publishing, Leo Cooper, Remember When, Seaforth Publishing, The Praetorian
Press, Wharncliffe Local History, Wharncliffe Transport, Wharncliffe True Crime
and White Owl.

For a complete list of Pen & Sword titles please contact
PEN & SWORD BOOKS LIMITED
George House, Units 12 & 13, Beevor Street, Off Pontefract Road,
Barnsley, South Yorkshire, S71 1HN, England
E-mail: enquiries@pen-and-sword.co.uk
Website: www.pen-and-sword.co.uk

or
PEN AND SWORD BOOKS
1950 Lawrence Rd, Havertown, PA 19083, USA
E-mail: uspen-and-sword@casematepublishers.com
Website: www.penandswordbooks.com

Contents

Acknowledgements

I am grateful to the thirty contributing authors to *Serving With Pride*, who have helped us make sure that the 'Gay Ban' is not forgotten. Your words here are an act of courage.

For much of this journey, I have worked in a close partnership with Royal Air Force veteran and pioneering first transgender officer Caroline Paige MBE. I shall forever be grateful for her support, in years when Caroline and I found 365 working days! Her support, fantastic humour and solidarity to this important cause pushed us on to success after success. Without her standing by my side and helping make the case in select committees, ministerial meetings, in Portcullis House and in the Ministry of Defence, we would not be where we are today.

Thank you to Ed Hall, my successor as Chair of Fighting With Pride, who was a pioneer of the fight to lift the ban with the leaders of Rank Outsiders. Thank you to the trustees of Fighting With Pride for their support to our mission. At times our trustees have backed me when the risks seemed high and the chances of success somewhat grey. Never faint of heart, they have backed bold action and done everything they could and kept their fingers crossed. Thank you also to our patron, General Sir Andrew Gregory KCB CBE DL, one of Fighting With Pride's earliest supporters and champions.

My particular thanks to Army veteran and incredibly talented multi-media artist David Tovey for permission to use his inspirational painting 'Isolated No More' for the cover of this important book. The work, commissioned for the LGBT Veterans Independent Review, depicts LGBT veterans marching in the National Service of Remembrance in 2021. This was the first occasion that the military family was complete in its solemn act of remembrance for all those we have lost. David's work in its many forms, has been displayed in Tate Modern, the Saatchi Gallery and galleries across the UK.

Thank you to Heather, Harriet and Jon at Pen and Sword Books. I might be a son of Nelson, but I am not a son of Shakespeare. Their support to this writing project has been outstanding, helping give a voice to these thirty Armed Forces veterans silenced by the ban. Our community is truly grateful for your painstaking work to put this important book on the shelves.

In 2021 I was lucky to cross paths with Jude Habib at the charity Sounddelivery Media, where she is a powerhouse of ideas and energy. Jude has been an amazing supporter of Fighting With Pride and has opened doors that have helped put our cause in the public eye, for which I am hugely grateful.

Thank you to Shan Veillard-Thomas for your infectious enthusiasm. A more tenacious squirrel I have never met in her search for opportunities for Fighting With Pride.

Thank you to the amazing veterans of the Royal Navy, Royal Marines, British Army and Royal Air Force who have pushed us to the front and cheered us on as their community champions. Despite all that has happened to them, they placed their trust in Fighting With Pride. Together we will win.

Thank you to Lord Terrence Etherton GBE KC PC, whose dedication to his work as the Chair of the LGBT Veterans Independent Review has helped shine a light upon the history of what happened in the years of the ban and of its enduring impact of the ban.

The rigours and traumas that many of our veterans have faced cause anger and upset. Fighting With Pride's community team, led by Kenny Bryce, has done everything possible to enable friendships and mutual support in this community, and with every day that passes there are more smiles and fewer tears. The work of Fighting With Pride's team has changed the future for LGBT veterans and those dismissed because they were perceived to be 'gay'.

Thank you to my shipmate Dave Small, our Pride in Veterans Standard (PiVS) Manager. In his time, Dave was the first 'out' warrant officer in the Royal Navy, when it was not popular to be so! I will always be grateful for his pioneering and rock-solid support to the cause of enabling change in the Royal Navy. By far the best 'sparker' I have met.

ACKNOWLEDGEMENTS

My greatest thanks go to my husband, Adam Mason, who has shared this journey with me for the better part of thirty years. With quiet dignity, he attended his first mess dinner on 25 January 2000, two weeks after the ban was lifted. He was the first gay spouse to move into married quarters, days after the Civil Partnership Act became law, and has been a stoic and at times courageous first amongst equals. I have always been proud to see him step over the gangway of the ships in which I served. Every day since we met on 5 February 1995, he has supported me and loved the Royal Navy – even when it did not love him! Adam has helped bring the impossible within reach in quiet but important service of the Armed Forces' communities.

Foreword

Lieutenant Commander Craig Jones MBE Royal Navy November 2024

It has been an honour and privilege to bring together the accounts of thirty remarkable veterans, who, like so many others, began their careers full of hope for a lifetime of service in our Armed Forces. They met every challenge faced by those who proudly wear the uniform and many are veterans of armed conflict and contingency operations all over the world. Yet in their time, they were not welcome and their accounts in these chapters lay bare the shocking treatment they faced.

Those suspected or found out faced arrest and harrowing interrogation, invariably without legal support, invasive medical procedures in military hospitals and court martial. At best they were dismissed from the Armed Forces, at worst they served up to six months in military detention or prison and were left with a criminal record. Some were subjected to debunked medical procedures, including electrocution conversion therapy.

On 19 January 2023, in his apology on behalf of the British people for these shocking acts, Prime Minister Rishi Sunak stood up in the House of Commons and said:

> The ban on LGBT people serving in the British military prior to 2000 was an appalling failure of the British State, decades behind the law of this land. In that period many endured the most horrific sexual abuse and violence, homophobic bullying and harassment, all while bravely serving this country. Today, on behalf of the British State, I apologise.

In the telling of their experiences and of the enduring impact upon their lives, these veterans have ended the silence of decades spent in the long shadow of the 'gay ban'. Their stories are at times graphic and unvarnished as they describe the damage done by a policy that was a horrific breach of the Armed Forces Covenant, the nation's promise that those who are prepared to stand in harms' way to protect our peace and freedom shall not be disadvantaged by their service. Yet this promise was broken as they were expunged in their thousands, excluded by a gay ban implemented more commonly with zeal than mercy. Each of their narratives is a stark reminder of the inhumanity so many endured as they were stripped of all they held dear. Through their words, we gain insights into the emotional turmoil, the struggles for acceptance, and the decades spent devoid of hope. With quiet dignity most have endured. These are veterans deserving of our compassion for the adversity they have faced and the courage they have shown, all while waiting to be heard and acknowledged. One of the most incredible groups of veterans are those who are not LGBT but were removed through a vindictive act or zealous suspicion. I have been humbled to see their incredible support of Fighting With Pride; we are indeed all of one company.

Our country has an illustrious history of protecting the peace and freedoms of our people and many beyond our shores. The vulnerable and those facing injustice have found protection by the command of our government and the actions of our Armed Forces. It is hard to fathom why generations of enforcers of the ban never challenged it and with each year that passed, more young men and women were removed for reasons which, in their own time, made little sense.

In 2020, I gathered the authors of my first anthology book, *Fighting With Pride* to begin to tell the story of this shameful period of military history, but in doing so I knew that beyond our reach were most of the lost legion of veterans, washed in the shame of unspeakable actions by commanders in whom they had placed their trust. With those authors on the twentieth anniversary of the lifting of the ban, I formed the charity, Fighting With Pride, as its first Chief Executive. The charity has become a beacon of hope and a champion of the cause of justice. As the story of the ban has been remembered, hope has risen.

After all they have been through, it is quite remarkable that for most, their loyalty to the armed forces has endured, and today, as they step forward to shake hands with Armed Forces leaders in acts of reparation, they have shown great dignity. Many have felt able to walk back through the doors of the military units from which they were removed to accept the presentation of berets, heartfelt apologies and a few moments of being recognised again as veteran members of our Armed Forces of whom the nation is proud.

Their service in Korea, Borneo, the Arabian Gulf, the Falklands War, Northern Ireland, Cold War Germany, the Balkans, indeed wherever our Armed Forces have been, has been remembered, medals have been restored and are once again worn with pride.

For too many years, without acts of reparation, this history which 'dare not speak its name' was at risk of erasure. Counter to that, here you will learn of the full force of the gay ban, lest we forget. Yet once in a while, you will see the flicker of the flame of hope. As they have stepped forward, they have found each other, they have helped each other and they have remembered that the values they held dear and were denied in their careers of service, have always existed in themselves.

In my five short years leading the Fighting With Pride charity, with Caroline Paige MBE and our trustees, I have seen remarkable acts of courage, as these veterans have returned to their darkest of days to help make sure that the service of LGBT veterans and the history of this wretched policy are not forgotten. The pages of this book are testament to that.

This community stands at the threshold of the opportunity for the restoration of justice, but will justice be done and fair financial recompense paid?

It is all too easy to stand in parliament and offer the words of an act of contrition, but far more difficult it seems for governments to recognise and recompense the damage done. We must restore for these veterans the comfort in later life we would wish for all veterans, but also the sense of justice that can be the catalyst of a burgeoning recovery and a watershed moment, beyond which we can say that the wrongs of the past were recognised and righted. Let us remember that whether they knew the rules or not, the policy that brought about their downfall was ruled an illegal act in 1999.

This book is dedicated to the tall poppies affected by this policy. I hope these incredible people will bloom again and that the justice they have stepped forward for will finally be done. I acknowledge that not all are with us today. We shall remember them.

Chapter 1

One Moment in Time: Discovering You're Not Wanted – and Not Even Really Knowing Why

— Claire Ashton —

Gunner Royal Artillery (to be) Ashton was caught by his mother holding a tea-towel around his head when he was fairly young. He didn't know why he was doing it. Many, nay most, of the women in the area waiting for buses or walking to and from work wore headscarves. He was to find out later it was to keep the cotton threads from getting in their hair in the mills. All the men, well, some of them, were covered in black coal dust and all squatted at the bus stops waiting to go to work. None of them walked to work, it was now too far, as the coal mines were closing by the day and the industry was heading towards oblivion in years to come.

I used to hug myself as I swayed with my headscarf on. I don't know why. I didn't want to be a mill girl, or a pitman for that matter, as they were old, and I was just a kid. I just knew I was different. I didn't even know what I was different from or to.

He was bullied throughout his childhood. He had something about him that signalled to everyone else he was a target. No one had difficulty reading the sign he appeared to carry around that read 'Bully Me'. That carried on into secondary school, Hindley & Abram Grammar School. Sounds grand. It wasn't and the bullying carried on. He can't recall his name. The bully caught hold of him near the bike sheds.

The bully waited until a suitably large audience had assembled, then started punching. This was a moment, a defining moment, a moment in time in his bullied life.

I'd had enough of this. I started fighting back. I don't actually remember connecting with any of my punches. It didn't matter as he was a good 9 inches taller than me and had plenty of bullying practice. But my spirit in fighting back seemed to turn public opinion and I felt myself being dragged away to safety. I think I was still mid-air swinging, minutes later. Why did this happen to me? But it felt good, fighting back. I thought I was a coward, but now I knew I wasn't. Not exactly brave either. But everyone else there that day thought I was, so that would do for me. For now, at least.

He hated gym. He hated sports and would do anything to avoid them. He began playing truant, or at least being so late he missed having to change with all the others. The others being boys of course.

I didn't know why I was different. I tried, without making it obvious, to always be in the corner or to be late getting back to the changing rooms. I feigned recovery from being out of breath. I made-up technical questions to ask the teacher. Anything not to be in the showers or changing with the others. I don't know why. I hated it. I supposed I was different. I didn't know how, or why, that was just the way it was.

After a false start as a 'press photographer', where he got the scoop of the Queen Mother visiting Wigan using a camera without a film in it, he got a job, a proper man's job, in construction. Motorways were springing up here and there. So, he found a job as a trainee surveyor. Transferring to the Lake District to work on the M6, he was now in his element. Until he found his digs consisted of four people to a poky room. Being late for catching the minibus to travel 60 miles to 'Tech' once a week mounted up. Exams passed but attendance to lectures below the required days attended meant a failed year. Failed Tech meant failed training and no job. Failed.

I'd have been ok if it hadn't been for the old problem of being frightened of being around others when changing or getting into bed. I liked girls, so I was ok on that score. Wasn't I horrified when hitchhiking back a few weekends ago when the driver put his hand on my knee? What I needed was a bit of discipline to sort me out. And I knew where to get it! The Royal Engineers had surveyors, didn't they?

Gunner Ashton, Royal Artillery (Bolton Army Recruiting Office thought the artillery was the destination for all their catches) made it to the depot at Woolwich. He could bull his boots, blanco his webbing, make and keep a bed block (sleeping under a sheet only meant the 'block' could sit square overnight, ready for morning inspection) and could strip and assemble an SLR and SMG with the best of them. But as he was different, he got the attention of the troop bully. No bike sheds here, only the washrooms. A torrent of abusive swearing presaged what was inevitably coming next. The beating started.

Body blows started it. The odd head punch was thrown in for good measure. It started before the audience gathered. A dim memory surfaced. Fight back. I didn't want to, but I knew it was my only chance. So, I got up from the floor and started swinging. I caught him with a punch to his face. It only seemed to make him madder. But once again my status amongst the onlookers went up a notch or two and the assault was stopped. When questioned by the training sergeant (he must've been told something?) I gave the really lame excuse that I'd slipped in the showers and that explained my bruises and split lip. I knew he didn't believe me, but he let it go at that. The funny thing was that from then on in training, I was a bit of hero. For standing up to the bully that no one really liked anyway. But, more importantly, for not grassing on him to the sergeant.

Luckily, no one else from Gunner Ashton's training troop went to 94 (Locating) Regiment RA at Celle in West Germany. Gunner Ashton was glad to see the back of training and its dozen or so beds to a room. Here, at least, Gunner Ashton was finally getting to the modern army, where he would have a small room and possibly even a bit of privacy. He could start again.

Wrong. The whole regiment was housed in one massive building. My battery, 156 (Inkerman) Battery, was on one complete floor. The barrack rooms held six or so at a time. Luckily, it looked as if a little customisation of your space was possible, but the washroom/showers were in one large facility for the entire battery. This was all going wrong for me. I couldn't understand it. No one else was bothered about it, but I was different, wasn't I?

So, Gunner Ashton's army career began in earnest. He'd convinced the posting people back at Woolwich that he'd to go to a locating unit as it was only there he'd get a place as a 'proper' surveyor (his words). A course was soon set up for him at Larkhill on Salisbury Plain. That was great as he'd seen a photo of the modern accommodation. Two to a room and en-suite toilets. Not great, but better than back at Celle. He learned to rock climb on the nearby large stones at Stonehenge. Yes, that's right, Stonehenge. This was pre-World Heritage Site, pre-'Keep Out' signs and pre-security patrols. A few weekend trips to North Wales for climbing was good as well. Top marks in the end of course exams and a substantial pay rise for becoming technician grade meant things were going well. Or so he thought.

Back to Germany. I was looking forward to day-to-day work, exercises, and nights out. On nights out, I had to go with the flow usually. I once tried to go out on my own but soon stopped when it was pointed out that only queers did that. I knew I was different, but not that different. So only trips to the bars and nightclubs with the boys were considered acceptable. I could drink with the best of them, down 'bratwurst mit frites', *could climb the back gate of the camp as a shortcut and could swear all the right swear words. I could even brag that I'd been electrocuted by faulty lighting wires when climbing the gates. But what I couldn't do was go into detail as to what I wanted to do with the* 'stripper' *that featured everywhere we went. I can't even think about it, let alone write it.*

Gunner Ashton had no first name back then, as he was just a last name. Convenient then, as it is now, as he never had a first name in his mind. He continued his career as any squaddie did, smoking his health away, getting drunk in the NAAFI as well as exercises to defend the Free World from the Red Army just across the border. It was common knowledge then that their battery, due to join a division's artillery units, would probably not get out of the camp gates before the forward units of the Warsaw Pact overran them. But they didn't care, they were paid in Deutschmarks, bought all they needed in the NAAFI bar and had their suits measured up and delivered within the camp. Gunner Ashton was even given the wink that promotion was on the cards. Then they got the orders to start riot training. For Northern Ireland.

What for? We're an intelligence regiment. We're all a bunch of [...], not the hard nuts from an infantry unit. Well, let's see if we can have a laugh and maybe we'll never get there anyway.

Wrong. They trained using pieces of coke, absolutely not with stones as they might have got hurt. Oh, they used empty drinks cans, but they were steel then, not your aluminium ones that wouldn't fly more than a few feet. They formed in squares, Roman style, with the officer and senior NCOs in the middle to be best protected. (How did Gunner Ashton and his mates know that?) Surrounding them were the riflemen with their SLRs and short shields and round the outside were the long shield carriers with a baton. Those shields weighed a ton; thank goodness no one even considered Gunner Ashton for carrying one of those. Luckily, he'd been 'best shot' in training and couldn't miss on the ranges in Germany so, unlike the army in general, who usually didn't do the obvious thing, Gunner Ashton was to be a rifleman. Carrying a short shield and a short baton as well. The rifles were to be carried in the hands at all times, and to ensure this the sling was effectively tied to one wrist so that if the 'enemy' got hold of it, they had hold of you as well. Gulp!

The battery was chosen to join with two others under the auspices of a Heavy Regiment RA. Off to another German camp for exercises and tests to decide where they'd be stationed in Northern Ireland. 156 (Inkerman) Battery RA drew the short straw by winning the competition. Border and Falls Road. The others got Peace Line. Who cares?

I loved the Border. Lying in quick release sleeping bags in ambush near a border station. Frost on the ground and not a sound or light anywhere. But, there's always a but, we were aware that 'They' knew we were there. 'They' knew that we knew that 'They' knew. So, it was potluck if we were attacked. Unlikely. But even more unlikely was that 'They' would attack the border checkpoint while we there, because 'They' knew that… '

The highlight was defusing the bomb, although it wasn't the first time I felt the gulf between the others and myself. The radio and TV mast in the middle of nowhere had an almost comic appearance. Sticks of 'dynamite' (commercial gelignite) were taped to the mast legs. Connecting them were long lengths of white fuse (detonating cord) and at their end a battery and detonator - an almost comical Micky Mouse alarm clock with two brass bells on top. My protestations were brushed aside. All that was needed was to cut the 'det cord' to disarm the system. After my fascination with all the rock cuttings explosives crews on the construction of the M6 through the Lake District, I was aware of how this all worked. The sergeant thought otherwise. He'd watched enough Westerns to know the fuse wire would 'fizz' and blow the 'dynamite'. So, the best thing to do would be to disconnect the activator, being the clock, which was ticking loudly. So, a tug here and a tug there and throw the clock away. All was ok, except the alarm rang while it was still in the air. Two seconds earlier and Mickey would've rung time on half our patrol. I suppose I should've been scared at that point, but even I could see the funny side, so I shrugged and returned to base at Newry. I also returned to deception, hiding my fear of the sleeping quarters holding all our troop and its communal living.

And so I thought if this how it is, I'll survive. I won't like it. But I'll survive. If it's like this for our whole tour of duty, I'll survive.

Wrong. Again.

The battery moved to Belfast on board a grey ship, the *Maidstone*, with grey paint and grey everything in a grey harbour. Gunner Ashton was given a grey bunk among what seemed like dozens of grey bunks with grey blankets in a grey ship's hold.

My memory of the grey Maidstone *began to fade almost immediately, so much so that I've had to research its name. I don't remember where we ate or what we ate. I do remember the food was plonked onto the all-in-one stainless-steel trays. No, I just remember the trays, nearly grey.*

Where we stored our rifles, or our kit has gone into the mists of time. All I really remember were the grey bunks above, below and to the side. I'd nowhere to turn. Nowhere to hide. And everyone constantly staring at me, staring at the stranger amongst them. No one ever told me why they stared at me, but then again, I never asked. I just knew that I was being crushed.

The monotony of the grey ship was broken when the troop was called on to go to the New Lodge Road area of Belfast. It was fired on in two separate attacks a short distance and time apart. The first time two of the troop were hit. Most weren't aware as they thought someone had used a starting pistol.

The second was as the 'Roman Square' moved down Lepper Street off Old Lodge Road. Amongst what was thought to be dozens of rioters, a gap appeared and then a machine gun was fired at the troop. One soldier was killed and others wounded. The soldier was the first to be killed in the Troubles. His name was Gunner Robert Curtis. Research shows that no one knew what sort of gun it was. Some said a Thompson submachine gun, others a Sterling submachine gun. Some said it was a 9mm, others a .45ACP. The troop took cover before moving the wounded into cover.

The first shots sounded like a pistol. Like someone repeatedly pulling a trigger. Perhaps it was a starting pistol? Although that was silly as they could get shot for holding something that looked like a gun. Still, the stones and half pavers rained in. I'm not sure we were doing any good, plodding down the middle of the street like, well, ducks. The noise was incredible, shouts and noise, clanking shields and noise, shouted orders and noise. Just remember you have a rifle. But what use was it? You can't shoot anyone for just throwing stones. The memories are fading now. I don't even know if it's light or dark. I close my eyes and all I can see are stones in the air. Only some. So perhaps it's dark? I can hear the noise, the noise of stones and half bricks hitting shields. I can feel something hitting my legs, I don't know what. I can feel we are moving, yet we're frozen in time. We're frozen in time awaiting, what?

'Whup, whup, whup, whup...' The sound of a stone on a length of rope being swung round by boys at play. 'Crack, crack, crack, crack...' Now that was a sound I knew. Automatic gunfire. The 'Whup' means they're shooting at me. I vaguely remember not being too bothered. After all, that's why we were there; to be shot at. I crashed down against a terraced house's brick wall corner. Just like a hundred terraced house brick wall corners back home in, where? Where do I belong, where is home? I suppose I belong here. With my ma? Are they my mates? Focus. I know where they're coming from. But I can't see anything. Why? I can't remember if it's dark or light, just I can't see anything. I glance into the street. Someone's lying there. I must go and rescue them. But I must stay and engage the gunman. But I must go and rescue them. Stay, go, stay, go. Stay.

I look but don't see. It's my job to see. I'm failing the others. I failed that day. I failed.

As we climbed aboard a truck and left the area one of the troop said he had a sore bum (although he put a little more plainly). I was amused, as were others, when we pointed out he'd been shot in the arse, but the levity ended abruptly we came to realise that one of our number,

Geordie Curtis had suffered a heart attack and died. It must have been the shock of being shot at, he died without a mark on him, what bad luck.

I was alright, though. I'd been shot at, not shot, and I'd not had a heart attack. I was alright.

I asked permission to go to the memorial service to Geordie on the ship deck. I thought I ought to, to ask permission that is. As an atheist, I was the only person in the forces I ever heard of having ATH on their ID card instead of CofE or RC. As I stood there silently during the prayers and hymns, I secretly wished I'd been shot. Not dead, like poor Geordie, but just enough to get me out of this dreadful grey ship with its dreadful walls and dreadful grey bunks and dreadful greyness. Tears began to trickle down my cheeks, just as they are now, when I'm writing this. I can't remember whether it was day or night. I can't remember what time it was. I can't remember what was said or what was sung. I do remember failing Geordie Curtis and wishing it was me.

Gunner Ashton moved with his battery to George Street factory, which was huge. But the entire battery was accommodated (squeezed) into what seemed like a small high storeroom. With grey bunkbeds tiered up four high. Each tier was about 18 inches apart, all standing on a grey floor surrounded by grey walls. The battery went out on patrols at frequent intervals onto the Falls Road area. While the previous residents of the factory, the Black Watch, had patrolled solely in the Pigs (wheeled armoured personnel carriers), 156 (Inkerman) Battery RA, surveyors, sound rangers and meteorologists, went out on patrol on foot. On the notorious Falls Road. And still managed to be given cups of tea and biscuits. For a while. A short while. In between riots with hails of rocks and nail bombs, grenades and all the rest.

We never knew when they started or why they started. We were never quite sure when they ended or why they ended. We just knew that it was potluck who got hit by shrapnel or by nails. I was grateful that 'They' used nails with heads, as one pierced my shield, only to be stopped by its head. Just as it scratched my nose. Odd, but solvable by later putting the shield on the ground and jumping on it to drive the nail out. What couldn't be solved, though, was the return to the grey bunks in between the grey walls. I'd have rather stayed on patrol. There, at least, I felt the same as the rest. Same uniform, same equipment, the same.

The bullying continued between the grey walls. When we all got body lice, I'd caused it. I nearly died when the medical officer insisted on full body examinations to see the extent of the infestations. The grey room got fumigated, we got fumigated. It was dreadful and it was my fault.

When the armourer found a round missing on a patrol's return, it was naturally my magazine it was missing from. What was amazing was the staff sergeant who slipped me a round to hand in to the armourer. I never found out what the armourer thought when I turned up with the 'missing' round when he probably knew where the original one had gone to. Details. Details I can remember because remembering them causes no real pain. Yet the grey bunks and grey walls hold no details, or if they do, then none seems to get through the mists of time.

Gunner Ashton left Northern Ireland with the battery on an unknown date by unknown means and returned to Germany. Post deployment leave, or whatever it was called, happened sometime after and Gunner Ashton left for the UK by unknown means for an unknown period.

At my home address near Wigan, home was the bed pillow my tears dropped onto, I told the stories of Ireland that needed telling in the way that they needed to be told. Mickey's clock was always a good story to tell. I was questioned at home about girlfriends, though how anyone could make friends with anyone while having rocks thrown at you, goodness knows. Underlying this questioning was the unspoken question. 'You don't like boys, do you?' Not an unspoken question, an unspoken accusation. Luckily it never got asked. Not that I would've said yes, but my truthful 'No, of course not!' would somehow have sounded a bit lame. I'd considered whether I was queer or not (forgive me, gay was still twenty years or so in the future then). I'd long dismissed this idea, even though 95% of my 'mates' were probably convinced I was. No crude stories of what I did to (yes, did to!) the local 'slapper' while on leave, whether real or made up. No stories of going out with the lads and getting paralytic. No tales a man tells a man about what men do.

Another tour of Northern Ireland was mooted to be in the offing for Gunner Ashton and the battery. 'Troubles' veterans who'd performed well (getting killed and wounded, I suppose) were in demand, so their turn would come around soon. But courses for their 'day' job still had to go on. Gunner Ashton was to be sent on another surveyors' course at Larkhill.

Great! Larkhill! Civilised! An unknown again?

Wrong.

The course was moved to Hohne in Germany. Bang went the 'Larkhill Dream'.

Hohne was another grey bunk in another grey room with some more grey walls.

Something snapped, then. The grey walls crowded in and suffocated me. I wished I were dead.

I was taken back to my unit, 94 (Locating) Regiment. RA, in Celle. I was put in the guardroom in a cell, for my own protection, I think. I'm not even sure if the door was locked. I just wanted to be myself. I wasn't a soldier. A male soldier. I couldn't bring myself to admit this to anyone, never mind myself. I was me. Please let me be me!

There was talk, from whom I don't know. There was talk of putting me back in the barracks, a fresh start. Training course failed. Again. Or off to a British Forces' hospital in Germany. To find out why...

...Why Gunner Ashton had had an episode. Off to the Hannover Forces' hospital, he thought. Papers mentioned Munster. Where's Munster? Once in a system, Gunner Ashton went where orders told him. Why? It didn't matter. Orders were orders.

Corporal [...] reports that Gunner Ashton was found to have a cut to his left palm while engaging in a woodworking class. Gunner Ashton was given requisite First Aid, etc.

I did indeed get a cut in a woodwork class. Why was I doing woodwork? Goodness only knows. But the chisel was blunt... ish. Nobody had said that pushing the blunt chisel along the wood with the right hand while the left hand 'steadied' the wood at the far side was dangerous. The predictable result? A cut the length of my palm almost through to my tendons. Yes, it hurt. I have now, and have always had, a low threshold for pain. Or so I thought. So, my palm was wide open with bits showing in the depths of the wound. But not to worry! Where better to be sliced open than in a hospital?

The doctor, a major, had the measure of me. He looked at me with steely eyes. He then started a short, curt, conversation. Well, more of a monologue really.

'You don't want any anaesthetic, do you.' It wasn't a question.

As he started on the first of six or seven stitches through the thick palm skin, he said, 'This will make a man of you'. It didn't then and it sure didn't now. I managed to withhold my screams as I looked through tearful eyes. He thought he knew. I knew my card was marked. He thought, no, knew, I was queer, and he was going to prove it.

I knew I wasn't. And if cards were involved, I held the trump one. If asked, demanded, interrogated on the subject of being queer, I could answer truthfully, straight into someone's eyes that I wasn't. Not only that, but I didn't like men or boys (it's always boys, isn't it?) and absolutely only had an interest in girls. Only girls? Yes, it was ok to have an interest in girls. Girls of any age, as long as they weren't boys. Girls good. Boys bad. I knew the answers to all the questions before they were asked. So, they saved me. More than once.

Shipped off to England, I fetched up at MH Netley. Or Haslar. Does it matter? It was a one-way ticket to Blighty and the mental hospital (is that what the MH stood for?). No going back for Gunner Ashton. No more serving his country. No more doing his duty. No more trying to satisfy his parents that he was worthwhile when they knew full well he wasn't. Gunner Ashton answered every question 'No, I'm not interested in boys' and, 'I didn't find a girl I could like' and' Of course I want to marry a girl' and 'No, I don't like boys, men, playing with boys, playing with men or playing with myself.' 'What's wrong with me? I don't know, you tell me. As far as I'm concerned there is nothing wrong with me.'

And there wasn't. But thank goodness they didn't ask THE question.

The question was, "Why did you hang around the WRVS room back at Celle? Why did she fascinate you? She was older than you, she was too young to be your mother. So why your fascination?'

It was simple. If I could've changed into the WVRS lady, I would've done it at a shot. She was me; I was her. It wasn't that simple then, and it's not really that simple now, but I would've done anything to wear the bottle-green uniform and speak with the soft voice that enveloped me on every occasion I could think up to be with her. Did I want her? Did I want to date her? No, I wanted to be her. Simple really. But no one ever thought to ask the question.

Now we can send you, Gunner Ashton, back to your Unit. That'll be ok, but they'll know what we thought what your problem is.

We can send you back and tell them we think you are a queer and to keep an eye out for solid evidence, or we can discharge you with a Medical Discharge.

There it was. Kicked out. No choice, the RTU was no choice at all. My life would've been hell. Not that it hadn't been hell already. Being put next to a soldier who was repeatedly taken for electrocution played games with my head. But truth was on my side and as long as THE question was never asked, I was safe. Thank goodness the question was never asked, as I couldn't not be truthful. Being truthful then kept me safe. Being truthful later, much later, got me into trouble, but at least I could look myself in the eye.

I was sent home with a Medical Discharge. I didn't fully take it in earlier when the doctors mentioned they'd contacted my parents to ask of early problems. I realised later when questions by my parents were never asked, when my parents floated over subjects, when my parents stopped asking about girlfriends.

My father died sometime later. I never quite connected with him. He was a flight engineer on Lancasters during the war. He did mention those who fell by the wayside who LMF and alluded to others who, well, the conversations ended there.

My mother also served in the ATS during the war on gun sites all over the vulnerable ports and cities. She was my mother and never asked searching questions. When I told her my name was Claire and her daughter loved her mother very much, she said she loved me too. That was all I needed to hear.

I never found out what the doctors had said to my parents and my parents never told me what the doctors had said to them.

The years went by for Ex-Gunner Ashton. Veteran? Never heard of it, them or whatever. Just a failed soldier, destined to fail in life. He soldiered on (no pun intended) for years. Hiding when necessary, hiding when essential and avoiding when necessary. Always there for family occasions, always there to help family. The questions were never asked. Was it because they already knew, or thought they knew, the answers?

One day Claire met her. It really was love at first sight. She loved him, ex-Gunner Ashton. He told her a sanitised version of his life, but never mentioned her life. That was really only just beginning and it would be years in the future before she really became Claire.

So, to spoil the plot for some and to cut the boring bits for others, we are now in real time, not the wandering thoughts of an imagination that tends to run away with itself, the real time of the real world. Where one moment in time is finally approaching. It's approaching fast. Faster than we would like, faster than we can control. The moment is the culmination of her army service, her seeking peace on the open road, her seeking of peace in the mountains, her seeking peace with seventeen years of police service.

Finally, she's found it. Why she had to look, I don't know. It was there all the time. The waking at night with the unheard screams on a Belfast street. The sound of bullets that made no sound. The body lying in the road that displayed her failure to protect him. The dreams that were there by day and by night. The dreams that never really went away. If only. The peace was there all the time. She did her best. She did her duty, as she promised she would.

Claire, the proudest veteran you could think of, was given the honour of carrying the Fighting With Pride standard at the 2023 Royal British Legion Festival of Remembrance at the Royal Albert Hall in front of our King and Queen. Fighting With Pride had been given the opportunity to be one of the Ex-Service Organisations to have their standard paraded there. She spent hours going up and down the steep stairs, carrying the heavy Fighting With Pride standard at the Friday rehearsals. Having literally no sleep at all that night, she prayed (a first) that she wouldn't trip during the Saturday performances. When the evening performance came in front of the King, her nerves nearly betrayed her. She avoided that fall on the stairs, but only just. She managed to gather herself during the rest of the event, carrying her standard down onto the stage twice more. At the end, as the dismiss was given to the service men and women, she carried her standard down to the main floor, gathered a few of the fallen poppy petals, and made towards the exit stairs at the far end. All the way down from her place behind the presenter and then across towards the exit, she'd been hearing very loud applause from the audience, assuming it was for someone else. Looking this way and that for Fighting With Pride members still at their seats, none could be seen. But her proudest moment was yet to come. As she started up the steep steps, she heard a loud screaming coming from above. She finally looked up to see dozens of faces peering down, all shouting and cheering. Then, Claire knew she was indeed the proudest veteran in the hall. All the faces she could see above merged into the thousands of LGBT+ casualties who'd had to leave their identities behind while trying to be loyal to their service and their country. And they, looking down at their standard, knew they'd all come home at last to their veteran family.

The following morning, fifty veterans from Fighting With Pride marched past the Cenotaph alongside thousands of other veterans. Some of them wore berets and a few wore medals, as they did the 'Eyes Left' at the Cenotaph. But all of them, including Claire, already had their LGBT flags held close to their hearts.

The dreams faded a little after that. Never really bad dreams, but enough to reassure Claire she'd done her best, done her duty.

She finally received her veteran's ID card and her small veteran's badge. They meant a great deal.

Yet what meant most of all was a passer-by, noticing the veterans' badge, who said 'Thank you for your service'. There it was. That was the one moment in time.

Chapter 2

Always Have Rebellious Hope

—————————————— Ruth and Ju ——————————————

My early life was spent in Porthcawl, South Wales, where I grew up the eldest daughter of Derek and Barbara, with my sister Helen and brother Michael. I loved being by the sea and many happy days were spent down at the beach, where I was a lifeguard. I was brought up in a Christian household and went to three services on a Sunday. I was an alter server, sang in the choir and rang the church bells. I loved the great outdoors, and being a Brownie, Guide and then a Ranger fuelled my passion. I'd decided early on that I wanted to join the forces; I felt I needed to get away before I was married off and doing an admin role somewhere. From a relatively early age, I knew I wasn't really interested in boys and instead had feelings for the female police inspector in the TV show *Juliet Bravo*, although I couldn't really understand why I had such feelings.

I went to the RAF recruitment office in Swansea and was told there were no vacancies, so I went next door and found that the army wanted me. In hindsight, it was a great choice. I had to go through several entrance tests, medicals and interviews, after which I was identified as potentially suitable to become an analyst in the Intelligence Corps and was invited to go to Ashford for two days to assess my suitability. In December, I had another interview, medical, basic fitness test and an interview at Guildford, the headquarters of the WRAC (Women's Royal Army Corps). When I arrived, I saw quite a few 'butch' women, but I rather liked it. I felt I wasn't alone; it was like a 'gay discovery'. I took my Oath of Allegiance to the Queen, which I took extremely seriously, and on 10 February 1987 started my six weeks' basic training at Guildford. I'd been interviewed quite a few times due to the high security clearance I needed for my job role and I was always asked if

I was a 'homosexual', to which I just replied 'no'. At that point, I can honestly say I didn't really know I was gay. Coming from a small town, with no books and nobody to ask about sexual orientation, I just had no real idea.

After completing the six weeks' basic training, I was then on my way to Ashford to join squad 113 'Sully's Rising Suns' (named after Staff Sergeant Sullivan) to start my Intelligence Corps training. We joined the men and were soon completing the same training as them, including the men's basic fitness test, the combat fitness test, and running for miles on end with a telegraph pole throughout Kent. There was a female PTI there, who always started our PT sessions with the cry: 'Round the parade square two minutes ...Go!' It didn't matter if you did in under two minutes, round you went again. I thought she was gay, but nobody mentioned it. After all, it was just something nobody talked about because you'd get 'chucked out' if you did. After successfully completing the men's training course, including firearms, those of us who were going to be analysts and linguists were sent to Loughborough. I can't say much about what this involved because it was Top Secret, but I completed all my training and found my first posting was to 13 Signal Regiment, in what was then West Germany.

I flew out at the beginning of December 1987 and was allocated a bed space, sharing a large room with a private in the Royal Signals. She was from the Valleys near to where I lived and helped me settle in. My 'gaydar' worked well and I got involved with playing hockey and basketball. One of the main sporting events of the calendar, the women's hockey competition, was held in Aldershot. This was a fantastic event and when I spoke to other WRACs I never said I was in the Intelligence Corps because they thought I was in the RMP (Royal Military Police) and was out to get them discharged. Once they started to know me, I was able to tell them where I worked. Playing hockey in what was a sort of gay 'safe space' was refreshing and even though you couldn't be seen with anybody, you felt you were with your kind of people and didn't have to be anybody else. In fact, if you were 'straight', you stood out like a sore thumb and could even be said to be in the minority.

Whilst in Germany, two of my female friends were seen kissing in the sitting room and an investigation followed where I was called in and told to say I'd seen them kissing. I was told not to protect 'these people' or they would think I was gay as well. This really frightened me, but I really hadn't seen my friends kissing myself so I wasn't lying and I certainly wouldn't have said anything anyway. It did make me think about how traumatic that experience had been and I knew I had to keep my sexuality as secret as possible. I had a few dalliances, but no proper relationships in Germany.

My second posting was to Northern Ireland with 225 Signal Squadron, 15 Signal Regiment, Lisburn. I didn't know it at the time, but this was where I'd meet my forever soulmate and the only true love of my life, Julia, known as 'Ju'.

Ju was born in Bristol to Ray and Angela and soon was followed by her sister, Sharron. They moved to Chepstow when Ju was about 3 years old to live with her grandparents and uncle in an old cottage on an acre of land. The cottage was divided into two and there was a log fire for heat. Ju used to love playing 'fighting games' in the orchard using bows and arrows and machine guns made from sticks. She'd wanted to join the army since she was 10 and at 17 she took the bus to the army recruitment office and joined the WRAC as a driver. In April 1989 she started her WRAC training at Guildford and completed her driver training at Leconfield. She was loving the army life and all the opportunities it offered, including her beloved sport. Her first posting was to Bovington, where she also got to drive tanks. After this she was posted to Lisburn, Northern Ireland, and continued with her sports, including playing hockey. She said she never really thought about her sexuality until a hockey match in Lisburn.

Due to my rank of corporal, I was given my own room in Lisburn. It was very small, with my bed on one side and my TV stand opposite it. I didn't need a remote for the TV as I could just change channels by slightly stretching over from my bed. I was on the second floor and the old sash single window was the width of the room, but it was mine: my safe space, as far as I could get it.

I continued to play hockey and got pretty good at it. One evening, we were playing against the WRAC from the RCT (Royal Corps of Transport), who had players who were very serious and fierce looking. I went to tackle the ball away from a woman I'd soon learn was called Ju. She seemed different, and as I closed in to take the ball away from her, something seemed to happen; we had a connection. Ju later said she thought I was 'cute' and that she 'gave' me the ball. We still laugh about this today, although I'm convinced it was my technique and skill that got the ball away from her. When people talk about love at first sight you just think, 'yeah, right,' but when I saw Ju something happened, some sort of electrical impulse of love in my heart. Ju could only describe our first meeting as being like 'something in her eyes just opening my heart and my soul. I'll never forget that first look.'

The next morning, I was having my cooked breakfast in the cookhouse (a large room where junior NCOs eat their meals), when I saw Ju walk in. She was dressed in civilian clothing for her driving details off camp and had such a smile and eyes that I just dived into them. She looked at me and I knew she wanted to talk to me – just as much as I wanted to speak to this gorgeous person. She said, 'My name's Julia, what's your name?' and I just tried to sound cool and said, 'Hiya, my name's Ruth.' Our eyes just locked. I was overjoyed, we'd made contact and now we'd be able to get to know each other. She was somebody I really wanted to know more about.

Shortly after this, I was due to go back to the WRAC at Guildford to complete my sergeant's course. I went over with the hockey team, including Ju, to Aldershot. Our PTI had seen the connection between us and let Ju drive me to Guildford. Ju gave me a cuddly mouse she'd nipped out to buy from the shop 'Athena' that said 'Thinking of you' on the mouse's t-shirt. This was the era of cassettes and the Sony Walkman, which Ju owned, so I asked if I could borrow it for my course. I had my own Walkman but didn't tell Ju that as it now meant I'd have to see her when I got back.

My time away was one of the longest two weeks, but I managed to speak to her once on the military line, just to check she was ok. She wanted to know how I was getting on but we couldn't say too much because the line was monitored. When I got back to Northern Ireland, I couldn't wait to see her and we met in my room that evening. I gave her the Walkman back and while we were sat on my bed, I put my hand on her knee and we kissed. Ju later said she was very nervous and had practised her kissing technique on an orange!

That was the start of our fourteen-month relationship. We knew we had to be careful because I was a corporal and Ju was a private. We both had totally different job roles and lived in different parts of the accommodation block. Ju said she loved me with every ounce of her soul. I just knew I wasn't going to let her go. We knew our relationship was wrong, according to the army at least, and we kept it a complete secret as best we could. We didn't even acknowledge each other on the camp. We had to defy the rules or risk losing everything. It was so difficult because you had to be two people all the time. It was mentally exhausting. You're not the person you want or were meant to be you have to remember to be somebody else. When you first fall in love with somebody, you want to tell the world, but we had to keep it secret because of our careers. It was like living a double life. Our relationship was against the rules: we couldn't tell anybody about our love, it had to be kept secret.

We saw each other when we could, whether it was in the NAAFI having a cup of coffee (milky coffee was as exciting as it got), or a pizza that burnt the roof of your mouth off. We saw each other if we weren't working at the daily circuit training at lunchtime but couldn't partner up in case we drew too much attention to each other. We did manage to get together some weekends and lived for our Friday and Saturday nights in my room. We had an ESB (emergency sleeping bag) on the floor in case we got 'raided' by the SIB (Specialist investigation Branch), the plan being one of us would get out of the bed we shared and into the ESB as fast as possible. We went shopping in Lisburn on Saturday morning and bought rolls, ham and coleslaw for our tea as we watched *Gladiators* and *Solder Soldier*. Our careers went well; I'd passed my Education for Promotion Certificate and was told I'd soon be promoted to sergeant. Ju was looking at promotion to lance corporal, but then it all came crashing down.

We'd felt we were being 'watched' as a couple. Ju told me her sergeant had left and their replacement had told the corporal he thought she (Ju) was gay and was going to 'get her out'. He put her on the worst driving details, late at night and weekends, which made seeing each other more difficult. He made her life hell. This rocked our world and we had to stop seeing each other as much as we'd done before. It was so difficult and really cut us up inside, but we couldn't show it. Then, within a week, Ju came back to say the sergeant was posting her out to Colchester and then out on a UN (United Nations) tour to Cyprus. We were heart broken and devastated. This was not the plan. I'd been asked to extend a year due to my work and specialist knowledge and Ju wasn't due a posting yet. We couldn't even say a proper goodbye because we knew we were being watched.

Ju was posted out within the week. We pledged our love for one another and exchanged rings. It's impossible to put into words how upset and devasted we were. Ju spent a week at Colchester and was then flown out to Cyprus to start her six-month United Nations tour. I was very proud of her. However, the job she was given when she first got there was the worst job ever, driving round the camps emptying the sewage tanks. This continued for at least two months, and she later said they were trying 'to break' her. We'd said we'd write to each other every day on what were known as 'blueys'. These were the same as air mail letters, but you didn't have to pay to send them out. We'd managed to agree beforehand that we'd use a code, with the word 'Chelsea' meaning 'I love you'. We'd mention places we'd been together, and when we talked about our pets saying how much we wanted to see and hold them, in reality the pets were us. After all, we knew our letters would be monitored and read.

The way Ju writes is the way she speaks and she used to draw pictures as well. That's what kept me going. After over four months with just the letters to keep us in contact (no mobile phones or internet in those days), I took some leave and flew out to Cyprus for two weeks to be with Ju for her R&R (rest and recouperation). Ju had booked us accommodation well away from prying eyes and had also rented a car. I was counting down the months, weeks, days, hours, minutes and seconds before I flew out. When the plane landed, I walked out onto the tarmac into the warm dry air and made my way to the terminal. I was only waiting for about five minutes before she found me, but it seemed like an eternity. We gave each other a massive hug and a kiss on the cheek, even though we really wanted to run at each other, kiss passionately and hold each other forever. We sat up in the flat on the balcony, hand in hand, together again where we should be, as one. The two weeks flew by and after swimming, snorkelling, eating, and walking all around Cyprus, we had to say goodbye again. My heart, which had just started to heal, had being smashed into a million pieces again. We'd discussed that once Ju was back in the UK we'd sort out me trying to obtain a posting back to the UK. We'd work something out.

I returned to Northern Ireland and started trying to get back to my routine of fitness and work, just to get me through each day. A day closer to seeing Ju again. After about a week, I came back to my accommodation block, unlocked my door and went into my room. I stood still and was in shock. The place had been ransacked: all my clothes were thrown out of the wardrobe; my paperwork and any letters were gone. My CDs and videos were all strewn around the room. I later realised two of the CDs taken were Erasure and the Communards – obviously gay! They'd taken my briefcase with all my personal papers in, including paperwork for a house I was in the process of buying. I turned around and saw two MPs (Military Policeman) who marched me away for interrogation. An interrogation, not an interview.

I was taken to a room that had a desk in with an Anglepoise light on it. I was ordered 'Sit down, lesbian!' I'd no legal representation. Two men from the SIB shouted at me saying they knew I was in a 'sexual relationship with Private Currey,' And that I was a 'disgrace to Her Majesty's army.' They made lewd, disgusting sexual comments about our relationship, stating it was 'unnatural' and 'shameful'. They continued to ask me, 'Are you having a sexual relationship with Private Currey?! You're gay and were gay when you joined the forces.' I'd always answer 'No comment' to the questions and statements. I've no idea where this inner strength came from, but I was determined not to be broken. They then showed me blueys I'd just sent out to Ju and said they knew when I mentioned cuddling 'Tiger' (my family's cat at the time), they knew I meant Private Currey. I just kept saying 'No comment'. They then showed me blueys Ju had sent to me that I hadn't even seen yet. Again and again, I kept repeating 'No comment'. This really wound them up and they continued to interrogate me for hours. Eventually, late that night, I went back to my room, feeling like I'd been violated and raped. I'd no way of warning Ju but would try in my letter I wrote that night. MPs are also known as 'monkeys', so I mentioned that my brother Mike had been to Bristol Zoo and that he didn't like the monkeys. It was obvious, but what else could I do?

When I went to enter my normal place of work, I was stopped and told I'd been transferred to another department. This was actually much better for me. I was working with a great group of guys and a WO2 (Warrant Officer 2nd Class) who knew my work was of a high standard and they were glad to have me there. They didn't care if I'd been investigated for being gay, because I could do the job and do it well. I was, though, continually harassed, victimised and bullied by the RMPs. Blueys from Ju were withheld for weeks, some were MIA (missing in action), in other words, confiscated. I knew the same was happening to the blueys I'd sent Ju, but we were stronger than that. We knew they were still trying to break us and it was nearly working!

I'd been told I was being promoted to sergeant soon and that it was 'guaranteed'. Yet within a few hours of receiving it, it was taken away. Ju was also told she'd no longer receive her promotion and would remain a private forever.

One of the wonderful guys I worked with could see what was happening and how I was continually being treated either to force me out of the army or to get me to come out so he said 'Fu*k this, let's get married. That'll get them off your back. You can do what you want then.' He was serious, but I said no. I didn't want them ruining his life as well. Before Ju was posted to Cyprus, a corporal who worked with her and had warned her the sergeant was out to get her said 'Let's say we are having an affair'. He was married and would tell his wife why he wanted to do it, but, quite rightly, Ju said no to this. This just shows what people thought about the Gay Ban.

After six months of being deployed to Cyprus, Ju returned to the UK. She'd been back at work for a day when she was approached by two men in suits who marched her away in front of her colleagues for interrogation. She experienced the same barbaric treatment I had, again with no legal representation. The questions were asked again and again but she didn't break. They had all the blueys I'd sent her and highlighted certain sentences. After she returned from Cyprus, they continued to harass her and go through her belongings. After the interrogation, nobody trusted her. We were both now being hounded out of the army and careers we so loved. We were under pressure to do our jobs professionally, as well as the immense pressure of suspicion.

The harassment continued for both of us, and Ju called me from a phone box one night to say she just couldn't cope anymore and no longer wanted to continue our relationship. We were both in such a dark place. To me this was an act of courage in the most desperate of situations. We'd both now decided to leave the military before we were 'dishonourably discharged'. We'd been 'gay hunted' and our careers were as trashed and broken as our rooms had been after the RMP searches. What a waste of money spent training us. We were good soldiers, we loved our jobs and all we wanted to do was serve our queen and country, but that had all been taken away. It was an impossible situation.

I was a broken woman. I couldn't talk to anyone. Looking back, I had a nervous breakdown. It was 1993 and mental health was still seen as a weakness, and I was in a very dark place trying to function. We felt everything we'd fought for had been thrown on the fire and the ashes of our beautiful love couldn't be put back together. In all honesty, we never thought we'd see each other again.

When I came out of the forces, I couldn't explain that I'd been hounded out for being gay. Instead, I said I'd just decided to leave, but in my heart and soul I was devastated; I was an empty shell.

We were both on the reserve list and Ju was later called up to Bosnia, where she went. It was incredible to think they were happy to let her to go to a war zone because they needed her skills. She trained up again as a soldier and drove lorries for what was initially a six-month tour, but she extended it for another three months. She loved been a soldier again and it also made her think about me, but the years that followed were empty for us both.

Twenty years later, in January 2015, Ju discovered Facebook with the help of Jewels, her best friend from school. Jewels asked Ju if there was anybody she wanted to contact on Facebook. Ju quickly said Ruth Birch and so Jewels checked Facebook and brought up my profile. Ju recognised me straight away. She's not very IT savvy and so asked Jewels to send me a message to see if I was ok and whether I wanted to meet up for a coffee. I'd only recently joined Facebook and had no idea you could receive private messages – I guess I wasn't very IT savvy either! It was over three months before I read the message and my heart skipped a beat again. I typed back that I was currently on a reality TV show on Channel 4 called *Coach Trip*. Ju couldn't believe that not only had I messaged back, but that I was on the TV. We started to text each other once a week and then twice a week and then we started to speak to each other on the phone. We didn't want to rush anything. After all, it'd been a long time. After six months, I asked if she wanted to meet me in Porthcawl for a fireworks display. She agreed and I waited nervously by the ice cream parlours on the corner of Coney Beach. I saw her walking towards me down the promenade. I couldn't believe this was happening. We gave each other a massive cwtch (hug) and a kiss. I felt like twenty-two years had vanished and we were back together again, where we always should always have been.

We talked all evening and it was like we'd never been apart. We started meeting up more regularly and I'd spend weekends at her flat with the mad spaniels Sky and Holly. We had a lot to sort out, but nothing was ever going to stop us being together again. We set up home in Porthcawl in November that year and on Christmas Eve, Ju asked if we could go up the tower in St. John's church. I was the 'tower captain' of the bellringers at that time and had the keys. We got up early and walked our dogs on Newton Beach. It was windy, cold and raining and I couldn't understand why she wanted to go up the tower, but she was insistent, so up we went. When we got to the top, she went down on one knee. She couldn't get the ring box open but proposed and tried putting the ring on the wrong finger. I was ecstatic and said, 'Yes!' Two years later, we were married in a registry office and then received a blessing in St John's with our friends and family.

We can't believe we're back together and even now we say to each other, 'Did that really happen?' We just count our blessings every day. What happened in the past was so wrong. You could say that we lost over twenty-two years together and that it was the army that took it away from us, but it's no good to be consumed by such thoughts. We need to move forward. We look at each other and can't believe we're actually back together again. It's an absolute miracle and how it happened is just incredible. I wish love and light to everybody because there is hope. We march together.

Chapter 3

Navy Days

———————— Terry Newton Laheney ————————

It started when I was 4 years old. My brother, fourteen years my senior, had joined the Royal Navy. I remember how proud my parents were of him. It seemed every conversation was about him: where he had been, what he'd achieved, how smart he looked… It was then I knew that when I grew up, I'd join the Royal Navy.

In June 1979, HMS Raleigh loomed. Exciting times – I'd made it. Training seemed to be in the distant past when my draft arrived: HMS *Fearless* L10, a landing ship, and boy did she turn out to be just that.

I celebrated my 21st birthday in San Juan, Puerto Rico, where the temperature was over 100°F! If only my school mates could've seen me. Then, in a news flash, we were suddenly preparing for war. Really? We were heading to the Falklands.

It was hectic getting ready. Not preparing, because the Royal Navy is always prepared, but back in Pompey we had to store the ship, paratroopers, and marines. There were strange faces, weapons, electrical stores and even body bags. That was the day we were issued with dog tags. It was all becoming real.

Goodbyes were said and Portsmouth disappeared into the distance. It was a view so many of us were familiar with, although everything was surreal and it rained. Shortly after sailing, news arrived that HMS *Sheffield* had been hit by an Exocet missile. Our war, the Royal Navy's war, had begun.

Being part of a ship's company means everyone becomes one, brothers in arms. You live and breathe together. It is the glue that bonds us together and the element that makes us who we are. It's a special bond, to serve as a fighting unit.

At 03.42 on the morning of 21 May 1982 (D Day), we were anchored in position in San Carlos Water. At 06.30, 2 Para and 40 Commando were on the beaches. By midday, after being sighted by an Aermacchi, an 'aircraft warning red' screamed out and all hell let loose. From 12.50 to 19.00, we came under heavy air attack and life would never be the same.

The war is well-documented and nothing should divert our eyes and minds from the casualties on both sides and to those who failed to return, and who are forever in our memories. God bless the souls who gave their lives.

I was lucky. I returned unscathed and to a hero's welcome. The country celebrated as the Union Jack flew over the Falklands. My father told me he was proud of me, but this is not a mantle to distract from the truth for something that happened earlier in my story.

I was 19, fresh faced and fit when I met *him*. I can remember those feelings. Those special feelings. I didn't know it at the time, but I'd fallen in love with a senior, older guy. My head was spinning, my body shook with anticipation and all the time, eyes were watching. We stole moments, whispers and breaths.

And then I was drafted and so was he. Shortly after joining my ship, I was visited by SIB informing me he had been 'dealt with' and asked, how I knew him? What did we do?

I was scared, confused and alone, very much alone.

They asked if I wanted a coffee, before knocking it out of my hands. I thought the whole ship's company would hear it crash on the deck. They then informed me they were going to visit my father at work and inform him that I was a queer. It took everything I had to stop being physically sick. The absolute shame I would bring on my family.

Darkness surrounded me. They left and to my surprise, no one asked what it'd been about. Had I got away with it? Got away with WHAT? I was angry, but nature and events took their course and I continued with the job in hand.

Time passed and eventually I told my parents and informed my seniors… Big mistake. My mother, bless her, said, 'Tell an officer, they'll help you.' Big mistake. My life spiralled from that point on…

I was handcuffed.
I was kept in solitary.

I was kept in a civilian holding cell.

I was flown handcuffed on a civilian aircraft in the presence of holiday makers.

I was screamed at.

I was incarcerated.

I was spat at.

I was verbally abused.

I was physically abused.

I was myself.

Further abuse and belittling followed, but by then I'd become numb and almost oblivious. I left the Royal Navy.

Many, many times my father asked me where my medal was. At one point he questioned whether I was actually in the Falklands. Each time I could feel myself folding into my body, trying to hide in my skin, so I kept quiet.

My father passed away ten years ago. I loved him and it hurt.

And I kept quiet.

Chapter 4

Never At Sea

———————— Vito E. Ward ————————

My name is Vito E. Ward and I was born on 12 July 1943. As soon as I could, at the tender age of 17, I proudly joined the Women's Royal Naval Service on 24 January 1961. After nine years of exemplary service, on the day of my discharge, I had risen through the ranks to become a petty officer based at HMS President in Kensington.

On that fateful day in January 1970, I was called by the third officer to collect my hat and attend the commanding officer's table, which was conducted in the first officer's office. I had no clue what was to come until she read out the charge of homosexuality. To my shock and horror, I saw on her desk photocopies of letters in my handwriting. At that split second, perhaps reflecting the values I had learnt and kept in my life in the Royal Navy, I decided to not lie. I preferred to be a lesbian than a liar and I wasn't sure my letters were evidence, as I'd always been careful. Still in shock, I was told that homosexuality was against the Naval discipline act and that I'd be discharged. I was then marched out of the room before being asked by my third officer, 'who else was like me?'

This was the biggest drama I'd ever experienced in my life. My service record was exemplary and I was respected and liked by those who worked for and with me among my fellow senior ratings and by my seniors. I was fortunate that the petty officer regulator (service policewoman) was a friend of mine. She'd been informed, knew the drill, and helped me as much as she could in the bewildering circumstances I now faced.

I couldn't tell my parents. I'd hardly any experience of civilian life as I'd joined the service aged 17, straight from my family home. I had to find somewhere in London, but had no income. It was a desperate situation. Against my principles, I was forced to lie to colleagues to explain my leaving as they forbade me from declaring my sexual orientation. Nor could I contact my friends who, like me, may have watched what was happening and been implicated – it was a desperately, lonely time.

Within weeks, on 7 February, I was out. I'd no money and my pension rights were to be denied. If it hadn't been for my friend helping me, I don't know how I would've survived. I'd no idea of the job market and the only accommodation I could afford was a tiny bedsit.

To add insult to injury, my service record reviews always showed 97% efficiency and an overall grading of Excellent, while the discharge entry showed only 60% and average. This was to serve as my reference for work, too; annotations that could've made the future years all the more bleak. I was 27 years old and not without a bit of imagination, so I managed to get an officer to give me a good reference. I doctored my documents and got a live-in job as a housekeeper in a hotel. The role was way beneath my skill level, but with time and therapies I moved on and retired many years later as a social work trainer and psychotherapist.

The road to recovery from the shocking impact of dismissal was not without its bumps. In 1982, rocked by the death of my mother, I suffered a breakdown. I sought the help of counselling services, but not from a military charity; those organisations weren't for people like me. The kind and helpful counsellor I was allocated told me my bereavement had triggered trauma from the years before – what we might now call PTSD. The news came as no particular surprise. I'd lost the two things that mattered most in my life: my career and now my mother.

In 2024 I celebrated my 81st birthday and, as I write, my pension has still not been reinstated and compensation has not been forthcoming. If, when you read this, things have changed, please raise a glass and toast to 'justice'. It is my most sincere hope this will never happen to anyone else. A national pardon and apology have at least helped some of my veteran colleagues, but what was done can't be undone and sadly many of my wonderful fellow veterans have faced poor mental health and some have not survived.

Chapter 5

The Cavalry Eighteen
— Simon Wallington, Terry Skitmore, Kalvyn Friend —

[Simon]

'I want a word in your shell like.'

I suppressed a laugh. I've never heard that one before, I thought as the Special Investigation Branch (SIB) officer continued his bad cop routine.

From the get-go, thanks to this guy's attitude, I found it difficult to take the whole thing seriously. How wrong I was going to be.

'What do you want to know? I don't know what this is about.'

It's late summer 1975, at Hyde Park Barracks, London. I'd been told to go to this little office in the main block of the barracks but was given no more information than that.

Two men dressed in civilian clothing were waiting. As I entered the room, they both produced their identification cards. The bigger one of the two got up from his seat behind an empty desk and introduced himself and his colleague; the good cop, as it turned out. They both had briefcases which they proceeded to take A4 note pads from.

'Sit down,' Bad Cop instructed.

I still didn't have a clue what was going on. My mouth was dry and I could feel my anxiety levels rising. All I was thinking, concerned about, was, 'whatever this is about, how long is it going to take?' My wife and I had a married quarter in Penge, south London, and had just got our first dog, Susie. We hadn't had her long so I was concerned about her being on her own for too long as my wife was at work in east London so it was down to me to get home.

'Where do you drink?' Bad Cop asked.

'A pub at the bottom of our road in Penge. Why?'

'No, what I meant was, where do you drink close to here?'

I began to understand what he was getting at; my friend Skip had been interviewed by the SIB a couple of weeks ago and I remembered him telling me about the questions he'd faced. Right, let's have a bit of fun, I thought.

'Oh, close to here. I don't, I live in Penge.'

'Ok, let me rephrase the question,' he said, getting angrier by the second. 'Where you drank when you lived in the barracks.'

'Ah, understood. *The Paxton*'s, why do you ask?'

Good Cop looked up from the notes he was scribbling. 'Can you just answer the questions as clearly and precisely as you can?'

I was more confident now, the initial nerves having gone, and even though Bad Cop was trying to intimidate me, he wasn't going to win. How little did I know.

'When drinking in *The Paxton*'s did you talk to civilians?' asked Bad Cop.

'Yes, sometimes, why do you ask?'

'Just answer the question as it's put to you,' said Good Cop.

'Why did you talk to these civilians? Were they gay? Are you gay?' asked Bad Cop.

'I've just got married,' I said. 'Why shouldn't I talk to them? It's not against the law, is it?'

This form of questioning went on for another hour or so. I was getting as irritated as they were. If it sounded as if I was being impertinent, I was, because I was telling the truth. Some of the questions were unbelievable, such as, 'Is there a telephone line into the saddlers' workshop?' and 'Who's running the vice ring?' I didn't have a clue what they were on about.

I was six months into my marriage, happily living in south London, working hard for the Queen's Life Guards. My wife had a job she loved with Royal Mail, while my ambition was to be trained as a farrier, do my nine years, then leave and set up my own business.

'I expect you want to get home, don't you?' said Good Cop.

'Of course I do. I don't know why I'm here in the first place.'

'Well, sonny,' said Bad Cop, 'we've got other people to interview, will they be mentioning your name, because if they do, you'll be back in here faster than your bloody horses can carry you, understood?'

I confidently nodded at him, as confidently as I could anyway. I felt sick to the core. I'd never been in this sort of situation, never even been on a charge. Feeling relieved it was over, all that was on my mind was getting home. I can't remember signing anything, but I remember discussing it with Pam (my wife) later that evening.

It was nearly 17.00 when I walked out of the big metal gates onto Knightsbridge. Loosening my tie, I hurriedly made my way towards the tube station on the corner of Sloane Street. At this rate Pam would be home before me, so should I get the train or the bus? The number fifty-two was waiting at the traffic lights as I crossed. That'll do, I thought. The sign on the front said Crystal Palace: I'll get this one.

In my favourite spot at the front on the top deck, we travelled towards Chelsea and the river Thames, the evening sun hot on the side of my face. Rolling my ticket as tight as I could between my fingers, my thoughts turned to the last three hours. Where did they get their information from? All their accusations were untrue. Well, I thought they were untrue. I certainly knew nothing about them.

'Crystal Palace!' the conductor shouted. 'The bus terminates here. Off the bus, please, unless you want to go back to where you came from.'

I'd done it again; fallen asleep. Staggering to my feet, I made my way to the steep steps down from the top deck. It was nice to feel the breeze on my face as I stepped from the bus; a ten-minute walk and I'll be home, I thought as I started walking down the hill towards Anerley Park. As I walked towards the small block of flats where our married quarters were, I noticed my mate, Colin, who lived in the flat above us. He was standing outside the entrance smoking a cigarette. Being in the same regiment, most days we'd take the early morning walk to catch a train to Victoria station to be in work at 06.00.

'Hi mate, what's happening?' he asked as we met at the communal door that led to our respective flats.

'Hang on, I'm just going to get the dog so she can have a pee, then I'll tell you.'

When I got back downstairs, I walked Susie onto the grassed area in front of the building; she was desperate to go.

'I've just spent two hours being interviewed by the SIB,' I told him as he offered me a cigarette.

'Oh, they had me last week, I wouldn't worry about it. What did they ask? Did you go in *The Paxton*'s and all that?' he replied, in a reassuring manner, which, sort of, made me feel better.

'Yeah, all that stuff. They also said they had more to interview.'

'Like I said, don't worry about it. Are you in tomorrow?'

'Yep, see you at five, don't be late.'

After finishing our cigarettes, we went to our respective flats. Susie had behaved herself so there was no mess to clear up. A short time later, I heard the key turning in the lock; Pam was home.

'Had a good day?' she asked as she walked into the living room of the very 1940s flat. The Army furniture didn't help: a green vinyl three-piece suite and black and white television in the corner.

'Not really, bit of a strange one. I'll tell you when we go for a walk.'

'Ok, won't be a minute, I'll just get changed.'

Our evening walk took us through Crystal Palace Park. I had two important bits of news to tell but needed her full attention.

'Fancy a drink on the way back?'

'Ok, why not? You're quiet, what's up?'

'I'll tell you at the pub.'

It was a nice evening, so we sat outside. Sipping my drink, I could hear the Bay City Rollers blaring out of an upstairs window a couple of houses away.

'First thing, good news', I said.

'What's that?' Pam asked.

'There's a flat available in Peninsular Tower, in the barracks. If we want it we can move in at the end of the month.'

'That's great, can we go and look?'

'Yes, I'm trying to arrange it for this Saturday. Then I thought we could meet Terry and Quiff for a drink, if they're available, which leads me onto the next news.'

'Oh yeah, what's that?'

'I've spent two hours this afternoon being interviewed by the SIB'

'What's the SIB?'

'It's the Army's Special Investigation Branch.'

'What do they want with you?'

'Well, I'm being accused of being involved with running a homosexual vice ring in the barracks.'

'That's ridiculous! why are you being accused of that?'

'That's what I want to talk to Terry and Quiff about, see what they know. The SIB said there were a number of people involved, so I need to find out more.'

'Ok, we'll go up on Saturday, then. I can't believe this, come on let's go home.'

The next day, after watering order (morning exercise), I asked Terry what his interview was like.

'Well, the SIB came down to Whitehall, it was while I was on guard.'

'Tell you what,' I interrupted, 'shall we meet for a drink on Saturday? Pam and I are looking at a married quarter in the tower block.'

'That's good news. We'll go down *The Paxton*'s after. Come up and give me a knock.'

Terry lived with his wife in a flat in the tower block a couple of floors up from the one we were looking at. Sneaking into the canteen during breakfast without being seen (we weren't allowed in there as we lived out), I grabbed a coffee and sat in the corner with Quiff.

'Have you been interviewed by the SIB?' I asked.

'Yeah, a couple of weeks ago. They came up to my room, went through everything.'

'Do you fancy meeting up in *The Paxton*'s Saturday, early evening? Terry's coming down, we can try and work out what's going on.'

'Ok, I'll be there,' he said, as I exited quickly.

The flat in the tower block of Hyde Park barracks was great: modern, warm, a little bit too warm for my liking, but Pam loved it and that's all that mattered.

'I'll tell them we'll take it, then,' I said to Pam as we made the short walk to *The Paxton's Head*. It was busy, as it always was on a Saturday. There must've been twenty troopers, mostly Life Guards, in there, all in various stages of drunkenness. I spotted Terry sat in the corner, a pint of Guinness in front of him, although I couldn't see Quiff yet. After getting the drinks, I joined Pam and Terry, Susie having already settled herself safely under the table.

'So, fill us in then. How did your interview go?' I asked Terry. He told us what had happened.

[Terry]

I was 17 and a half when I joined the Army, innocent of worldly experience, never giving a thought to my sexuality. I'm not that tall, but I was fit; the training at the Guard's Depot held no fears for me and I embraced the challenge. I initially signed on for three years, wanting to make sure it was right for me. I soon settled in, completing my training with no problems. After passing out of the Guard's Depot, I was posted up here, to Knightsbridge, where, like all of us, I went through months of riding school, passing first time, no problem. Following three years' service with no negative accounts of my performance, along with many of my comrades I decide to leave, to go back home, to Wiltshire. After six weeks of civilian life, I was missing the regiment and my mates so much I asked if I could re-join. They accepted me back immediately and within two weeks I was back, back in my old troop. This was the second time the Army accepted me; I couldn't have been that bad, could I?

Jump forward to 1975, Simon and Kalvyn were 'uptown' now, ('uptown' was what Hyde Park Barracks was known as). I was on guard in Whitehall, a state trumpeter. I was lying on my bed reading a book when the guard commander called for me. Pulling my boots on and stretching as I stood up, I was curious what he might want. I descended the old wooden stairs and knocked on the large door of the guard office.

'You wanted me?' I asked the corporal of horse who was sitting at his desk, looking out over Whitehall.

'Yes, the SIB are here, they want to talk to you, they're in the room next door.'

As I stood at the door to the room, I had no idea what it could be about. I hadn't done anything wrong, nothing that came to mind anyway. On entering, two men were sitting at the old wood and metal table that had, it seemed, been placed in the middle of the room in front of them, with a chair on the other side.

'Sit down,' one of them ordered as he nodded towards the vacant chair.

As I sat, I was thinking, what can this be about? I was on my own, no representation, no warning. It was a pretty unnerving situation.

'What pub do you drink in?' the first one asked.

'*The Paxton's Head,*' I dutifully replied as I suddenly realised what this was all about.

'Why that pub?'

'Because it's the nearest pub to the barracks.' I'd decided by now not to play their game.

'Are you aware that the pub is frequented by homosexuals? Have you ever spoken to any of them? Are you one?'

'One what?' I asked.

'A queer, a poof. You know what we mean,' the second one now said.

'No, I'm married, happily married. I live in the married quarters.'

'With these civilians at the pub, do you or have you ever been invited to parties? Have you ever had sex with a man?' the first one asked.

The questions were coming think and fast; he was being quite aggressive and threatening. I remained calm and continued to answer in the negative, and after about two hours, they left. I was left in that office, alone, shaken and wondering what the hell it was all about. I remember thinking, my sex life is my own business and no one, not even my comrades, ever questioned my sexuality, so why should they? I kept thinking, if I've done anything wrong, why am I not being charged or even accused?

On the day I was dismissed (services no longer required) my experience was exactly the same as Simon's and Quiff's: marched in, sign here, goodbye! My 'red book' read the same as well: 'He has found it difficult to adjust to military life, more suited to civilian life.'

All was lost: job, career, plans, friends, home, pension. I would've died for Britain, if necessary, but all they were concerned with was who you may or may not have slept with.

[Simon]

Quiff had joined us now. We'd first met when we joined the Junior Guardsmen's Wing at Pirbright in 1972. Our career path was very similar; both junior non-commissioned officers, both looking forward to our future in the military.

[Kalvyn]

I was in my room on the fourth floor of Hyde Park Barracks when, this is going to sound familiar, two SIB people came in. They searched all my lockers and personal belongings.

'What are you looking for, maybe I can help?' I asked.

'Evidence, evidence of homosexual activity.'

One of them had found my address book and was flicking through it.

'This name rings a bell,' one of them said to his colleague.

'How do you know George Harvey?' he said, directing his gaze in my direction.

'I've played squash with him. I've also been out with his daughter a couple of times. Why, what's wrong with that?'

'Why don't you let us be the judge of that?' the younger one said as he continued scrutinising my personal belongings.

Like you two, they were in my room for about two hours, arrogant twats, left me to clean up and put everything away. Whatever they were looking for they didn't find it. It wasn't a great experience, though, two of them, me on my own. I don't mind telling you, I was quietly shitting myself.

[Simon]

We continued talking for another hour or so, in the end we all concluded that it was probably nothing and that we'd do a bit more snooping, see who else had been interviewed. I knew Colin had, but that was all. As Pam and I left, the pub was filling up. It was early evening. Most of the customers were cavalry, senior NCOs downwards. This wasn't unusual; it was the local pub, exactly what we'd told the SIB.

Months passed and everything appeared normal. Pam and I were living in our flat in the barracks. On Friday 27 January 1976, a bright, sunny afternoon, Terry and I were sweeping up at the entrance to Three Troop. The horses were restless, waiting for their last feed of the day. A long row of hay nets sat in a row along the length of the room. It was a busy scene, echoed across all Three Troop rooms. All the troopers were dressed the same: green work trousers, shirt, topped with a heavy-duty jumper and a red and blue stable belt. I could hear the telephone ringing in the tack room on the other side of the long corridor connecting the troop rooms. A couple of minutes later, our troop corporal of horse emerged from the tack room signalling towards Terry and I.

'You two, you're required up on the parade square. Get your caps and get up there.'

As you do, we did as we were ordered, and as we walked along the freshly swept corridor, the afternoon sun was flooding down the ramp towards us. I noticed other soldiers coming out of their troop rooms and joining the growing precession. Up on the square, a line of green and Khaki formed a line facing towards the row of offices that sat below the other ranks' living quarters. Looking around, I spotted Quiff a little further down the line.

'What do you think this is all about?' I asked Terry.

Before he could answer, the squadron corporal major marched across from the direction of the colonel's office. Everyone, automatically it seemed, came to attention and the muted conversations stopped.

'Right, you lot,' he started, 'you'll be in front of the colonel this afternoon, one at a time, starting on my left.'

I glanced to my right; I was forth in the line. I still didn't have a clue what was going on. Butterflies were churning in my stomach as I wracked my brain as to what it could be. The first of what I later discovered were eighteen of us were marched in. It was Colin, who still lived in Penge, who had just had his first child with his wife. One by one the three in front of me were marched in, then it was my turn. Two NCOs screamed orders in my ear until I was in the office and stood to attention in front of the colonel's desk. He was sat behind it, and behind him were five other officers forming a semi-circle. On the desk in front of him was an A4 sheet of paper. I noticed as this grand entrance was going on that he didn't look up, but just kept staring at the piece of paper. After standing there for what seemed ages, he eventually looked up, straight in my eye, a look of pure distain etched across his face. I was still none the wiser as to what was going on, until he spun the paper round to face me and simply said, 'Sign this, your service is no longer required, either in this regiment or the Army. Your last day is today, there's no need to return to duties.' No charge, no explanation, and no opportunity to defend myself. I couldn't focus on the piece of paper. I just stared at it; it was if the world had stopped.

One of NCOs lent in and whispered in my ear, 'Sign it, son, you're dismissed.'

I couldn't talk and was finding it difficult to breath. After being marched out, I turned left towards the riding school, leaving the remaining fifteen men to their fate. On the parade square I saw Terry and Colin, who, like me, were in shock. We were all young men; Colin, Quiff and I were 18 and Terry was 22, but we were now jobless and soon to be homeless. All I could think was, how am I going to tell my wife, my family, my friends? And so there began a lifetime of having to live a lie, not because I wanted to, but because the Army put me into a situation where I had to. The shame was immense.

Later that day we all sat in a very busy *Paxton's Head*. Still confused, Terry concluded that all of this must've been linked to the earlier interviews with the SIB. As he talked, I looked around the pub; lots of strange faces were milling around asking complete strangers questions – it was the press. We decided to go somewhere else, none of us were in the mood.

The next day their presence was confirmed when the national papers ran a story about gay soldiers running a 'vice ring' in Hyde Park Barracks. This, as everyone knew, was the biggest load of nonsense ever written. If it was true, why weren't we charged and court martialled? As the papers ran their stories to increase sales, we were all faced with the problem of how we were going to explain to family and friends why our military career had come to an end. In the case of Quiff and I, both our fathers died not knowing the truth.

To add insult to injury our 'Red Books' (discharge books), read that our conduct had been very good and that we, 'without doubt had ability but were more suited to civilian life'. This is an Army that had signed Terry up twice and had allowed Quiff and I to serve since we were 15 and a half. In fact, Quiff had just signed on for a further six years at the Army's request.

Eighteen men's lives were ruined that day. The British Army lost good men, potential leaders and a lot of talent. The three of us have remained friends over the past forty-eight years, and all three of us are curious as to what happened to the other fifteen. We wish them well.

Chapter 6

(Un) Friendly Fire

Sarah Sloane

'Sloane. Get yer arse over 'ere!'

The drill sergeant shouted loud enough to be heard two football pitches away, let alone the two paces he was standing away from my ear. But I'd been warned of the 'tough time at basic' by my father, who had done his National Service in the 1950s. He also said I wouldn't like the army as I didn't respond well to discipline. But here I was nearing pass out. I just jumped the 2 inches to the right as required.

As I boarded the civilian plane to my first posting, I had mixed feelings about doing the trip solo. No comrades to have a laugh and a joke with, no one for support. It was almost as though I was part of a secret army that wore civilian clothes, although the regulation two black suitcases would be a dead giveaway. As the plane descended and blue skies gave way to grey and rain, I got my first glimpse of the industrial city of the 'North Rhine-Westphalia', bleak and wet just like I'd left it in England. But that didn't matter, I was on the adventure of a lifetime, and who knew what lay ahead?

The barracks were located right next to the airport, so I soon found my way to my new home. It was nearing the weekend and the camp had a quiet air about it. I'd been allocated my own room in the main building, with ample space and wardrobes and a shared bathroom across the hall. For a moment the anxiety came back like a wave washing me up the shore against my will. But these worries started to disappear as soon as I saw my uniform laid out on my bed. It had survived the journey fairly well and would only need a tweak with the iron. The rest of my kit was in a large wooden crate that had already been delivered to the camp ahead of me and would be brought to my room once I'd been to the stores and signed for it. For now, I had the weekend to settle in and familiarise myself with the barracks and maybe even meet some of my new colleagues in the corporals' mess.

Although recently turned 19, I'd not lived away from home before and the six weeks' basic training at Guildford with 200 other women had been a shock to the system. But I soon learned to fit in, although I'd had a few close calls with the training corporal as I tended to answer questions literally. For example, when, on finding dust on top of my wardrobe the corporal barked, 'What's this, Sloane?!' My reply of, 'Dust, Corporal', had not gone down well and I thought I'd be up on a subordination charge. However, the corporal let it go, this once. I really hoped I wasn't going to rub others up the wrong way on my first posting and was keen to make a good impression.

My trade training at RMPTC (the Royal Military Police Training Centre) in Chichester had been six months' long, where, along with the gruelling physical routine, I'd also learned interview techniques, note taking, military law and above all, the corps' motto: *Exemplo Ducemus* (Lead by Example). I'd joined the military police as my grades were good enough and I had a strong sense of justice. However, it wouldn't be long until I realised that not everyone upheld the corps' motto and values.

There *were* things that irked me about joining a 'men's' army, which I found out after signing up. For one, it appeared that the Equalities Act of 1975 didn't apply, and I was often told, 'You can't do that. You're a woman!' For instance, when I requested to learn to ride a motorbike as I'd already passed my car driving test before joining, they refused, saying 'Women don't have the aptitude.' I was later to prove them wrong, but only after leaving.

Likewise, I soon found out that women were paid £2,000 a year less than their male counterparts of the same rank at their first posting. When I questioned this, I was told it was because of the 'X factor', i.e., the guys were expected to be on the front line and shoot and be shot at. However, they still taught weapons training at RMPTC to all the WRAC provost personnel and on my first posting I was expected to carry a side arm, which I presumed I'd have to use if I was shot at.

My first weekend was a blur. I was forcibly dragged out by the WRAC provost sergeant who said I HAD to go out with the girls on a night out at the weekend. At first, I just wanted to fit in and be one of the gang but after many large glasses of strong German beer and then countless shots of even stronger spirit, I knew that drinking games weren't my thing. I tried to keep up as they went from bar to bar and didn't remember getting back to my billet. Only the room spinning and having to run to the bathroom to be sick over and over in the night; I felt like I was going to die. No one came to look out for me, I just had to clear up the mess and hope that by Monday morning I was able to stand upright.

Thankfully, it was a training day on the Monday and it was fatigues and just jimmying around with safety drills and reading. I don't know how I managed to get through the day and was glad to crash into my bed with another training day ahead. (We were on a rota of four days, four nights, two days off then two nine to five training days and then starting all over again.) Being an emergency service, we also worked 24/7, unlike some of the other trades who had a regular nine to five (when not on active duty). There was precious little actual time off except pre-booked leave, but I still managed to fit in some sightseeing; usually on my own, as my colleagues were either too busy or asleep.

My first formal parade in No. 2 dress (the next best uniform down from ceremonial No. 1 dress) was with one other WRAC provost and nine male colleagues. The platoon commander was a moustachioed, gruff staff sergeant who made it clear he didn't like women on the team, and that WRAC stood for 'Weekly Ration of Army C*nt'; not the Women's Royal Army Corps that I was proud to be a part of. I'd pressed my No. 2 dress (a very easily creased material that was a lovat green skirt and jacket) to its best, exactly as done to training camp standards, but it wasn't good enough for my new line manager.

'What the f*ck are those, Sloane?' as he pointed to my chest. 'F*cking mammaries on my parade?' None of the line up let out a sound as he berated and verbally attacked me.

The staff sergeant became predictable in his attempts to bully me whenever the opportunity arose, and I was glad to get out on patrol and away from him once the daily parade was over. My colleagues were either fearful of him and/or they were just looking out for themselves. No one backed me up whenever he lurched forward and dressed me down with a torrent of abuse.

I wasn't very worldly wise and was still inexperienced at dating and matters of sex. Most of my colleagues found it fun to have a private bet that whoever got to bed me first would be rewarded with a crate of Grolsch. Each week that passed and I remained intact, it'd go up by another crate. I was grateful when another provost girl came from depot and they focused on her instead. I'd nearly reached the camp record of six crates of Grolsch and four litres of whisky. I even fleetingly thought to try to persuade a male colleague to say he'd 'done the deed' and split the proceeds, but after the alcohol-fuelled arrival, I didn't want to see another drink for a long while to come!

I tried to keep a thick skin as my father had told me to do, but the staff sergeant's insistence that my breasts were distracting him on daily parade and comments about the suspenders showing through my skirt were degrading. It took me some time to realise he was interested in conquering me where my colleagues had failed. He was a married man and in a position of authority, but this didn't seem to mean anything to such a predatory guy. Queen's Regulations stated that 'relations between higher or lower ranks' were strictly forbidden, but this didn't seem to deter him. I was learning, sadly, that there was culture of turning a blind eye to sexual harassment.

Now out of training, I went straight to the NAAFI and ditched the standard issue suspender belt and stockings for all-in-one nylons and I hoped this would keep the staff sergeant at bay. Yet he seemed hellbent on conquering me for some unknown reason. If it wasn't my uniform, it was my hair or the smell of my soap that day. Again, I couldn't fathom what his problem was and tried to keep away from him as much as I could.

When I signed up, I'd never been told that homosexuality in the forces was a no-no. It wasn't even covered in training. So, it came as a shock to me to find out one night shift when myself and the other provost girls were called down to Joint Head Quarters (JHQ) to go on a midnight raid. These were the infamous 'witch hunts' that I was beginning to learn about. We were quickly briefed by the SIB (Special Investigations Branch) sergeant that we were to go through every drawer, locker and space in the four-man rooms occupied by the WRAC. We were looking for photos, letters from one woman to another, anything that could be used as 'evidence'. I was taken aback. Even though I'd never really thought about same sex couples, I'd no objection to it and actually wondered if I wasn't that straight after all, as I'd rebuffed every approach by every male colleague to date. I believed no one should be persecuted for their choice of partner, but I knew I had to keep this quiet.

The room I was allocated to search yielded up plenty of photos and letters as briefed, but instead of bagging things up, I put the 'evidence' on the bed in front of the shaking victim and told the whole room to 'make it disappear before the sergeant comes back in'. On returning with the SIB sergeant, he questioned me in front of the victims and was surprised I'd found nothing I kept a poker face and told him, 'Nothing here, Sergeant.' I had no idea where the evidence had gone, but it had likely gone out the window. I didn't have any further encounters with the SIB until I was in Northern Ireland, where these raids were a common occurrence. It was said the SIB did it when they had no murders to solve or nothing better to do, and having a high number of WRAC such as at JHQ in Germany, it was easy prey.

Like all the other WRAC I had signed up for twenty-two years' service, but I knew I wouldn't last another month with this constant barrage of puerile nonsense and constant wearing down by my platoon commander.

I felt I had no option but to put in a formal letter of request to see the officer commanding (OC) of the unit. I was then put through the mill and denied my right for some weeks, being harassed by the regimental sergeant major, (RSM) who would march me into his office daily, shout at me that I didn't want to see the OC and send me out again. This continued Monday to Friday (for he only worked weekdays, office hours,) for over a month. It wasn't until a kindly older captain (who'd worked his way up the ranks) asked me what was going on. I told him the truth and the next week I was in front of the OC. However, I might as well not have bothered as he was weak and insipid and would take no action when I voiced my complaint.

I even sought a second opinion and requested an interview with the visiting WRAC provost officer from the UK who did a tour of Germany once a year to visit any provost woman who wanted to see her. She was as useless and unsympathetic as my unit OC. She just got mad with me and said, 'Oh, you girls are always thinking of yourselves and not the service!' I asked her what she meant and she implied I had to 'Lay back and think of Britain'. Sadly, this was the final nail in the coffin.

Being on a notice engagement, I would have to wait until I'd done eighteen months' full service, then had to give eighteen months' notice to leave. I marked in my diary the date to make the first step and requested another meeting with the OC to start the process. The day came around and the weak arse didn't want to deal with me, so it was down to the second in command (2IC), who was the friendly captain. At least I was spared having to deal with the idiot OC again.

Once the papers had been submitted to Manning and Records, where all admin was kept in the UK, I then just had to sit it out until I was posted away from this crazy situation. In the meantime, the staff sergeant continued his nasty comments and would harass me at any turn. I wondered if I would go mad!

My nights became restless and I'd feel like death warmed up on parade. I was glad when I read in daily orders that I was to be taken off general police duties for two months and run the corporals' mess bar. At least I'd be away from HIM, as anyone above the rank of full corporal had their own mess bar and wasn't allowed in ours unless by strict invitation. I enjoyed working in the bar, although the late nights were a bit of a drag, as I had to stay until the last person left. There was also all the cleaning, food prep, ordering and going to collect drinks stock from the NAAFI. But truly, it was better than being with the man who was making my life hell. Oddly, my colleagues who'd tried to seduce me before behaved well, and although the language was as blue as a navvy's on some occasions, they at least became more relaxed when off duty and knowing the staff sergeant wasn't around.

There was one occasion when the staff sergeant was in our mess, along with the other sergeants, staff sergeants and warrant officers, as there'd been a regimental dinner and the higher ranks were invited in. But this did not bode well for me either as the RSM decided to verbally attack me in front of all my colleagues. He said I needed a 'good seeing to' and this would solve all my and their problems. His tone of voice was the same sneering rebukes he'd shouted at me before in his office, when he tried to get me to withdraw my request to see the OC. He was just as bad as the platoon commander and I was counting the days until I would walk out the front gate and not be under the thumb of these nasty bastards.

Whilst working in the bar I heard that the staff sergeant was to be posted to Northern Ireland. I never found out whether it was a result of my complaint, but either way I was glad. Even though I was on 'other duties', he insisted the whole platoon have a goodbye drink with him and he organised an informal get together, but one we had no possibility to refuse as it was at the end of his last day with us. He provided the crates of beer, from which each of us reluctantly took a bottle. You could cut the atmosphere with a knife. No one wanted to be there, we just wanted him gone and hoped his replacement would be a better boss.

However, the staff sergeant started to get very drunk. He took me outside the room away from the others and walked me up and down the underground corridor leaning on me, with his arm over my shoulders. He said to me in his slurred beery tones, 'Why don't you like me, Sloane?' I replied curtly and truthfully, 'Because you're a dick, Staff.' We reached the end of the corridor and he suddenly turned and pinned me up against the brick wall and stuck his tongue in my mouth. I pushed him away and saw that he had an erection. I was in shock but knew well enough to lay a finger on him would mean serious consequences for me. We returned to the training room and he carried on as though nothing had happened. I was glad when, a few moments later, he dismissed us and I made my escape. I speed walked all the way to my home off camp and hoped I'd never see or hear from the man again.

Life in Northern Ireland was not too bad. At least it was away from my abuser, although the rules and regulations were a bit odd at times. As a woman soldier, in Northern Ireland there was an unwritten protocol with the IRA (Irish Republican Army) that they would not (knowingly?) shoot a woman in the services, as they knew she was unarmed. A flak jacket and 12-inch baton were all that was issued. I wondered how the IRA would know a uniformed soldier was a woman from a distance, especially if dressed in fatigues or combats (trousers rather than the skirt uniform). Whereas barrack dress (skirt, shirt and jumper) on patrol in the streets of Belfast was a little easier to spot? Generally, this was the dress of the day in the towns and cities, but often we'd go out on patrol in smaller towns and rural locations in trousers. It all felt a bit like Russian roulette on some patrols.

There was a rule that intelligence would know if there was likely to be a flare up in a particular location, so the WRAC wouldn't be deployed that day if it was thought there'd be any 'trouble'. However, this wasn't foolproof!

On one occasion, when the intelligence was wrong, I had to bolt for the back of the 'pig' (armoured vehicle) I'd alighted from, as an angry mob gathered where we were doing a house search with the UDR (Ulster Defence Regiment). I dodged the petrol bombs and bricks (some being thrown by kids as young as 6), but my 'colleagues' from the UDR were quick to save their own skins and the vehicle I'd come in was already shut. I looked round desperately for another but one by one they shut the back doors of their armoured Land Rovers. I just about made it into one before they shut the doors. I wondered what kind of men these were, who were themselves armed, but appeared to ignore my need to get onboard. Perhaps the kindest explanation is that the UDR men were dis-organised and not as efficient as the British Army.

Unusually, in Northern Ireland the provost girls were housed with the non-provost girls. Normally we were kept very separate as the RMP were hated by most of the army, just as the civil police are treated with suspicion by some people in civvy street. But here it was a bit more relaxed, and I enjoyed sports and being in mixed girls' teams for rounders. There was also an athletics team and I got to do the physical activities I excelled at. However, the 'green hats' and 'red hats' weren't actively encouraged to mix socially, despite working quite closely together.

Whilst waiting out my last eighteen months' service in Northern Ireland, I'd hooked up with an old school friend who was now at university in London and training to be a lawyer. I arranged a long weekend's leave in London and my friend took me to my first ever gay bar, where I was spotted by some of the green hats from our base in Northern Ireland. Some of them recognised me as a provost even though we were all in civilian clothes. They wrongly assumed I was on covert, plain clothes duties and ran from the bar, but one brave WRAC woman remained. Whilst I'd loved my day-to-day job in the Army and had felt I'd like to stay the full term, the encounter in Germany had shaken my belief and I felt betrayed by the 'system'. So, I didn't think too much about breaking the rules and having an intimate liaison with the green hat who'd been brave enough to stay when her 'mates' had fled the scene.

On our return to Lisburn, there was another 'witch hunt' kicking off and the SIB seemed determined to hunt down and throw out as many lesbian WRAC as they possibly could. I was ordered again to attend to assist the SIB and had to sit in on the long, tortuous 'interviews' with the accused WRAC. The methods employed by the SIB were nothing short of medieval: barbaric, inhumane, callous, threatening, demeaning and truly 'witch hunts' in every sense of the word. All because a woman loved someone of the same sex.

The warrant officer (WO) leading the interviews was a particularly vindictive and spiteful man, who I later found out was not well liked by his colleagues. After a week of interviews, the WO called me into his office, alone. I decided I was prepared to lie if asked a direct question, so, when he said to me, 'Your name isn't going to come up in this is it?' I did my poker face again and said, 'No, Sir.'

I'd briefed the one person I trusted, the WRAC woman with whom I had spent the night in London, to tell everyone who was dragged in to say nothing and admit to nothing as it was their 'confession' that was the only evidence in a case against them. Even with photos, letters and other 'incriminating' items, it was only the WO's word against theirs. Unfortunately, one woman caved in and named everyone she'd seen at the gay bar in London, including me. Sadly, it was a common technique with the SIB to say, 'Give us some names and we will go easy on you.' Many fell for it, but usually they also found themselves on the street with no more career.

I was soon pulled off duties, off the case, off my promotions course and confined to my accommodation. I was escorted to and from meals by a colleague who'd come to collect me. Everyone had been briefed to have no interaction with me whatsoever. Once in the dining hall, I was sat on my own, watched from across the room and returned in the same style after I'd finished my meal. I felt like a pariah. I knew a few were sympathetic, but the company commander ruled with an iron fist and it seemed no one dared be associated with me or outwardly express their support.

My own room was searched, but there were no letters or 'incriminating evidence'. Although my copy of the feminist magazine *Spare Rib* (I still have the copy today of that featured, anonymously, one of our own Fighting With Pride WRAC) was confiscated (but later returned). Oddly, no one commented on this, even though there was a two-page spread about women such as me being thrown out of the army.

When the actual interview day came, I was in a room alone with the WO again. I sat opposite him and tried to keep my cool. My only aim was to get through the experience as quickly as I could and hope I'd soon be on my way to civvy street. Although I still had another eight months to serve of my eighteen months' notice, I was ready to leave at the drop of a hat. But I wasn't going to give the WO or anyone else the satisfaction of knowing this.

I sat through the most embarrassing forty minutes of my life to date, listening to the prepared statement the WO had written before my arrival. He then asked me to read it out loud as he'd done with other suspects. As I did so, I wondered about the satisfaction he seemed to get from listening, day in day out, to young women read out the details of their sexual activities. I'd cringed when I was in the witness chair the week before and felt any intimate sexual act was a private matter for those involved. Yet here was this guy who seemed to be getting off on this stuff.

After reading out the statement, I duly signed it and hoped that was it. I was escorted back to my accommodation and I waited for a decision.

A week passed and no news. I was just into my second week of waiting when I was ordered back to the SIB WO, but this time I was to be accompanied by my WRAC provost captain, whom I greatly respected. Although I already knew she'd have no say in the proceedings, I was curious as to why she was there this time around.

Once in the WO's office, Captain H sat just behind me, and I had to go through the whole process again of reading out loud the sexual acts I'd 'committed' and to sign the statement all over again. I was perplexed but did it as I wanted a get-out-of-jail-free card ASAP. I handed the three-page statement over to the WO, who snatched it out of my hand, placed it in a drawer in his desk and locked it tightly, pulling at it to make sure it was secure then placing the key inside his jacket. His face was like thunder. Me being me, I couldn't help but ask, 'Why did I have to sign this all over again, Sir?' The WO became apoplectic, and spat out, 'I don't know who you know, but the first one went missing!' I laughed inwardly and took my leave. I thanked the captain for being there as a witness, but felt truly embarrassed, as much as she probably did. I looked up to and respected her and she had always been fair with her command, although sadly she had little to do with our day-to-day work but was there mainly as a figurehead. She and I had played doubles tennis on occasion, and she knew the pain I was in. We'd discussed, very briefly, in the past about gay women in the army and I knew it wasn't an issue for her, but she had to be seen to be upholding the rules. We shook hands and went our separate ways.

A week later the decision was made and I was finally given my marching orders and a plane ticket back to the UK. Initially to a holding centre where 'bad apples' were sent and where I completed the formal paperwork for my discharge. I then took the train straight home to my father. I didn't tell him what'd happened and why I'd left early, but he did know I'd put in my notice to leave. He was the old-fashioned Victorian type and personal matters weren't usually expressed out loud or discussed, so I didn't have to go into the details.

I was finally able to obtain the scant records of my service that remained, thirty years later. I was glad that under 'reason for discharge' my 'red book', or army discharge record it just said, 'QR 1975 para 9.414: Services no longer required' rather than 'sexual aberration'. I was angry that the (male) OC of my unit had downgraded my conduct from 'exemplary' as it had said on my temporary discharge paper to 'very good'. This was a discretional change by the OC and the OC only. However, I knew I wasn't the only one to have been downgraded in this way. (I'm fighting to get this changed with the written apology and other reparations that are due 2024/25.)

I remember the last words my father said to me as he put me on the train for Guildford forty years ago: 'If it doesn't kill you, it will make you stronger.'

Dedicated to all those who died before their time at the hands of their own government. And in memory of Gunner Jaysley Beck, a 19-year-old soldier who took her own life as recently as 2021. An investigation took place after sexual assault by a warrant officer and sexual harassment by her boss led to this fatal action. No one was there to keep her safe.

Notes/postscript

To this day there are no records of my regimental records, the assault I reported or any evidence of my being interviewed and dismissed for 'sexual aberrations'. The only thing that remains is this latter charge on the SIB computer system against me, with my name, rank and number. I have a letter, as others do from the MOD, that in 2010 The Police Defence Committee decided to 'protect' those who'd been dismissed for being homosexual, and that the ban had been lifted in 2000 and that records were destroyed 'for their benefit'. Of course, this was just another way of preventing the outside world from really knowing what had/not been reported. I've recently found out, by a further direct SAR (Subject Access Request) that ALL my regimental records were destroyed, not just those relating to the 'offence' of being gay, but everything written about me during my service with the RMP.

I was discharged/Services No Longer Required in 1985. It would be another fifteen years before the 'ban' was lifted and gay personnel were able to openly serve.

Chapter 7

Pride and Queens

Tremaine A.O. Cornish

It was in late 1970 when I visited the recruitment office in Bristol, seeking to join the Army. I would've been just 15 years old. After the conversation about options and a medical, I was sent for further medical checks to a military hospital in Wiltshire due to numerous operations I'd had as a boy. I formally enlisted on 9 September 1971, aged just 15¾. I was granted four days' unpaid leave and given a day's pay for the sum of £1.44, plus a travel allowance of 33p and a further refund of fares of 40p, amounting to a grand total of £2.17. Oh, and I was also given the Queen's shilling for signing on, along with a travel warrant to get me to my training depot.

The goodbye from my parents was formal and cold; I'm sure they were pleased to be shot of me. The last of us had flown the nest. We all escaped as soon as we possibly could. For my part, I was pleased to be away from them, to find a family the recruiting sergeant promised and one I so dearly wanted, needed and desired; one that appreciated, encouraged and nurtured me.

I'd signed up for six years' regular service and six in the reserves, to formally commence on my 18th birthday in 1973. So, including 'boy's service', I'd pledged a little over fourteen years of my life, which would've taken me to 1985, but as my career progressed, I know I would have signed for a full career.

On 14 September 1971, off I went with a little bit of pride on becoming a soldier in the Army. My new home was to be the Junior Leaders College, Blackdown Barracks, Deepcut, Surrey – my new family. Arriving at the train station I, along with several other young lads, was herded onto a bus, and transported a short distance to what was to be our new home, where we were assigned to our respective platoons. I was in Cutforth, in B Company, with Corporal A.D. McIntyre as our instructor and Lieutenant A.D. Bentley as our platoon commander. We were shown how everything was to be done. Once we were issued our uniforms, for the first weeks, no civilian clothes were to be worn, not that we had much time to relax as just about every minute was accounted for. Military training and education proceeded at a pace. I remember doing particularly well in nuclear, biological and chemical warfare, military law and maths, as well as a number of sports such as orienteering, trampolining and judo, so much so that at the end of the year I was awarded a silver cup for perseverance.

In October 1972 I finally took the short trip across the county border to Aldershot, Hampshire, where I joined a handful of others who transferred to the Army Catering Corps (ACC) at St Omer Barracks. Shortly after, we commenced trade training. It should be said that my end of term reports generally read 'good but away doing ...' which was usually yet another outdoor activity, be it Ten Tors (which I did in 1973 and 1974), training for the Nijmegen Marches, or the Welsh 3,000 in June 1973, when I lacerated my knee yet still had to walk the 6 miles to a vehicle to get me to A&E, or the Outward Bound mountaineering course in Eskdale in March 1974.

On 15 January 1973, I signed to change my contract of engagement on reaching my 18th birthday to serve for nine years, with three in the reserves, with the option of serving the full twenty-two years. I had every intention of serving the maximum, so much was I enjoying my time in the Army; I had found what I thought was my forever family.

Life in junior service wasn't only spent doing adventure sports, however. From log runs before breakfast, to cleaning before bedtime, our time was fully occupied and somehow the all-important trade training and education was squeezed in as well. Whilst there I took part in the Hotel Olympia Catering Competition, where in a number of sections, the overriding question wasn't who was going to win, but who in the Army was going to win, such was the prestige of the ACC in the catering world.

Trade training took place in the infamous tower block, with each floor having six kitchens. Those under training each had a workstation, with the instructor's work station at the front. One instructor who particularly stands out when I think about this journey is Bill Jenner, a former WO1 who would regularly recite the following ditty in class:

My pride and joy is an ACC boy,
with a bum like a cushion on springs.

Recently, I've been reliably informed that even six years later, he was still inviting selected apprentices to his home for special instruction. I was never invited, thankfully. We were 16- and 17-year-old lads, children in the eyes of the law, and the Army was acting 'in loco parentis', but it clearly failed in its duty of care.

Shortly before the passing out parade in August 1974, we were issued our trade badges to be sewn onto our uniforms, having each passed our city and guilds' trade exams. After this, Field Marshal Sir Michael Carver, who'd taken the salute, awarded me with a silver cup in the awards ceremony for 'Outdoor Activities'. Even though my parents were in attendance, they made no comment about this achievement, but I felt some pride for it.

Earlier in the term we'd each been asked where we'd like to be posted for our first unit. I recall asking for Singapore, Germany or Belize, so I was informed that I was off to RAOC Bicester in Oxfordshire. Shortly after arriving there, I received a letter from our catering science tutor at the college, informing me of my exam results. I had gained a First, with 89%, and was the top in the country by a clear ten points. I was overjoyed, and not a little chuffed! Over the Christmas period, most of our time was spent preparing one grand buffet after another, sometimes three a day, as well as feeding the troops their regular meals. It was incessant but rewarding.

In the November, I'd been informed that I'd been selected for the four-week pre-commando course, to start in January. Whilst in juniors, a corporal who was on advanced training at St Omer gave a presentation about chefs in the commando forces and although it hadn't been on my radar, it sounded right up my street. Accordingly, when we were informed of our first posting, and others had received overseas postings, I'd been a little dejected, but now I needed to get fit and ready – and pronto! I was passed fit for the course on 2 January, so off I went to Plymouth. The entrance to the Royal Citadel, home of 29 Commando Regiment, Royal

Artillery, which'd been standing for some 300 years, was and is imposing. So, I, along with some thirty or so others, entered to begin the intensely gruelling selection course. Many withdrew, others failed, I passed.

After this came the Commando Training Centre Royal Marines (CTCRM) in Lympstone near Exeter, Devon, to commence the all-arms commando course. What had we let ourselves in for? Thirteen weeks of intense training and testing, from which at least 50% are generally expected to drop out or be dismissed before completion. It's designed as a test of fitness, but also of character, not to mention a test of courage, agility and the determination of the candidates. Including speed marching, endurance courses and more, it tests the fortitude of the person to the limit, who must be cheerful in the face of adversity. In March 1975 I received the coveted green beret and commando dagger, which is worn on our uniform to indicate the accomplishment. A feat to be proud of for sure.

A quick trip back to Bicester to pack my remaining belongings and an immediate posting to 29 Commando RA, HQ Company in the Royal Citadel. This was to be my home for a while, starting off in the main kitchen or, as they termed it, the main galley, which prepared meals for soldiers below the rank of sergeant. Staff Sergeant Alex Brennen was my boss. He was a decent guy who taught me a lot, although two lessons stand out. The first was 'clean as you go, no clean, no go', and the second was that after I'd shown him my work, he'd show me once more and if I messed up, he'd show me again. If I messed up a third time, then I was being stupid. To my mind, he gave me permission to mess up, albeit with limits, and the opportunity to learn.

I was soon put in with two other chefs, who I only rarely met, where we would 'run' the officers' mess and the sergeants' and WOs' mess. One day, I was called over from the officers' mess to see the boss. What had I done? What was wrong? I needn't have worried, however, as it was just that a member of the unit's team, which was partway through the annual Army Cookery Competition, had fallen sick. An immediate replacement was needed and would I be interested? My response was, 'But you want to win, don't you?'

'Exactly,' he replied.

Bearing in mind I wasn't so long out of training, there was no real way I could decline. I was informed what I'd have to do, and the particular dish I'd be responsible for, and that I was to practise it at every opportunity. Serve it up every day, if necessary, but get it perfect, and fast. The dish was a baked milk pudding in an oval dish, topped with an edging and cross-hatched meringue with alternate apricot and raspberry jam puree in the diamond spaces. I got through so many eggs making that dish, getting the timing down to the minute, making sure the custard was set perfectly and my piping skills were up to par and at speed, so much so that I was sick of the sight of that pudding in quick time.

Later in the year I, along with the other three in the team, returned to St Omer for the finals. Throughout the event one of the examiners would wander about the kitchen checking our progress, making notes as they did. As well as working on my own dish, I was assisting Staff Sergeant Brennan with his work by prepping garnish and clearing away all mess, all the time keeping in mind his rubric, 'clean as you go, no clean, no go'. All too quickly I head, 'Time's up. Stand away from your workstation and bring your dishes to the front.' It was over.

That done, one of the examiners asked about my details, particularly about all the sports I'd listed, to which I confirmed that, yes, they were all correct. I don't recall if it was then or later that he commented that on every occasion he'd come to our workstation, there was never any mess, no vegetable peelings, no dirt, no eggshells, nothing. I'd always cleaned them away. So, we left the kitchen to await the results. I proceeded to pull my own work to pieces: the custard wasn't quite set properly, there were two diamonds of jam missing and there were holes in the meringue. I trashed all my efforts! Alex was relaxed and said we were fine. I really wasn't so sure.

When the time came, we all assembled in the gym where I'd taken my catering science exam about a year earlier. We were in the Category One section, so we wouldn't be kept in anguish for too long. Well, we only went and won! Gold medals for the four of us. The room was filled and in the audience were many of the staff from junior service, including the commanding officer and my company commander. I felt so damn proud as they looked up at me. Oh, and the name of the dish I'd made? Queen's pudding!

It was around this time, given the letter I'd received earlier concerning my exam results, that I looked into extending my knowledge of the science of food. I'd found an external course, which I could attend at a college in Plymouth, and received approval from my boss to do it. However, this was thwarted in May 1975 with an internal posting up to 7 Sphinx Commando Battery, attached to 45 Commando RM, in Condor barracks in Arbroath, Scotland. There, I started working in the main galley, in charge of making the desserts for a few hundred marines and soldiers, and later being sent to work in the officers' mess.

In January 1976 we packed up and set off for the frozen north of Norway. The temperature on arriving in Narvik was a balmy -25°C. As it was my first time there, I joined other newbies on an arctic survival course, which my skiing experience certainly came in useful for. Over the three months we were there, the temperature dropped to -40°C. I loved it. Each week, there was a film show, where all those not on duty attended a screening of a newly released film. One showing stands out to me, so much so that to this day, I smile at the idea of Booty (the affectionate term for Royal Marines) dressing up in tutus, suspenders and high heels to sing along to the music of that film. You've got it, it was *The Rocky Horror Picture Show*.

October 1976 saw me back in Plymouth, again working in the officers' mess. One day, I was told to report to a portacabin, but not told why. I was confronted by two sergeants from the Royal Military Police, Special Investigation Branch. Whatever was this all about? After confirming who I was and that I worked in the officers' mess, they proceeded to interrogate me. Did I know anything about missing clothing from the room of Lieutenant Sally Hutt, the only woman in the unit? No, I informed them, before explaining exactly where I worked, which was on the ground floor at the rear of the building, and that my only access to the main part of the mess was up the back stairs which led to the serving area on the second floor and nowhere else. A string of questions ensued, all aggressive, antagonistic and degrading. I again explained that I only had access to the galley and the serving area and nowhere else. I'd been in the dining area and on the second floor outside of the dining area, but only when on duty for special functions. After more questioning, I returned to my work. The investigations continued.

It was clear to me that only those who had access to the bedrooms in the mess should be interviewed, which would include her fellow officers and any staff who cleaned the rooms. Nevertheless, I was called back on many occasions over the following months and grew heartily sick of the nonsense. On 7 December 1976, the least aggressive of the two SIB sergeants, when on his own with me, stated that they'd been told I was, and I don't recall the term he used, but it wasn't homosexual, but that's what he meant. It was degrading, demeaning and downright offensive. I was sick to the back teeth of all this BS!

I knew their rationale was that gay people in HM Forces were a security risk, and that we'd be subject to bribery on account of our sexuality. What was I going to reveal, my secret recipe for Queen's pudding? I mean, really! I knew such a threat would only hold up if I, and others, sought to hide it, and that if one was prepared to admit it, any threat would immediately evaporate. Whilst I didn't sing it from the battlements, and it wasn't something I openly declared, neither was it something I was ashamed of. So, I responded, YES, I am. It was a matter of integrity for me. Unto thine own self be true! Well, to this day I don't know if he was just trying it on, seeing what might stick, or if indeed someone had suggested that I might be, but it kicked off an entirely new shit storm. I've recently been told by a retired ACC major that most in the service at the time really didn't care what I and others did in bed, and that a senior colleague of his was known to be gay and no one cared a jot. So much for the integrity we'd heard so much about.

Anyhow, a new level of offensive, derogatory and insulting questions ensued. Did I like wearing women's clothes? Who had I been with in the unit? Which officers? What role did I take in sex? Did I like cock? Did I like the taste of cum? On and on it went. They told me they needed to search my locker, to which I informed them it'd already been searched. Well, I was told, this time 'they' would do it, and do it properly! So, off we went, and my officer in charge (OIC) of the chefs joined us. The SIB sergeant, the more obnoxious of the two, went through everything, noting as he went that he could tell it'd recently been searched on account of it being so tidy. My OIC immediately informed him that it was like that when he'd searched it. He clearly didn't like hearing that, and so took away letters, my address book and some fitness magazines. Over the following months there were more interrogations, more checking, more agro! There was absolutely no one to whom I could turn, no padre, no colleagues, no one. I was completely and utterly alone. No one offered any guidance or advice, no one informed me of my rights. No one even informed me that I *had* any rights. It was soul destroying in the extreme.

Any sense of self-worth, of purpose, of personal pride was completely destroyed.

It became clear that the SIB weren't happy with me. They wanted proof. Proof that I really was a poof! That I wasn't just saying it to get out early. They continued to push. Who had I been with? What were their names? Where had I met them? On and on they went, taking turns. Was I mad, was I deranged, was I trying it on? No, I wasn't mad, I was bloody furious! Eventually I broke, telling them yes, I'd been with a soldier, that he'd picked me up in a bar in Dundee when I was stationed in Arbroath. That he was an RMP! I didn't know his real name, yet somehow, they worked out who he was. To this day I'm so bloody angry at myself for revealing this, and for drawing him into the whole horrible farrago. I'd like to apologise to him for that. Many years later, I found out his surname and service number (they're in my record of service) on the application for the discharge of a soldier which was completed by my then-commanding officer.

On Thursday, 9 December 1976, I was sent to the Royal Marine barracks where I was 'medically examined' by a naval doctor looking for 'signs of homosexual activity': the results were negative! Confirmation of my stay at the hotel in Dundee was attained by the RMPs, after which I was again interrogated on 14 December 1976. According to the official report by the SIB, I was then informed I'd reported where their guy was on leave from, namely Hohne, in Germany – a complete fiction on their part.

Prior to the discharge application being completed, from mid-March 1977 I spent just over three weeks in the military hospital in Plymouth with a gastric problem. I recall a member of the RMPs visiting the ward and talking with the ward sister. A day or two later, I was sent for a physical examination by a surgeon lieutenant commander, who performed a very intimate physical rectal examination, later reporting that I had a tight anal canal and that there was no medical reason why he'd need to conduct the examination. I felt completely violated. So, even though there was no medical reason to do this extremely intimate examination, he still did it. As far as I'm concerned, I'd been sexually assaulted, and it'd been sanctioned by the State, and I'd had no say in it. There was absolutely no one to whom I could turn. No one. I was broken yet had no option but to somehow carry on.

I occasionally worked in a local pub as a barman, and to my utter surprise, on one evening, the more aggressive of the SIB sergeants came in. I had to serve him; I had no choice. He was pleasant and asked if I was now a civilian, to which I chose to be honest and told him, 'No'. This would've been around the time Her Majesty the Queen visited Plymouth on her Silver Jubilee tour around the country. I'd watched her pass by the Royal Citadel from the battlements. Everything that'd been done to me had been done in her name.

Shortly after the incident in the pub, a clerk from HQ offices called over to the officers' mess galley to inform me that 'my friend' was on site and was being interviewed by the RMPs. There was nothing I could do. It wasn't as though I could pop over to ask him for a chat, to apologise, to get his details or anything. I was so very annoyed at them, and myself at the time, that they'd got him, too. I didn't really understand why the clerk had come over to tell me at all. If anything, as far as he could be, he seemed almost kind.

On 20 June 1977, my commanding officer completed a report stating that I was 'A very good cook who takes care of his work. Willing to learn…. Appears quite happy in his job. Always keeps himself clean and well turned out,' and adding that I was 'A willing worker who gives no cause for complaint in either his behaviour or his work. Can be relied upon to produce good results without supervision.' In my records I see that he also added another comment that completely baffles me: 'Has recently applied for a posting to BAOR, expressing a preference to serve with an RMP unit.' This is something I would never have suggested and I can only assume it was the CO's way of having a dig at the RMPs.

The following day I was sent for a psychiatric evaluation at the Royal Naval hospital in Plymouth. Was I spinning a yarn? Did I just see an opportunity to get out without a penalty payment? Was I mad? No, I wasn't, I was still bloody furious! Surgeon Commander J.A. Cameron RN, the consultant psychiatrist, reported that I'd been referred to him with no proper medical referral from a doctor, which complicated matters, and that there was no circumstantial letter detailing any alleged misdemeanours. He further reported that he presumed it was merely his duty to report on my mental state. He asked several questions about my family background, all of which I was particularly vague about. Looking back now I see that much of what he did report about my family and background he mostly got wrong. He did note that my sexual maturation would seem to be directed towards the homosexual, acknowledging that I freely volunteered my orientation to the executive authorities. He noted that in his opinion, although I was vulnerable and somewhat self-consciously pathetic (sic), I was not psychiatrically ill.

Diagnosis: No Gross Psychiatric Disorder.

Recommendation: 1. Category P2 M2 S2 (fit for duties).

He added a hand-written note stating, 'Any further referral of this matter should come through a doctor and with some circumstances', which supports my belief, then and now, that it was requested by the Military Police as part of their investigations. I hate them for this. No one should be put through such an ordeal, particularly anyone who is prepared to lay down their life for their country.

On another occasion, the clerk called over again to inform me that my promotion to lance corporal had been blocked, having been published in Part One Orders but not translated to Part Two Orders. I didn't talk to my boss about it. What was the point? My career was over. Yet, at the same time, I was expected to just carry on making meals for the officers as usual. I had zero support, zero guidance, and zero idea if or when I was to be kicked out. I was completely and utterly dejected. I'd worked hard, was respectful and respected, conscientious and diligent, and for what?

I recall it was late July or early August 1977 when I was told my discharge date and informed I had to use up all my acquired leave beforehand. I didn't know what to do or where to turn. I was a ship without a rudder. I took myself off to London, with no particular plan in mind. Once there, I sought out the few pubs known to gay servicemen and their admirers, and it was there I connected with two former guardsmen, to whom I confided my sorry tale. They told their landlord, a general practitioner who was also in the pub, who informed me he might have a place I could stay. We chatted briefly and he told me that a group of them were going away that weekend and suggested I join them. I guess it was to check me out. Not really knowing what I was letting myself in for, I agreed. At least it would save me some money and give me time to properly relax. I remember getting extremely drunk, and the following morning feeling that I'd blotted my copy book in some way. However, I was assured I'd nothing to be ashamed of. After the mini trip, I was given the address details and a number to call to make final arrangements, such as when I knew I'd be back in town, etc.

On 1 September 1977, having finished working the officers' mess the previous day, I handed in all my kit and packed the majority of my personal belongings into a trunk. I was given a lift to Plymouth train station, ready to have it transported the next day to London Paddington. I'd also been given my final pay packet, meagre as it was. How was this enough to pay for accommodation, food and anything else until I found work, however long that might be? I really could've done with the pay instead of the leave to help keep me going, but then, I wouldn't have found the rooms I had. That was a lucky break, or so I thought.

On Friday, 2 September, I took the train to London to seek my fortune. I'd been escorted to the main gates and was now out on my proverbial. My Certificate of Service book, which I destroyed long ago, had recorded my military conduct as being exemplary, with my commanding officer writing that, 'As a cook he has proved utterly reliable and carried out his duties in a conscientious manner. He is quite capable of running a mess catering for more than 50 SNCOs without any supervision and I believe this experience will assist him in civilian life.'

My new home was in the Barbican, in central London, and I walked to the GP's surgery, only to be informed that I needed the door to the side. There, one of the two guardsmen let me in and showed me around. He then went with me back to Paddington to collect my trunk and informed me that he hoped I hadn't got anything sorted for that night as they were taking me out. I was told that they, the two guardsmen who I'd met previously, as well as the doctor and others, were meeting up just off of Compton Street, in the West End, in the pub where I'd met them previously. They knew I needed to get drunk. I was a naive 21-year-old, raised and trained by the Army, who knew nothing of civilian life. I'd just been discharged from the only life I knew, that of an Army chef with a green beret, but after getting me right royally drunk, they took me back to our digs and raped me. I was in shock. Numb. I coped, though I don't know how. There was no thought of reporting it to the police, not in the 1970s, so I buried it.

Where now? What now? Who could I trust? Was there anyone? I certainly didn't feel like there was. I didn't know anyone. There was no one I knew who I could trust or even begin to confide in. I knew absolutely nothing about surviving in civilian life. The Army WAS my life. I needed to sign on, but how did I do that? Where did I go? What did I need? I knew anyone leaving the forces was given a period of 'resettlement training', informing them how and where to sort these sorts of things out, but clearly that wasn't for the likes of me! It'd been made abundantly clear to me that the service charities, those that were part of that service family, who had been so lauded to us as new recruits, wouldn't welcome the likes of me. There was no point going to the Royal British Legion, or SSAFA (Soldiers', Sailors' and Airmen's Family Association), as all were run by former service personnel. I was completely alone. Again. So much for that promised extended family. I was, to all intents and purposes, an orphan.

I never told my parents what'd happened, or even that I was no longer in the Army. To this day I don't know how they found out. Had the SIB told them? I've since learnt that they told people's parents as a matter of course, but they, my parents, never said anything about it to me. I knew that Mum was completely cool with it. Once, when I was on leave from the commando forces, she told me that whilst she was at an RAF training unit during the war, there was a contingent of male ballet dancers in a group of the recruits, and that it was these men alone who didn't get blisters on the route marches. It seemed clear to me that she was telling me she understood you could be gay and still be tough, and that for her, being gay wasn't a problem. She did, however, tell me this whilst Dad wasn't around.

On the Monday after being thrown out, I registered at the job centre. Even though I had a small amount of savings, which I couldn't readily get my hands on anyway, I was told I'd not be getting any money to live on and was referred to a specialist office for catering staff. As it turned out, thankfully, jobs were available and I was referred to a commercial catering company. However, I was informed that the contact person was a former captain of the Army Catering Corps, which filled me with complete and utter dread. What would his reaction be once he found out why I was no longer serving? Well, though I've no doubt he checked me out through his contacts in the Corps, I got a job and started working within a couple of weeks of discharge. Phew! That was a lucky break.

In my professional life that was to follow I enjoyed both career and academic success. I've many degrees and citations, but none of these endeavours brought me the pride I experienced in my Army career. The loss of the chance to serve was an enduring injustice in my life, which until recently was deemed not worthy of apology. The route to remedy began in 1993 when I read about a meeting in Earl's Court for former service personnel who'd been thrown out on account of their sexuality. The name of the group was Rank Outsiders, which I found out had been formed in 1991, the same year as John Major, the then-Prime Minister, had lifted the ban on homosexuals serving in the Foreign Office, and particularly from being in the Diplomatic Corps. I went along with a good deal of trepidation, but I needn't have worried. I was immediately made welcome with open arms. At long last I was among friends, friends who got it, who understood completely, who knew where I was coming from. What we hadn't appreciated back then, any of us, was how severely damaged we all were as individuals. Lives lost, lives lived, rarely to the full. The common thread? We'd all been broken down during basic training, then rebuilt into effective members of the military family. We had a shared trauma from suddenly losing our careers, homes, friends and self-worth overnight, with no support. Cast out but broken again.

One year, several of us attended that year's Gay Pride march through central London. Many decided to wear uniform, only to be spat at by others on the march. How could any self-respecting queer consider wearing a military uniform? Our argument that it was about equality of opportunity, regardless of one's sexuality, fell on deaf ears. It was made very clear that many LGBT folk didn't like us being there. We were an anathema to them too!

By then, one of the Rank Outsiders members, Ed Hall, had written his book *We can't even March Straight*, which was followed just two months later by Peter Tatchell's book, *We Don't want to March Straight: Masculinity, Queers and the Military*. It's a tad ironic that years later, it was revealed Tatchell had himself attended the army officer selection course and received an offer to attend officer cadet training at the Royal Military Academy Sandhurst.

Sometime later, I was elected vice-chair of Rank Outsiders, something of which I was rather proud. Among my responsibilities was to craft most of the press releases for the campaign, which I did up until shortly before the ban was lifted on 12 January 2000. Early in 1996, however, a cohort of us attended the Defence Select Committee in the House of Commons, to argue our case.

In 1997, we in Rank Outsiders applied to the Royal British Legion to join in the annual Remembrance Day parade in Whitehall and were delighted to be accepted. Shortly before the date of the parade, I visited the basement of their old HQ on Pall Mall, where I was informed that the secretary of the RBL wanted to see me. My immediate thought was, 'Oh, here goes, more bloody grief!'. Thankfully, I was greatly mistaken. The chap who greeted me was, I believe, a former colonel, who first offered me a drink before asking what our intentions were regarding the parade. I informed him that we were there, like all others on the parade, to honour our fallen brethren; the lesbian and gay service personnel who'd given their all in the service of our nation. Perhaps it was my quiet manner, or that I was besuited, or that I was respectful in my conversation at all times, but whatever the case, he seemed placated and proceeded to engage with me, asking what I'd done since serving. He was particularly gracious to me regarding my work at GOSH and that they (the Army) had lost a considerable asset. He did ask me about Peter Tatchell, what dealings we'd with him and whether there might be any demonstration from him. Whilst I hadn't had direct dealings with him, I was at least able to ease his mind on the matter of potential distractions from the principal purpose of the parade. I would later meet this man on several occasions prior to subsequent Remembrance Day parades, and he was always charming, gracious and engaging.

For my part, it's taken huge amounts of personal work to overcome that deep sense of anger, embitterment and rage. To begin to find a small morsel of pride in my service and to try to find some courage to declare 'Yes, yes, I served. Yes, I am worthy. I'm actually a nice guy.' We also gathered the strength to submit our personal evidence to the LGBT Veterans Independent Inquiry, conducted by Lord Terence Etherton, former Master of the Rolls and the first openly gay member of the senior judiciary.

On 19 July 2023, with the publication of the Etherton Report, Prime minister Rishi Sunak made an apology on behalf of the British people.

As a guest of the Minister for Veterans, I sat in the Strangers' Gallery and listened as he described much of the inhumane treatment I'd experienced.

Remembering these events from over forty years ago, memories long since buried through self-preservation and survival instinct, has been extremely challenging on so many levels. It's been both traumatic and, to some extent, cathartic. Life never comes with guarantees, but reading through my testimony, I return to the same question: Given my record and achievements, if I'd been allowed to serve my intended twenty-four years, man and boy, what might I have achieved?

Chapter 8

Kicked Out

Anne Myles

I joined the Royal Air Force in 1977, enlisting for the minimum nine years at age 18. On 8 March my father put me on the 08.00 train at Leuchars bound for RAF Hereford. Our Scottish contingent of three had agreed to meet on the train and begin our trip south, together. I was both nervous and excited about my future.

A uniformed corporal met us at Hereford station and checked us off her list as we boarded the RAF bus for the ten-minute drive to RAF Hereford. I collected my belongings (case, tennis racket, hockey stick) and committed a cardinal sin – I stepped on the grass! The corporal bellowed at me to get off, which I did with lightning reflexes. We followed her into the block where she opened the door to one of its four dormitories to be silently greeted by eighty girls staring back at us, patiently waiting for the Scots to arrive. The time was 20.15.

Over the next few weeks our worlds were turned upside down. Our weight and height noted, vaccinations administered, a mountain of clothing issued (two uniforms, two head-dress, two ties, four shirts (why not five?) flat and court shoes, kit-bag, trench-coat, hideous PT gear, etc.) followed by visits to the tailor for alterations. Making a bed-pack, 'bulling' shoes, tying a half Windsor knot and endless queues for an ironing board as we tried to master the art of ironing a shirt was all challenging, but none more so than witnessing all your hard work being pulled apart during a kit inspection. A high number of casualties found this new way of life too much and the queue for the single payphone in the block was long with everyone calling their families, crying and saying they wanted to return home. I made that phone call after just three days. My father, who de-mobbed in 1974 having served twenty-two years in the RAF, told me to buck up my ideas. His unsympathetic words affirming that I couldn't return home. I had to make this work.

None of us knew how to march. A great many thought 'camel' marching was the way to do it. It most certainly was not! Marching had to be mastered and so our drill instructors put us to the task immediately. Uniforms were being altered but shoes had to be worn. Marching in civilian clothing was a sight, with the 1970s having some questionable fashions: flared trousers, maxi skirts and Afghan coats. Striding out in shoes, which were instruments of torture, meant blisters burst and bled and everybody's feet were in tatters. Nevertheless, the shoes had to go back on the next day. Thankfully the NAAFI was well stocked with plasters.

My home-life culinary experiences were dreadful and so I didn't mind the mess food. Get in, eat, get out and get back to ironing and bulling shoes. However, nobody was allowed to saunter back to the block after the mess, oh no, we had to assemble after each meal and move about the camp as 'E' flight. If you were a slow eater that had to change!

We were paid fortnightly, £46. Many of us headed to the NAAFI bar. Boys weren't allowed in the WRAF (Women's Royal Air Force) blocks nor were they allowed to set foot on the path that lead to the block's front door. If any airman dared test the principle a voice would boom at the poor boy leaving him in no doubt he was to proceed no further.

My trade was WRAF admin so I was tasked with taking control of the flights, marching to and from the mess, the block and the parade square or, if it was raining, the parade hangar. I was stunned that I was in charge of a huge group and was expected to move them around the camp when I had no idea how to do it, what to say and when to say it. I think I was given this role so that, as WRAF admin, I might one day become a drill instructor? To make life easier I got the flight to sing (under their breath) to David Bowie's 'Sound and Vision'. The rhythm kept the flight in step and it worked a treat.

Easter fell in early April and the camp was shutting down. I was shocked I had to go home. The long journey made it a short visit to my parents' new, Dundee, home. I had no welcome embrace, fanfare or curiosity about my new life – I felt more at home with my RAF equals than I did with my own family. My return to Hereford couldn't come quickly enough.

Our passing out parade was soon upon us. Families and friends travelled from Aberdeen, Guernsey and Belfast to see their girl in uniform for her big day. It was hugely exciting, filled with adrenalin and hope that it would go well and the rain would hold off, allowing us on the parade square and not the drill hall where the reverberation made it difficult to hear commands. Everybody was in Number 1 uniform wearing white gloves and highly bulled shoes. Camaraderie burst from every pore, nobody wanted to put a foot wrong and let the others down. It went like a dream and was highly emotional, easily the proudest day of my life.

None of my family came.

I had changed trade to supplier and so stayed at Hereford for trade training and was then posted to RAF Lyneham. I stepped off the train at Swindon, was put into a car for the 12-mile trip, and then delivered to the station's guardroom. It was 4 July and a beautiful summer's day, which found me struggling up the camp's main drag with a tennis racket, hockey stick and now two suitcases (two uniforms and much more RAF paraphernalia). This was before rolling suitcases. It took a while! I reported to WRAF admin and was allocated to a 'four-man room', which I shared with two other girls.

The following day I 'arrived', which meant being sent from the general office to many sections, such as medical centre, guardroom, gymnasium and supply squadron, with a blue card to be signed at each area (the same process was done when posted elsewhere – 'clear'). This was all on foot at the UK's largest RAF base. That also took a while!

On 6 July I reported for duty at Supply Control Accounting Flight, an office full of computers. There was no guidance as to what to do and why, I had to figure things out myself. I took to the computers quickly and worked out the prescribed templates' functionality. I soon managed to understand what I was doing and why.

I moved to many sections of the squadron, keen to learn, always keeping my uniform pressed and shoes highly polished. A year on, working on the Hercules line servicing squadron, I met a mechanic whom I got serious about, he proposed and I accepted.

One Sunday evening one of my friends asked me to drive down the M4 with her to pick up RAF Lyneham's physical training instructor (PTI) who'd broken down in Uxbridge. I fully expected to be back on camp in a few short hours. When we arrived, I had an uneasy feeling. I felt awkward and aware that there was a bit more than 'friendship' going on with the PTI and her civilian friend, whom I'd been introduced to. This was my first encounter with the homosexual world. I was told that we were staying the night, sleeping on the floor. That was when a 'pass' was made at me. I was horrified, shocked and questioned what my friend was doing, because I was going out with a man! I lay awake all night, terrified and desperate to get back to camp. We left very early, allowing for a shower and change into uniform before work at 08.00.

I spent six months struggling with what had happened. What was I to do? Was this what I wanted? What about my career? I called off my engagement and, after much soul searching, I came to realise that, yes, it was what I wanted. I relinquished my single bunk and we moved to Wootton Bassett, hoping for a *normal* life away from the threat of the Special Investigation Branch (SIB) or Military Police. The move lasted six months, until she was posted to Germany and I moved back to a four-man room.

The terror of the SIB can't be over emphasised. Whenever I saw a black Ford Escort estate my heart would beat faster. Whenever a call came to go and see the WRAF admin warrant officer, my heart beat faster still, expecting to see a black Ford Escort estate parked outside her office. However, despite the dread of the SIB being all consuming, I met somebody else. We'd drive anywhere hoping not to meet anybody we knew, trying to be a couple visiting London's gay discos, staying at hotels in Weston Super Mare and Bristol.

I soon became aware that homosexuals got kicked out and it was not 'normal'. So I convinced myself I wasn't 'normal'. I felt forced to go along with the heterosexual banter, commenting on a good-looking guy. I played a lot of sport and always made sure I was in a corner of the changing room with my back to everybody so as not to raise suspicions that I was checking people out. I've always been passionate about music and, coincidentally, I preferred male musicians; it was their posters which adorned my walls. I know how ridiculous that sounds today but, in my desperation, it was ridiculous things which I naively hoped would help keep me closeted.

The 'one foot on the floor' rule was in Queen's Regulations and was designed to enable you to *prove* you weren't homosexual. Periodically, accusations cropped up about so-and-so being gay and what you'd do if they tried anything on. The only right answer was to say, 'Smash their face in' (or terrible words to that effect).

My life had become compartmentalised consisting of my heterosexual life, my homosexual life, my work life and my sporting life. In all compartments, at all times, I feared a knock on the door from the SIB. The mental strain was indescribable.

Out of the blue my squadron leader summoned me and my alarm bells rang, but I quickly realised my fears were groundless. Instead, I was offered a commission to become an officer. I had indeed been viewed in a positive light, but I couldn't see myself as officer material, so I declined.

A few weeks later, on 1 February 1982, my squadron leader again wanted to see me. 'This is it', I thought. A black Ford Escort estate will be with him. He arrived alone. He said he was 'delighted' to inform me I'd been promoted to corporal. WHAT? The supply trade's rate of promotion to corporal was approximately seven to eight years, I had done less than five. How could this be? Desperate for a long overdue posting abroad, my initial devastation at missing out turned to delight when he returned seven days later to say I was also being posted to Cyprus.

On 10 August I boarded a VC10 aeroplane at RAF Brize Norton bound for RAF Akrotiri, Cyprus. I was assigned to the Bulk Fuels Installation, which issued and receipted aviation fuels. The F222 was the daily calculation of fuel capacity of all four installations and was a notoriously cryptic form and a mathematical anathema to most, but I quickly mastered it. I was feeling confident and comfortable in my rank; my future was with the RAF and so I signed on for twelve years.

I soon got to know the station's PTI and, in February 1983, we formed a relationship. We both had cars and finished work at 13.30 on Fridays which allowed us to head off for weekends across Cyprus, staying in hotels as a couple.

I had a good relationship with my sergeant, for whom I would babysit. One day, in June 1983, he called me to his office to inform me that the SIB had visited him, asking questions about me. I thanked him; we both knew nothing more needed to be said. Finishing work that day I came across an old oil drum at the back of the WRAF block. My partner and I gathered letters, cards, photographs, anything that was remotely incriminating and watched as years of memories, many photographs of drunken nights with friends, burned. I couldn't risk anything being misinterpreted.

The next morning at 10.30 a black Ford Escort estate arrived at my work. I approached the two sergeants, knowing 'this is it', and asked if I could help. They asked to speak to my sergeant, so I took them to him and I collected my head-dress and bag knowing what was coming. My sergeant told me to let him know if I needed anything, but I remember thinking there would be no point because homosexuals were routinely removed from camp within twenty-four hours, never to be seen again.

I sat in the back of the car, my heart thumping, my mind racing. How could this happen? I thought I'd always been careful. My career was over and the future looked horrific. I was taken to a room and asked why I thought I was there. I pleaded ignorance. I was told I was accused of homosexuality and that my partner had been questioned that morning and confessed. The male interrogator did all the talking, saying that she'd been lifted first because they thought she'd be 'easier to crack', words which have stayed with me. They had also identified and spoken to previous boyfriends and knew I'd stayed in certain towns and hotels across Cyprus. I knew it was hopeless. After five hellish hours of questioning, I could deny no longer. At no time was I offered legal counsel, support, food or water.

The interrogation was suspended for the day and chaperones had to be found for us. We were both corporals, therefore our chaperones had to be corporals, which presented a problem as there were so few of us. Shifts were altered and two were found.

My chaperone and I were sent to The Princess Mary Hospital, located in a remote part of the camp. We were allocated to a cold gloomy room, which clearly hadn't seen a patient in many years. It had a toilet attached, which wasn't great for my chaperone as shock began to set in causing me to have sickness and diarrhoea. I can still recall being on my hands and knees over the heavy porcelain toilet, wondering when the retching would stop. I'd had no food so only bile was coming up.

On day two the interrogation resumed and despite repeated bathroom breaks, the sickness and diarrhoea continued for several days. Alarm bells should have been sounding for the SIB to take me to a doctor, but no. Instead, the SIB (female) sergeant took me to the block and my single bunk where my officer commanding (OC) WRAF was waiting. I watched as my room was ripped apart in the hope of finding any incriminating evidence. The sergeant always took a back seat during interrogation, she later told me that she was the only female police officer on camp and was ordered to take the case. She also played sport and the only two females she knew on camp were the two she had to interrogate.

The accusations the male sergeant put to me were relentless and vile. He said that I visited London's gay orgy scene, that I was involved with WRAFs at Lyneham, sharing each other, performing group orgies, and acting out fantasies portrayed in pornographic magazines. He also asked did I use sex toys, my fingers, was I dominant or submissive, who played the male role (because he said there had to be one), did I perform cunnilingus, was cunnilingus performed on me? This questioning continued day after day, month after month. I felt I was being verbally raped, every single day. His colleague never intervened.

Then came what I was waiting for; if I gave him names of other gay WRAFs, I might be able to save my career. I'm ashamed to admit that, for a nanosecond, I did consider the offer if it meant saving my precious career. Yet, how could I knowingly subject others to what I was experiencing? What sort of person would that make me?

The investigation was, again, suspended and we were allowed back to the block. I remember returning, braced for the backlash of name calling and abuse which I knew I was powerless to address. Instead of abuse, the dozen or so WRAFs I socialised with greeted me with a fierce wall of protection. Their curiosity was easily more manageable than the SIB. A week passed, why was I still on the island? I dared to wonder if I'd keep my career, which only increased my anxiety.

I had to return to work to the tongue lashing from men. There was name calling, innuendo, and predictably 'a good shagging would sort her out'. However, the most shocking of all came from my warrant officer. It was the sergeants' mess summer ball and he asked my sergeant who was babysitting his two very small daughters?

'The girls are', (myself and partner) he said.

'But they're lesbians', said the warrant officer.

My sergeant said he was happy with his choice of babysitters before walking away. And there it was; the paedophile accusation. I thought fighting for my life, job, pension, career, future and happiness was bad enough, but now I had to convince people that I did not molest children! A label, like a curse, which remains today.

I was still receiving mail from family and friends. Every letter was opened and read before being summoned to the SIB. I was given each letter then interrogated about its contents, repeatedly seizing upon any morsel which could be twisted into an abhorrent accusation. The most memorable was regarding my youngest sister. She and my other sister (then 20 and 22 respectively) thought they'd exploit the opportunity for a cheap holiday and could they visit me in August? This enabled the male SIB to go further still with his repugnant questioning. I can easily recall the following:

SIB: 'Who is Sheona?'
Me: 'She's my sister.'
SIB: 'What is she to you?'
Me: 'She's my sister!'
SIB: 'What relations have you had with her?'
Me: 'SHE IS MY SISTER!'
SIB: 'Have you ever had sex with your sister?'

I asked him, 'Are you a pervert, are you getting a kick out of this?'

I knew my calls were being listened to (clicks could be heard on the line) and it was difficult to talk them out of coming to Cyprus without telling them of my situation. I was trying to avert a family crisis. With each phone call I would be summoned, leading to further questioning such as, if they both come over would I share a bed with them? Both at the same time? My sisters' lack of understanding of the enormity of my experience irretrievably scarred the relationship I have with them both.

Legal support was never offered. What was offered was being escorted into a squadron leader's office and asked if I wanted psychiatric help. This was the military's answer to dealing with homosexuality. I said no. The UK law deemed male homosexuality legal in 1967, however, UK law has never ruled female homosexuality to be illegal, but the UK military did.

I had previously booked August annual leave with the intention of using one of my flight allowances to return home. The SIB said

I wouldn't return to Akrotiri but I impressed upon them that I had to go home to tell my mum why I was getting kicked out. Reluctantly, they let me go.

I flew to Lyneham where a friend met me, she was uncharacteristically quiet. I wanted to see the much respected and revered Warrant Officer "Dev" Devine, who was in her office. I tried to be as cheerful as possible, which was tricky as everybody knew of my situation. She asked how I was getting to Swindon (train from Swindon-Crewe-Edinburgh-Dundee) and I told her X would take me. Our conversation still remains very clear:

> 'It's a bull-night', she said (meaning the block was thoroughly cleaned then inspected).
> 'That's alright, I'll give her a hand', was my reply.
> 'But you're a corporal', she insisted.
> 'Not for much longer', I said.

That was the last time I saw Dev, although I always kept in touch with her. She taught me how to be professional, respectful and always be a proud, responsible person. To my great sadness, she died January 2022.

I arrived in Dundee the next morning. Not wanting to bombard my mum immediately, I left it two days. Just as I was about to tackle the matter, the phone rang. It was my ex from Hong Kong (also being investigated) who was in London on leave. She asked if she could come up, I said absolutely not because I had to tell my mum what was going on. Mum asked who was on the phone, so I told her.

'Oh, tell her to come up', she enthused.

My heart sank. The month before the investigation, Mum had holidayed in Hong Kong where my then partner showed her the sights. Up she came, spending the duration of my leave in Dundee until my return to Cyprus. I had failed.

September came and my partner's parents, with two friends, decided to holiday in Cyprus. We were ferrying them to and from their hotel in Limassol and all over the island, in between interrogations. It was a very long fortnight! I continued going to work, being the complete professional, irrespective of my warrant officer's contemptible comments. I gave him no reason to question my performance, which remained exemplary, scoring 'Special Recommendations' for annual assessments. He never spoke to me again.

I had to do something about returning to the UK, believing that if I couldn't get a job in London, I couldn't get one anywhere. I rang a friend, told her what was going on and asked if we could stay with her until we got sorted. Finally, seven months after the investigation started, we were told we were leaving on 12 January 1984.

Thousands of pounds had been spent training me; full car and HGV driving licences, health care, accommodation, mobilisation, uniforms, etc. All gone, because of a vicious lie. The basis for my dismissal was because we were allegedly seen at a party, on camp, holding hands. Having spent every fibre of my being avoiding anything which might raise suspicion about my sexuality, the "party" was fabricated. I put this to the female SIB sergeant and OC WRAF who both agreed it was farfetched. However, OC WRAF had to sanction the investigation because, had the truth come out later, and she'd ignored the allegation, her career would've been in jeopardy. I bear her no malice and to this day we remain in contact. She has never revealed who was behind that lie.

12 January 1984 was horrendous. Emotions were made worse because many WRAFs took time from work to see us off. From Brize Norton we went to Swindon and caught a train to RAF Innsworth, Gloucester, to clear from the Royal Air Force. Hungry and extremely cold, we arrived at the WRAF block to be greeted by a chalk board instructing corporals Myles and X where our rooms were. Separate rooms of course. Suddenly, I saw my ex from Hong Kong. What on earth was she doing here? There'd been a cock up with her paperwork and she should have cleared before I arrived.

The next morning, all three of us cleared. When I handed over my uniforms, I thought I was going to throw up. I wasn't allowed to keep a head-dress, nothing. I had worked so very hard, worn my uniform with pride and it was being thrown on a pile of dirty, ripped clothing to be scrapped. The interrogation was bad enough but stripping my pride, my uniform, before the final blow of handing over my F1250 (identity card) was worse. The only thing asked of me at Innsworth was a forwarding address.

My mum and I used to write to each other every six months or so. Close to when I was leaving Cyprus, I wrote to her thinking I had six months to get organised in London and then go home to tell her why I was a civilian. However, if she did write sooner, the RAF had a forwarding address for me. Or so I thought. A few weeks after securing a job and accommodation, my ex from Hong Kong contacted me to say, 'You had better ring home – your mum knows'.

My mum had replied to my last letter almost immediately and instead of forwarding it to me, the RAF returned her letter stamped NO LONGER IN THE ROYAL AIR FORCE. She was frantic. My eldest brother rang RAF Innsworth and was told they couldn't divulge any information as to my whereabouts. Detective work ensued and a phone call was made to my Hong Kong ex's mother in Lancashire, who blurted out:

> 'Oh, don't you know? They've all been kicked out because they're queer.'

Outed to my family, and I had no idea.

I rang my mum, who made it clear I should go home 'alone'. I arrived at 23.00 the next day. My mother's Catholic faith was extremely important to her, more so since my father died two years earlier and, at the time, the Church opposed homosexuality. I told her what had happened (extremely edited), but never told her how long the interrogation lasted. I was ashamed, embarrassed and, above all, I felt worthless. I had disgraced the family. We talked until 05.00. Trying to defend myself was futile, I knew I was getting nowhere. Mentally I was spent.

Finally, I asked her, 'Isn't it important that I'm happy?'

'No', she said.

How could I follow that?

The brother who'd called the RAF regarding my whereabouts visited me in London in mid-1984. He took me out for dinner and I'd barely got myself comfortable when he referred to my discharge, saying:

> 'It's a disease, I've read it in books and it can be cured.'

It's a sentence which will go with me to my grave. I got up and left. Apart from a handful of words at my mother's funeral (in 1999), I've never spoken to him since.

And so, how has the SIB investigation impacted my life? That is an easy question to answer; it destroyed me.

As noted, my military career was going from strength to strength. An offer of a commission, my rapid promotion and much sought after posting. I was extremely successful and from success came confidence. There was no self-doubt and pride oozed from every RAF pore until, in June 1983, my world imploded. I was accused of not only paedophilia but also incest. My whole personality and very being changed. My discharge papers read 'Services No Longer Required'. Subsequently, I have never had confidence in anything I've done, professionally or personally, always assuming I was going to be dismissed for something, always readying myself for disappointment. No matter who told me I was good at my job, I never believed them. Why would I?

In August 1984 I began a lengthy BBC career as a sound engineer, initially at Broadcasting House in London until, in 1992, I was transferred to Glasgow. In 2007 I became audio lead for a new Glasgow digital HQ and was also in great demand for staff training in Edinburgh, Aberdeen, Stornoway and Inverness. Throughout my time at the BBC, I struggled to comprehend why a great many staff had neither loyalty to the organisation or pride in their work – military values which have stayed with me. When my line manager intimated to me that perhaps I lower my standards, I knew it was time to leave.

In 2022 I applied for my military police records, because I wanted to see what had been written during the most harrowing period of my life. I was told the police records were destroyed in 2010, but I did receive my (heavily redacted) military records. I can't put into words the sickening sense of loss when I read my promotion to sergeant was formally under consideration, after just seven years. Who can tell me I was not an asset to the Royal Air Force?

In 2019 I completed a four-year degree course BA(Hons), something I never dreamed possible. Growing up, my father repeatedly told me I was "thick", so to this day I have to pinch myself that I have a First Class Honours Photography degree.

I watched Prime Minister Rishi Sunak's live apology to LGBT veterans on behalf of the British people on 19 July 2023. When he said, 'I apologise', I burst into tears. I was shocked at my reaction but suddenly felt vindicated, my heartbreak and debilitating outrage had been acknowledged. I shouted at the television:

'No, I didn't do anything wrong.' I didn't.

My mum died in 1999 and spoke often and affectionately of my father's twenty-two-year RAF career. She never mentioned mine. She wasn't interested in seeing photographs of me in uniform, the same was true of my BBC career because she never asked what I did. As for partners, I believe she was as equally disgusted with them as she was with me. Since 1984 I've often wondered what my mum would have thought of me had I been able to tell her of my sexuality on my terms, and had I been able to achieve my intended trajectory to the rank of warrant officer, serving as a valuable member of the Royal Air Force until I was 60?

I believe my story would have a very different ending.

Chapter 9

The Six and a Quarter Pence Per Day Soldier

— Michael Pitchford —

I grew up in North Nottinghamshire in a working-class pit village with an abusive father who'd served in the Army throughout the Second World War. He made me leave grammar school in July 1964 and forced me to work in the colliery. Joining the Army was my escape, but not until I'd spent two and a half years 3,000 feet underground. Roy Gilbert, who worked with me in the colliery, joined up at the same time but entered the Royal Green Jackets. Even so, he'd play a pivotal role in my fall from grace. I joined the Royal Electrical and Mechanical Engineers (REME), signing on for nine years. After basic training in Arborfield, Berkshire, I went to the School of Electronics Engineering (SEE) to train as a telecommunications engineer, after which I was promoted to lance corporal.

Soon after training I was posted to Hong Kong for two and a half years and was stationed in Sek Kong Garrison in the New Territories, near the Chinese border. My job included regular inspection and maintenance of the early warning system that was installed along the 20-mile border. Weekends off were spent in Kowloon (YMCA) or across the harbour in Wanchai on Hong Kong Island (the China Fleet Club). I led a heterosexual lifestyle, until in 1971 I met a US Navy Pilot called Captain Mike who was on R&R from Vietnam and staying at the Peninsula Hotel. I was 23 years old. We agreed to keep in touch by letter and would meet up every two or three months. My life became somewhat unsettled and to maintain the smoke screen, I continued to sleep with women occasionally. Late in the year I met up with Mike in Kowloon and he brought the unwelcome news that it was his final R&R: his tour of duty of Vietnam was almost over and he'd soon be returning to civilian life in San Francisco. He asked me to buy myself out of the Army and go to San Francisco to live with him. It was a moment that could've changed my life, but I was refused permission: the Army had spent far too much money on my training and so Mike and I parted with some sadness at the end of his leave. However, my life recovered and some weeks later I met the dashing Captain Peter Kelly, a BOAC pilot who became the focus of my weekend escapes.

In April 1972 I arrived back at RAF Brize Norton, having completed my tour. I was greeted by Peter and stayed for a while at his home in Richmond-upon-Thames. It would be the start of a long and lasting friendship until his death from cancer in 2007. Through Peter I met several other BOAC pilots – there must've been something in the water – and I placed their names and addresses in my address book, which was what we did before we had iPhones! I had accumulated eight weeks' leave and while in London, I stayed with my various new friends. I began a relationship with Mary Buettner, a lawyer from West Berlin who worked at Lincoln's Inn. Berlin would later become my 'second home' and I made frequent trips across Checkpoint Charlie, smuggling Deutsche Marks to Mary's friends trapped in the East.

In June 1972 I began my upgrading course for my pending sergeant's stripe. I still had three of my nine years left and, knowing I couldn't do it, I once again applied to buy myself out and was once more refused. One morning, in desperation, I reported to the sick bay, where I confessed to a very considerate and sympathetic retired RAF doctor. He told me that if it were up to him, he'd happily give me a medical discharge. 'But that's not possible', he said, 'are you quite sure you want to continue?' I told him I had no doubts whatsoever. Later that morning I was summoned to the CO's office and formally charged with homosexuality. Two MPs ordered me to open my locker and I watched as they emptied the entire contents on the floor. They found my address book, and so the interrogation commenced.

Some of the details were horrible and remain with me to this day. They told all and sundry on the base that I was a 'Queer'. I was immediately removed from my course and given menial and demeaning tasks before being shipped out to Coleraine Barracks, where the Royal Green Jackets were then based.

Armed with a rail pass from Euston to Liverpool, together with a ferry ticket to Belfast, I spent my last weekend with Mary before she tearfully waved me off at Euston Station. The overnight crossing to Belfast was crowded with drunken soldiers. I was at my lowest. I'd convinced myself I was on a journey from which I might never to return.

During my time in Coleraine Barracks, I did electronics in the workshop repairing equipment. Strangely, no one ever confronted me, but I was sure they knew.

Every second night I reported to the guard room at 18.00, where I signed for live ammunition to lead six young infantrymen as their patrol commander for a twelve-hour patrol. Our HQ was a house on a council estate and the whole thing was daunting. I was thankful the young soldiers looked after me that first night, with no hint of knowledge of my fall from grace. While there I crossed paths and exchanged pleasantries with Roy Gilbert, whom I hadn't seen since 1967. The time for him to do his worst would come.

During my time in Belfast, the RMP had sent their investigators far and wide and soon I was returned to the mainland where my nightmare began. There were frequent and harrowing interrogations by the SIB, who demanded names and a confession for having sex with other male members of HM Forces. They screamed at me, 'Three years in Colchester Prison for you, you queer bastard!' Other disgusting labels were spat at me, but I stood my ground. To this day I've no idea where I found the courage to withstand that dreadful period in my life, but I did.

Every Monday morning, I was ordered to report to a colonel psychiatrist in Aldershot at 09.00. I was assigned a young private to drive me in a Land Rover from Arborfield. Upon entering the psychiatrist's office, I came to attention and saluted. He was sitting behind a desk, while I remained standing.

'I think you're lying in order to get out of the Army', he said. 'I have your medical records from Hong Kong. You contracted gonorrhoea in 1970 from a bar girl in Wanchai by the name of Anlo. Is that correct?'

'Yes, Sir.'

'You're a lowly corporal. How come you have details of Major Peter Hughes in your address book? Is he a fucking queer also?'

'I wouldn't know, Sir. We are quite simply friends.'

'How many other soldiers have you had sex with?'

'None whatsoever from HM Forces, Sir.'

'And this captain in the US Navy?'

'I broke no laws in my relationship with him. He was a member of the US Forces in Vietnam.'

'You're facing three years in Colchester Prison. Now I want names of your bum boys.'

And, so it continued, week after week. Ostracised, I ate alone in the cookhouse each day, subjected to sneers from other soldiers. Shunning the NAAFI in the evenings, I preferred the solitude of my own room. My days were filled with worthless menial tasks, as well as frequent spells on guard duty overnight.

During a weekend leave in August I met John King, a director of associated newspapers in Fleet Street. He lived in a quiet mews off Belgrave Square and was a kind and gentle man who was appalled by my situation. He invited me to stay each weekend, letting me have the spare bedroom, and soon quickly warmed to Mary.

As the weeks turned into months, my resilience was weakening. The ceaseless interrogations by the SIB, the accusations and vile name calling, the dread of each Monday morning were all beginning to take their toll upon me.

During one of my weekend escapes to John in Belgravia, he asked my permission to speak on my behalf with Arthur Gore, 8th Earl of Arran, who John knew quite well. The earl was instrumental in fighting for homosexual law reform (his younger brother, who was gay, had committed suicide), so I happily agreed to John's kind offer and told him I'd come to London the following weekend.

It was then that John handed me a sealed envelope, on the front of which was written 'To whom it may concern'. John told me I was to hand this to the psychiatrist when I saw him the following Monday morning.

'I'm not privy to the contents', he told me, 'but I'm sure this might help you.'

For the first time in months, I slept soundly that night and reported as usual at 09.00, handing the colonel the envelope. 'This from one of your queer boyfriends in London?' he smirked. I didn't respond. As he read the letter, his face filled with fury and rage. 'Get the fuck out of here!' he screamed.

On my way to the barracks, the sergeant in the guardroom called me as I stepped from the Land Rover. 'Corporal, you're wanted at the CO's office immediately.' The CO and his adjutant were present, faces like thunder. 'I want a cheque from you for £250. Go and hand in all your kit and get your queer arse off this base. I want you gone by midday!'

'Exactly what I wanted to do six months ago, Sir', I said.

I hurried to my room and wrote out the cheque. Gathering up my entire military paraphernalia into my Army issue suitcase and kitbag, including the clothes and boots I was wearing, I quickly donned my civvies and packed my other belongings in the enormous suitcase I'd purchased in Hong Kong. I then reported to the stores and handed over each item as the sergeant called out the list. I returned to the adjutant's office and gave him my cheque for £250. Thank God I'd had the tenacity to set aside some of my weekly pay in Hong Kong.

Alone on the platform at Reading station, I was suddenly overcome with sadness and fear for my future. Thanks to John, however, I began working immediately at Roy Brooks Estate Agents on the King's Road, Chelsea. Roy was infamous for the outrageous ads for some of the properties he had on his books. I'd arrive at my desk each morning at 08.30, keen and eager, but the joy of my new life didn't last long and two weeks later, I received a bombshell when my sister, Marie, called me on the phone.

My mother had a passion for horse racing and would go into the village bookies several times each week and place small bets. One lunchtime, as usual, she was in the crowded bookies and noticed Roy Gilbert Senior. 'When you write to your Roy next', she said, 'tell him Michael's now out of the Army.'

'Yeah, we know', he replied loudly. 'He's flogging his arsehole down in London.'

A stunned silence fell upon the room and Mother fled in shame. Young Roy Gilbert had written this lie in a letter home – a rumour no doubt started by the RMP.

My sister begged me not to jump on a train. 'We know it's a complete lie', she said. 'Don't give him the satisfaction of coming up here and confronting the bastard.' I took her advice and remained in London.

I never did return home. The gossip spread and four of my five sisters disowned me. My homophobic brother delighted in fanning the flames of the rumour. My father banished me from the house.

Quite soon after this the second bombshell arrived in the form of a large manilla envelope marked 'Ministry of Defence'. The enclosed letter informed me I was now an 'A' Reservist until I reached the age of 45. I was to be paid 6¼ pence per day in the form of a monthly GIRO for £1.93. I was devastated. John said, 'They're never going to let you off the hook. You've truly annoyed them. They now want their pound of flesh.'

Realising I was still subject to Military Law, I'd been humiliated by a pay award of 6¼ pence per day. I wasn't a free gay man. My health began to suffer as I experienced, stress, loss of appetite (PTSD had yet to enter our vocabulary) and disturbed sleep. Meanwhile, Mary had returned to West Berlin to begin her new practise as a fully qualified lawyer, so I threw myself into my work, fuelled by cigarettes and coffee. At the end of December, I arrived at a momentous decision and handed in my notice to Roy Brooks. I needed to find somewhere far away, somewhere out of reach of the Army, somewhere to heal.

Following a rough Channel crossing one Sunday afternoon, I disembarked in Boulogne and made my way towards the railway station. I'd succeeded in getting a place at the university in Aix-en-Provence to study French, so I boarded the night train for Avignon at 18.00 and was shown to my sleeping compartment by a friendly guard. 'The dining car is now open, Monsieur', he smiled. My stay in France was to be the happiest six months of my life.

Armed with my diploma in French Language from L'Université d'Aix-Marseille, I arrived back in London filled with determination and vitality.

While I was away, the GIROs from the MOD had piled up so I cashed them at the Post Office in Sloane Square and deposited the frugal amounts into various charity boxes on display. I continued this habit until I received the final GIRO in 1979.

Fairly quickly, I was successful in getting a job with Berger Jenson & Nicholson in Berkeley Square, London, part of the international Hoechst Group in West Germany. My boss, Ron Cross, encouraged me to take evening classes in accountancy and was a huge support to me.

The company had factories all over the world, including Paris, Breda and Sunderland, and Ron pushed me and persuaded me to visit these factories and carry out audits. For a time, life was good until the next manilla envelope dropped on the mat.

In July 1974, Turkey invaded Northern Cyprus. I received my call up papers for active service and showed them to John. 'You mustn't go', he implored me. But I had no choice unless I wanted to be incarcerated inside Colchester Prison. Active service on 6 ¼ pence per day. Luckily, my boss came to my rescue. He'd served in the Army in the 1950s as a commissioned officer and knew Queen's Regulations inside out. 'Students can't be called up for active service', he told me.

'But I'm not a student.'

'Yes, you are! You study at home in the evenings. Leave this with me.'

Miraculously, he succeeded in getting me off the hook.

At that time, my only contact with my family were the occasional visits to London by my sister, Marie, and her workmate in the factory, Barbara, who'd known me all my life. Barbara was a force of nature. Widowed prematurely and left with three young children to raise on her own, she feared nothing and no one. She'd often confront people in the miners welfare or when shopping in the village and always defended me against the vile lies. Although my mental health was suffering, I chose to bottle everything up.

A combination of stressful work, particularly when Ron sent me away to the factories for weeks on end to investigate suspected fraud, as well as the never-ending treadmill of study and exams, added to the shame and guilt I still carried and resulted in a debilitating attack of violent headaches. I sought help and was referred to the Atkinson Morley Hospital in Wimbledon, where I was diagnosed with trigeminal neuralgia and prescribed powerful medication.

The problem didn't improve and so with huge sadness, I handed in my notice at the beginning of January. I was halfway through my third year of ACCA, with two more years of exams ahead of me. Ron begged me not to leave. 'Take off as much time as you need. We'll give you full sick pay until you're fit and well.' My mind was made up, however, so I left and began a new career as a freelance bookkeeper. I soon had several clients and was earning more money than I'd ever known. Most of my clientele were interior designers and fabric companies. One year later (1977) I went into partnership with an interior designer and took over his failing building and decorating company. I was thriving, but the headaches continued and sometimes I'd even collapse. In 1979 I was referred to the neurological hospital in Russell Square. It was my sixth referral and yet not one had bothered to X-ray or scan my brain. This time, the neurologist in Russell Square happened to discover I was an Army Reservist and succeeded in getting me a full medical discharge. I was free at last!

Two weeks later I received an income tax demand from HMRC for tax on the 6 ¼ pence per day I'd earned for the previous 6 and a half years. I ignored it. By now, Thatcher had the keys to Number 10 and it was time for me to go east! With the help of my friends from Sydney, His Honour Justice Donald Stewart and his wife Maybelle, I obtained a full Resident's Visa and emigrated to Sydney, unaware of what tragedy lay waiting for me. Just before I left Blighty, my sister told me that Roy Gilbert Junior was living in Melbourne employed as a prison officer.

As the plane soared into the summer sky, I gazed down on the patchwork of southern England and bade a silent farewell, thinking I'd never see it again. I settled back in my seat for the thirty-two-hour flight and reflected on the previous six and a half years. Mary was much on my mind as I thought back.

I'd rekindled my relationship with Mary in 1973 and made my first trip to West Berlin, where she was well established in her own law. The Berlin Wall encircled the Western Sector, which was controlled by the USA, UK and France. Meanwhile, Soviet troops controlled the Eastern Sector, forming part of the GDR, which was ruled by the hateful Erich Honecker. Mary was overjoyed that I was finally a civilian, albeit still shackled to the Army Reserve. She introduced me to her closest friend, Hansjorg Saladin (affectionately known as Sali), who was a producer for the classical station on West Berlin radio. We connected instantly.

Like all West Berliners, Mary and Sali weren't allowed to venture into East Berlin, where several of their friends were trapped. They easily persuaded me to make my first foray into East Berlin and my accomplice was their friend Adriano, an Italian hairdresser who lived and worked in West Berlin. He'd become a seasoned smuggler of West Deutsche Marks to Mary and Sali's friends in East Berlin. In 1973 the official exchange rate was 1 West Deutsche Mark for 11 East Deutsche Marks. We were each given 300 West Deutsche Marks, which we concealed inside our underpants. Adriano assured me it'd all be fine!

When the American soldier checked our passports at Checkpoint Charlie, Adriano explained that we were tourists. Further along the checkpoint, we were stopped by two East German soldiers, where we had to exchange the West Marks for East Marks on a one-to-one basis. Adriano had primed me in advance and we informed the guards we were day trippers and only wanted to exchange 10 West Marks each. Our passports were stamped and we crossed into East Germany.

Situated on the corner of Alexander Platz was an underground public toilet. Adriano explained that, once we were inside, each of us was to find a vacant cubicle wherein we could safely transfer the money from our pants to our pockets. A palatial men's WC adorned with Dresden tiles greeted us. Several uniformed GDR soldiers were lined up at the urinal. I almost had a heart attack. I hurried inside a cubicle and locked the door. I heard Adriano do the same. After transferring the 300 Deutsche Marks into my pocket, I waited a few minutes before flushing the toilet.

Back up on Alexander Platz, Adriano winked conspiratorially and grinned at me. 'Well done, Michael', he said. 'Let's head off to the bar.' A short distance away, down a side street, we entered a gloomy bar with only a few customers. In one corner, prearranged by Sali, a young man and woman called Gottlieb and Renata were seated at a table.

Adriano introduced me and over a beer, as we surreptitiously passed our booty beneath the table, I began to relax. I'd later make several more risky ventures into East Berlin on my own; it seemed the right thing to do. After all, back in London, the ugly rumours instigated by Roy Gilbert were never fully laid to rest, so I'd resigned myself to never seeing my family again.

Later that year, on one of my regular visits to the Westside Gym in Kensington High Street, I met the hugely successful Australian writer, Russel Braddon. Russ had been a POW in the Far East and suffered unbelievable cruelties at the hands of Japanese soldiers. Miraculously, he'd survived his ordeal and was released from Changi Prison in 1945. After the war he'd been unable to settle in his native New South Wales and so boarded a ship for England, where he wrote and published his memoir *This Naked Island* in 1952. Over a period of time, Russ coaxed my story out and a lasting friendship was formed.

By 1977 I became aware of rather frightening changes in my health. One such occurrence took place early one evening when I ventured into The Coleherne, a leather bar in Earl's Court. I purchased half a lager and, as I made my way towards the wall and away from the crowded bar, my legs gave way. The room began to spin and I ended up semi-conscious on the floor. I was gently picked up and cradled in the arms of a very tall drag queen. Despite the heels upon which 'she' tottered, she managed to push through the crowd and carry me outside where she gently set me down on the pavement. 'Has anything like this ever happened to you before?' she asked.

'Once or twice', I replied.

'I think you ought to have it checked out at a hospital, Love.'

She helped me to get a taxi and, to my lasting shame, I failed to ask their name. I tried to put the incident behind me, however, mainly because the doctors had assured me there was nothing seriously wrong. Yet, something told me otherwise.

When I confessed to Russ that I'd decided to live in Australia, he hid his disappointment and, instead, put to me a proposal. Once I'd settled in his hometown of Sydney, I was to introduce myself to his accountants, Price Waterhouse. Russ was keen to invest in the property market Down Under and saw how capable I'd become in my building and decorating business. I was humbled by the trust Russ had in me. He was a true friend and I was determined to prove him right to trust me.

His Honour Justice Don Stewart and his wife had made their annual pilgrimage to London in 1979. They helped me celebrate my release from the Army after twelve long years. The following day I gave my passport to Don and Maybelle as they went off to meet with the Australian High Commissioner and lunch at The Savoy. When they returned that evening, inside my passport, in all its glory, was the stamp for a full Resident's Visa. Don and Maybelle flew home to Sydney two days later, and I agreed to follow as soon as I'd wound up my business.

I arrived in Sydney on 31 July 1979, and the realisation hit me: I was on the same continent as Roy Gilbert, who was just 500 miles to the south. I decided there and then that, once I was settled in Sydney, I'd make the journey to Melbourne and confront my accuser. I wanted to look him in the eye and ask him why he'd told such lies about me in 1972. Less than an hour later, the taxi dropped me outside Don and Maybelle's imposing house on Darling Point Road. They were thrilled to welcome me to Australia and insisted I stay with them for as long as I wished. The following day I was to start working for friends of theirs, Max and Robyn Stokes, who owned a factory next to the airport, making neon signs.

The next day I arrived in good time to meet Max and Robyn, who I'd already met in London the previous year. Their accounts system was quite simply non-existent. Drawers were filled with cheque stubs, bank statements, suppliers' invoices and letters haphazardly stuffed out of sight. To say I was shocked would've been an understatement. Downstairs from their office, a small workforce beavered away in the factory, creating neon signs for customers throughout New South Wales, completely unaware of the mess I was facing upstairs. The task ahead didn't phase me. I'd had similar clients in London who ran their businesses in the same cavalier manner. I decided to give Max and Robyn one month of my valuable time, setting up a transparent and efficient accounting system and giving them a full and honest appraisal of their business, before interviewing candidates for the role of bookkeeper.

One month later, I'd completed my task in the factory, but my assessment was that they were broke, and sadly, the business would go bankrupt not long after.

By the spring, I was familiar with the city and its suburbs. I'd concentrated on the Bohemian suburb of Newtown, 4 kilometres south-west of Sydney's central business district. It remained somewhat of a backwater, far removed from the glamorous eastern suburbs where I'd found a two-bedroom flat to rent in Yarranabbe Road, Darling Point, a mere stone's throw from Don and Maybelle. Each morning from my bedroom window, I looked out at Rushcutters Bay and beyond to the magnificent Sydney Harbour Bridge and Opera House. I'd struck up a congenial relationship with an estate agency in Newtown, who alerted me each time a suitable property came on the market. A Victorian terrace house sparked my interest. It was in a sorry state and vacant, but I immediately spotted the potential. The guide price was A$45,000. Having arranged my first visit to Price Waterhouse Accountants in the city, they welcomed me warmly. I presented my detailed, costed proposal for which they gave me the go-ahead. The purchase of the Newtown property went without a hitch and my bid of A$40,000 was accepted. I'd bought a second-hand Holden van in which I loaded a new set of decorating tools. For two weeks I'd been working as a labourer for a builder called Miguel, who Don and Maybelle knew well. I got on extremely well with him and offered him his first contract with me. Within eight weeks I transformed the sad and neglected house back to its former glory. The estate agent was bowled over at the speed in which I'd accomplished such a professional restoration and was happy to list it in the next auction (properties were bought and sold in auctions in those days), with a guide price of A$75,000. I'd spent A$10,000 on the renovations.

I was astonished to achieve a selling price of A$80,000 at the auction. A handsome profit after fees for both Russ and myself. I was up and running. Nothing would stop me now. Or so I believed.

After purchasing a rundown Victorian terraced house, I renovated it before selling it at auction, making a profit of A$30,000. I quickly found the second property and my good fortune continued. The New Year could not have started better. I'd turned 32, was solvent, lean and tanned. I felt invincible. Through contacts of Maybelle, I was introduced to the owner of one of Sydney's top modelling agencies and, with a little pressure, I agreed to go in front of the cameras. I was a Pommie immigrant with a regional accent. I felt like an imposter. The agency concentrated on putting me forward for TV and cinema adverts: the highest paid work. My first gig was an advert for Captain Morgan Rum. Filmed over four days aboard a luxury yacht berthed in Middle Harbour, I had to be on set no later than 05.00. Each morning, before leaving my flat, I'd be physically sick with nerves. The rewards were huge, however: I was paid A$100 an hour, and as no day was shorter than twelve hours, I was in no position to turn down such lucrative work.

The year had raced by, but I still hadn't made the journey to Melbourne, despite the constant nagging inside my head to face 'the one' who'd been the cause of so much anguish in my life. I therefore made the decision to fly south early in the New Year.

Sunday, 2 December would prove to be life changing. The previous day, I'd worked a full twelve hours on the latest renovation project. Utterly exhausted, I headed home for a long, hot shower and some food.

By 10.00 I was strangely buzzing and not in the least bit tired and so decided to go out for a few beers. It was 02.00 when my head hit the pillow and I fell into a deep, deep sleep. The telephone ringing on my bedside table woke me the next morning at 09.00. That call was to save my life. It was my friend, Bob, and although we hadn't seen each other for several weeks, he told me to get up and be ready in fifteen minutes. 'The surf's up. Let's go catch a wave on Tamarama Beach.' The small inlet along from Bondi Beach is renowned for its huge waves, and as I clambered into the passenger seat of Bob's car, my next memory was standing on the beach in my bathing trunks hearing Bob call, 'Let's go, Michael!' I clearly remember racing into the roaring surf, but nothing more.

Apparently, we caught a wave and surfed expertly onto the beach, but as I lay on my towel, I immediately went into a seizure. When I came to, I was in a bed in St Vincent's Hospital. A drip was connected to a vein in my left arm and beside the bed was a young doctor asking me questions. I couldn't make sense of any of it and suddenly began to fit again.

The pain of an epileptic fit is unbelievable. Each and every organ inside the body rattles fiercely against the skeleton. Breathing in is impossible. The diaphragm, the major muscle of respiration, contracts involuntarily. As air is forced from the lungs, the entire body shakes violently. Relief comes after a few minutes when the patient loses consciousness.

Despite the Valium drip in my arm, I was having as many as twenty fits each day. It was imperative for the doctors to bring the seizures under control so they could get me on the MRI scanner. Some days I'd fail to recognise friends who visited me. Conversely, my brain fooled me into believing I knew complete strangers. I was adamant that the young Australian registrar had grown up in the pit village I hailed from. Eventually, they were able control the seizures and I was taken to the scanning unit. Later that day, Bob dropped by after work and sat next to my bed. 'Michael, brace yourself. The doctors have asked me to speak with you. You have a brain tumour.'

'Thank God!' I exclaimed. 'All these past six years I was told by doctors there was nothing wrong with me. I knew I wasn't imagining it.'

After two weeks I was stable enough to undergo brain surgery. I was speaking throughout the six and a half hours of the craniotomy, whilst

Mr Connelley expertly performed brain surgery on me. I've absolutely no recollection of the time I was in theatre, but I remember waking up in the Intensive Care ward with tubes in almost every part of my head and body, feeling like I'd been badly beaten up. Maybelle was at my bedside assuring me the operation had been successful. The following morning Mr Connelley arrived to check me over. I told him I was ravenously hungry. 'Any chance of a slap-up meal?' I murmured. He consulted with his medical team and it was agreed that most of the tubes could be removed before I was taken down to the ward and fed heartily.

After two weeks in hospital, Mr Connelley agreed I could go home, with strict instructions to take things easy. 'I was unable to remove your tumour', he told me. 'It's attached to your left optic nerve and removal would've left you blind. In simple terms, the tumour is a sac that was filled with gunk. Once I'd removed the top of your skull, above the left frontal lobe, it popped out as big as a golf ball. It was this pressure inside your brain which caused you to have fits. You're only 33 and it might well take another 33 years before it fills up again. I'm afraid you've been left with epilepsy, but this can be managed and controlled by medication which you must start taking today. I'll see you again for an outpatients' appointment in two weeks.'

By now, I was painfully thin: in a matter of four weeks, I'd lost almost 3 stone. Maybelle collected me from the hospital and drove me home to my flat, where she'd filled my refrigerator with delicious and nutritious food. The following morning, when I looked in the mirror, I was shocked; my ribs were sticking out. Most of my muscle definition had disappeared and my eyes appeared quite large in my shaven skull. It was time to start anew.

My follow up appointment with Mr Connelly was scheduled for mid-January (1981). Arriving at his outpatients' clinic, his secretary presented me with a very detailed invoice of costs. It'd never dawned on me I'd have to pay any medical charges. When I first arrived in Sydney, Maybelle had marched me round to the local pharmacy and insisted I take our private medical insurance. At the time I was 31 and appeared fit and healthy, so my insurance plan was to cost me A$30 a month. The small print clearly stated that cover only applied to the first 75% of any medical bills and the remainder was the responsibility of the person named on the policy. But when would I ever need medical insurance?

The total costs for my stay in St Vincent's Hospital, including scans and surgery, amounted to over A$100,000. I was stunned. I was liable for costs of A$27,000. My income over the past three months had been zero. Fortunately, I'd saved some money in the bank and so had a bit of a safety net.

Mr Connelley was pleased with my progress. However, he said it was his duty to inform me that the Australian sun would aggravate my condition and so advised me to return to the UK.

I needed to start work again. During my hospitalisation, a labourer I'd worked with called Miguel had come good. He and his crew had done a magnificent job renovating a bungalow, overseen by an employee of Price Waterhouse, who were rightfully protecting Russ' interests. The property was listed for the next auction in early February. Manual work was out of the question as I was still as weak as a kitten, but I soon saw an advert in the local newspaper for a full-time bookkeeper with a building company in Kings Cross. It was easy work, but tiring.

I eventually confided in Bob, who was upset about my decision to return to the UK. Nevertheless, he managed to get me a cheap flight and I was able to return to London after almost two years in Australia, having failed to meet with Roy Gilbert and get answers to questions that had tormented me for almost ten years. I arrived in London on 15 April 1981 and my dear friend, John King, was waiting as I walked into the Arrivals Terminal at Heathrow.

Chapter 10

Forced Away

— Lesley Davison —

I had a deferred offer from Dartmouth PE College but had to stay on at school for another year, on top of my two extra years at A-level, in order to pass another A-level. Mum and Dad couldn't afford for that to happen, and, to this day, I've no reason why, I went to the Army Careers Office to join up as a physical training instructor (PTI). It was the best thing I ever did; I wanted to teach PE and I certainly did.

In November 1978 I entered the Women's Royal Army Corps (WRAC) Training Depot in Guildford for six weeks' basic training. We weren't allowed home for the first four weeks of training but, because I used to I play netball for Sussex, I was allowed to attend the game at week two.

My training corporal was an Army netball player and she introduced me to the Army team, which I became a part of immediately.

I was a real tomboy at school and usually played with the boys rather than the girls. We used to ride our bikes, play football and hang out together. I'd no idea I was gay or even knew anything about gay people back then.

I was signed on (contracted) to the WRAC for twenty-two years but, after eighteenth months I could give eighteenth months' notice to leave; so a minimum of three years' service.

In January 1979 I started my seven-month PTI course at the Army School of Physical Training (ASPT): the first course ever to amalgamate male and female PTI training. This was where I met my first gay partner. As I've said, I'd no idea I was gay or the concept of what I was feeling at the time. How did I not fancy men? I was still only 19 years of age and trying to find my way through my own sexuality.

I really don't know how I found out it was illegal to be gay in the Army, but I did, and the realisation was devastating. I was trying to cope with thinking I might be gay and what my own thoughts were of gay people; if I was gay, how was I going to tell my parents? I didn't want to be a disappointment to them. And now I couldn't love this person I loved. How did I love her? It wasn't right, and yet, I did. I couldn't change that. It just was. How could I, though, without fear of losing my new career teaching physical training?

In August 1979, our PTI course came to an end. My partner and I were posted to the same gym in Aldershot. I was in 10 Company and she was 3 Signals Regiment. We both used the same building, same NAAFI, same cookhouse and same gym. Of all the ladies on our PTI course, we were posted together. It was obvious to us that someone upon high knew about us and wanted to keep us together.

Something happened at the end of our PTI course. Something to do with the instructor and one of the ladies from the course. This 'event', whatever it was, caused the Special Investigation Branch (SIB) to visit Aldershot, where we worked at Duchess of Kent (DoK) barracks. This was very bad news. The SIB were hellbent on catching anyone they suspected of being gay; whether they were or not. There were several ladies in the DoK barracks who were gay, and the ripple through the barracks was palpable.

My PTI sergeant at 10 Company was gay, as was the sergeant PTI from the Training Depot in Guildford. She would come to our gym, about 10 miles away from her camp, and they would sit at my sergeant's desk writing notes to each other, passing them across the table. It was obvious they didn't want to talk in front of us and were concerned about the SIB being in the building. This note writing would go on for hours, over weeks. My partner and I used to go up to the NAAFI and play space invaders for hours, but those paper conversations they had would cost us a fortune.

Unfortunately, this is what really made me understand how fearful I should've been of the SIB. Two sergeant PTIs communicating with each other by writing notes, in front of us. How terrified they must've been. Perhaps they were maybe trying to protect us, too? It was at this time that I knew I had to protect myself; and the start of me becoming deceitful and having to change my normal personality traits. It was horrible to have to learn a new way of being me, just to survive in a chosen career I was good at. It was something we just had to do.

There were rumours that some ladies were being investigated and then were never seen again. They'd obviously been discharged by the SIB for being gay. This was very scary for me, for a lot of us.

During the next year my partner and I would borrow the camping kit for weekends away in New Forest. It was a chance for us to be together, away from the Army, away from prying eyes and ears back at barracks. It was a joy to be ourselves just for a few days, spending time together, not just because it was a new relationship, but a new sexuality, which sometimes, I didn't always feel was right.

My partner's sister, who was also in the Army, lived 'out', meaning she lived out of camp in a shared house. We took every opportunity we could to spend nights with her so we could just be together and be ourselves.

Over time we developed a really good group of friends in the barracks and Thursday night was drinking night. Most of us were gay but it wasn't an 'us and them' situation. I don't know how we knew if ladies were gay or not, but our gay radars were working well. It was an evening of drinks and getting to know others in the corporals' mess. Those evenings were very special.

In DoK, nobody was allowed into each other's bunks, never mind sleeping in each other's bunks. We did, though; two of us, in a 3-foot Army bed, sneaking around trying not to be seen or found out. The barracks were very big and we lived on different floors, many corridors away. After a while we certainly mastered the art of tiptoeing and stealthily getting around the building. I'm sure others knew about us, but everyone just ignored it.

Within five months of being in the Army I was selected to play for the Army netball team. I felt as though I belonged. I was very proud at this early stage in my career of being selected to play for the Army in the annual Inter-services competition. We won. It was fabulous.

Many, but not all, of the team were gay. As a team we used to go to Aldershot to train over the weekends as we were posted all over the UK, including Northern Island, and Germany. We'd go out to a gay club quite often as a team, gay or not, on the Saturday night in Camberley. I forget the name of the club, but we had some good team-building drinking sessions then.

After about a year of being together, my then partner and I decided we were strong enough to tell our parents about us. It wasn't an easy decision. Things were different in 1980. Our family didn't know anyone who was gay; they certainly didn't know I was gay. How were they going to take it? Would they still love us?

We went to Plymouth where my partner's mum lived. We arrived on the Friday night, but didn't and couldn't get the nerve to tell her until 9pm on the Sunday night, even though we still had to drive back to Aldershot the same night. I remember it so well. The film *Love Story* had just started on TV. She said, 'Mum, I've got something to tell you. Lesley and I are going out together.' Her mum replied, 'That's nice dear, where are you going?' Well, that floored us and we've laughed about it for years. Once we'd explained it to her, though, she took it very well. She was very supportive and we spent many good times with her in Plymouth after that.

When I told my parents, well, my mum, we were both sat on the end of the bed. I started to cry I was so scared. I continued and said, 'I've something to tell you.' The first thing Mum said to me was, 'Are you pregnant?' I started to cry more and said, 'No.' Then she said, 'Is it your close friend?' I told her it was, and she said, 'Me and your dad had thought so.' She went on to say, 'I can only cope with this if it's just a phase you're going through. I don't want anyone else to know and don't tell anyone.'

They still loved me but were ashamed of me; at least that's what I thought. They confirmed the fact that I 'wasn't right', I wasn't 'normal'. We agreed on this course of action of not saying anything, and it held for some fifteen years until one day, my mum, who worked at Gatwick for First Choice Holidays, was trying to pair me off with a lady she used to work with! It was only at that time I finally came out to my sister and brother's families, assuming Mum had finally accepted me. Over the years, Mum and Dad welcomed my partners warmly with open arms. This was such an amazing comfort to me, having my family to support me after decades of hiding who I was.

My partner owned a car, an Austin Allegro, and one evening we went for a drive and found a car park where we could be together. We were kissing when suddenly, lights lit up the car. When we looked it was the Royal Military Police (RMP). Oh my God, no, I thought. We've been caught. In an attempt to explain why we were there together, I poked myself in the eye so hard, it looked like I was crying and she was consoling me. Then we realised the RMP wouldn't know we were military or not; unless they knew our car registration, which we supposed was possible. We were so paranoid at that time and scared of being 'found out', our feelings were amplified by rumours the SIB would sit outside gay bars and clubs watching people walking in, and if they were recognised then careers ended. These were just some of the tactics they used to 'catch' people.

After about eighteen months working at 10 Company, I was posted to Royal Artillery (RA) Training Depot 17 Training Regiment, Woolwich. This was the first time my partner and I had been apart in two years. It was awful. I was in southeast London as a PTI and she'd transferred trade and was now a training NCO in WRAC Training Depot, Guilford. We'd travel up and down during the week on a Honda 50cc motorbike. The A3 road and south circular were dangerous places to be in the dark and rain, but we did it so we could spend more time together. There were no mobile phones in those days.

In the Army, it was a real pleasure to work with wonderful, professional ladies, to play sport with them, to 'stag on' in the duty room, to live and eat with them; it helped us form a real feeling of camaraderie. To suddenly find out that someone was being investigated was horrific. At the time we heard stories the SIB would search everything in a person's room. Everything. Your photos, books, records, wardrobe, dirty washing bag; everything was searched. We heard they'd keep you for hours, even days, just keeping delving on and on into even more personal, disgusting lines of questioning until they got what they wanted. I often feel I was so very lucky. I knew I had someone looking out for me, but I still feel 'survivor's guilt' to this day and my writing here has brought that to the fore. I know so many friends who were 'kicked out'. It's heartbreaking. The amount of money spent on their training, on uniform, back filling recruitment. The amazing members of our armed forces lost in a second. It's shocking.

My partner and I spent years being happy together, even when we were both posted to other regions of the country. We decided we wanted to live and be together. We knew we couldn't do that in the Army, so we decided to leave. We were living in such a frightening, false, oppressive environment, and although we didn't want to leave our Army life, neither of us wanted to live like that, with the constant fear of being found out.

Just think about that for a moment. Your job and career at risk because you said the wrong thing, hiding who you are for fear the wrong person might find out, not being able to share stories of your life with those around you unless you made your partner a 'he' or 'his'. It was like walking on a verbal tightrope. I had to become this person who lied and made up stories. It was like living in a spy movie, but it was real, and scary.

What else could we do? We both put in our eighteen months' notice letter, which meant we had eighteen months left to serve. Eighteen months of being careful and not getting caught. Our emotions were torn about leaving the job and the life we loved. Why should we have to? I couldn't help loving the person I did. I didn't judge others who were having affairs with the girls from the block. I didn't get involved in their private life. I felt so bitter. I left on 29 February 1984, at least the first time....

We'd bought a house in Devon where I had a job selling insurance and even had a company car, a Panda. After a few months, and for various reasons, we decided not to be together anymore. I blame the stress and fear we'd suffered and been subjected to for so long. It took its toll on our relationship and we never really settled to civilian life because of the bitterness we felt having lost the life we loved and the friendships we'd lost. Worst of all, though, we'd lost each other.

I didn't know what to do with myself. So, rightly or wrongly, I applied to re-join the Army. By now, the higher ranks of the WRAC knew I was gay. My application was accepted and I rejoined in October 1984 as a sergeant Army recruiter, just after a bomb had exploded at the Tory Party conference down the road in Brighton. I believe the only reason I was accepted back was because I was of value to the WRAC as a very good sportswoman. I played Army netball, badminton, volleyball and squash, as well as being a sprinter and high jumper in athletics. I'd even been training as part of Great Britain's handball team and played in the World Cup in Germany. Whatever the case, I was back in the life I loved, but this time without the person I loved to spend time with, laugh with, travel with, explore with; just being with and loved.

Despite this, life as a recruiter was a good one. I lived in an Army quarter, which consisted of a four-bedroom flat to myself on the old Territorial Army and Pay Corps site, just outside of Brighton (it's now a large housing estate). Brighton is a very gay city and I had a great time there. I started playing Army netball again and basketball for a local civilian team. I even met a new partner; a serving captain in the WRAC based in north London. We knew of each other but became close after our shared interest in volleyball; I played it, she was officer in charge (OIC) of it. Every Friday night she'd drive down for a weekend together and then back again early Monday morning. Weekends were fabulous. We'd walk the dog, find a gay bar and meet new local, civilian friends. We'd cook roast dinners, watch movies, listen to vinyl. It was almost like we were properly living together, even though we weren't, of course, as we were living in an Army quarter, but it still felt good.

The highlight of my career in the Army must've been when I captained the netball team. We won, like we did every year I played, and I went up to receive the trophy. I was so proud of myself of having the honour to represent and now captain and accept the winning Inter-services' trophy. What a special moment for me.

As my new partner was a captain, she'd attend formal WRAC officer functions. One evening, I dropped her and her captain friend, who we were staying with that weekend, at the Training Depot in Guildford for a function. It was a meeting with a meal to follow. They looked fabulous in their Army dress with red sash. Apparently, one of the items on the agenda was 'How are we going to get rid of lesbians from the WRAC?' She said she looked round the room and about 80% of the people there were gay. What a two-faced, absurd agenda item. This is how ridiculous life was back then. We were wanted and hounded out. For whatever reason, the Army wanted us, but, to be seen coming out of a gay club, you'd be investigated and thrown out. The very top of the WRAC had their fair share of gay women; all the way up to colonels and RSMs. Why would that be an agenda item? It was clearly just paying lip service to the MoD in the guise of addressing the issue. I bet, at that time, if the SIB had caught all gay women and thrown them out, there would've been no more WRAC. It would've been decimated. But that's just my opinion.

I left the Army, for the second time, with my captain partner in October 1987. We lived in Leicestershire, where I became a driving instructor, and we became famous for hosting wild parties with our friends. We finally split up in early 1989 when I backpacked around the world on my own.

I'd been planning such a trip for the best part of ten years, and although she said she'd wait for me for the six months I'd planned to travel, she moved on very quickly while I was away. This really made me believe I'd made a big mistake for having left the Army again for a relationship. I was originally intending to meet up with my first partner's sister in New Zealand and backpack back together, but this never worked out due to her mother being diagnosed with incurable cancer. Consequently, she went straight home and I travelled for four months exploring New Zealand's North and South Islands, the east coast of Australia, Singapore, up through Malaysia and some of the wonderful islands it has, and then up through Thailand to Bangkok. It was a trip of a lifetime which taught me, even at the age of 30, some valuable life lessons.

At the end of 1989, I once again drifted for a while, with no clue what I was going to do. I knew I had to find a job as I'd completely run out of money and had had to borrow from the bank of Mum and Dad to get me home from travelling. I walked into my local Federal Express and asked for a job doing multi-drop work and started the very next day. Life was very different. I did the job for about six months and was promoted to a mobile recruiter for home delivery work around the London area. Four months later I was contacted by a friend I used to play Army netball with, from 1979 to the early 1980s. She was working in the USA as a bodyguard and asked if I wanted to come join the team? Of course I did. I'd no partner, nowhere to live on my own (I was living back with Mum and Dad) and my job was always going to be a stop gap. What was stopping me? The added bonus was the team were all people I felt comfortable around, ex-military and more like-minded, with a warped sense of humour.

I spent about four years working as a bodyguard, based in Washington DC and around the world for the Saudi Royal Family. I'd met my now-wife during this period and we'd been together about a year when I decided to leave the job, live with my partner and go back to study for a new career. So, in 1996, at the tender age of 36, I attended Manchester Metropolitan University.

During my one-year postgraduate diploma in Human Resource Management, I was invited to the wedding of one of the princesses I'd previously worked for in DC, in Riyadh, Saudi Arabia. What an opportunity. The European ladies were picked up for free on a private jumbo jet in Paris, where I met several ladies I knew who'd boarded the plane from DC. We were in Riyadh for three days and were transported around by police-escorted buses. We had free use of hairdressers and makeup staff, who'd work their magic to make us look gorgeous. I was even allowed to choose a designer dress from the palace to wear and keep. I had so much fun, bearing in mind we didn't have any alcohol the entire time.

Reflecting back, I believe I should've stayed in the Army; both the first and the second time. But the fear of being 'found out' was too much and I left before I was pushed. I wanted to live my life as a free person and not constantly have to look over my shoulder. To have to talk in riddles and not give away names, places, or myself to others who may be listening. It was a time of fun, sport, laughter, camaraderie and enjoyment, but I couldn't be me. I couldn't be Lesley Davison. Not fully. My love of life back then was tainted with fear and apprehension, of constantly being 'on guard' because I didn't want to say the wrong thing and have the wrong person hear you. It was torturous. Why did I re-join, and put myself through that again? I suppose it was the place I felt most comfortable, despite everything I've said about being afraid or of being caught out. I know, it makes no sense to me either. It was a huge dilemma for me.

I carried the feelings of hiding myself into my future civilian careers, too, fearing to tell my colleagues for fear of losing my job, them not liking me, making my life difficult, etc. From the end of 1987, when I left the Army for the second time, I can honestly say I've never had any negativity, slander, bad words, or direct abuse from anyone in any of my jobs. Even today, at the ripe old age of 64, I still don't tell people very easily. The fear and pain have stuck, good and fast. It does loosen sometimes but I'm still guarded. Still battle scarred from 1979, some 45 years later.

I recently met my old sports officer from Woolwich, from way back in the early '80s. She told me that if I'd have stayed in the Army I'd have made a full career and easily received my commission, probably reaching the rank of major. Just think what my life would've been like if that had been anywhere close to being true. Sadly, it wasn't, just because of the person I loved. I missed out on playing sport at a high level, status and salary and pension.

I knew many ladies who were 'kicked out'. Shocking, horrible, disgusting investigations often, nearly always, resulting in the end of their careers. I was lucky. I honestly believe that someone, during my nearly nine years of service, was looking out for me. Kept me safe. I was careful, I was always careful, but I can't help but think what my life would've been be like if I could've just loved the person I wanted to, without fear of recrimination, loss of self-worth, career or pension.

The Army is like an insurance policy: one never needs it until an accident or event occurs. We're always there, ready to protect the nation, but many were never allowed to be because they loved someone of the same sex. The Army had in place an illegal policy against homosexual people serving in the armed forces and it ruined my and many of my friends' lives, too.

I know life in the armed forces is very different nowadays. There is full integration and you're fully accepted for who you are and who you love. I do feel bitterness and sadness for the way I had to live my life. The people I lost because we were in the Army. But that bitterness is completely taken over from the pride I still have for having served. Served my country. Whenever I can I wear my WRAC cap badge and veteran's badge with absolute pride.

Sometimes I can't help but wonder what could've been, if only. This is my story. I can't change it, but I'm glad life has now changed for those LGBT+ people serving.

It wasn't until becoming involved with Fighting With Pride (FWP) that I fully realised how I did feel about it all. It's very strange writing things down; it really makes you think about it more deeply. Thank you, FWP. I love being part of you all.

I would like to thank my wonderful wife for helping me write this. To try to capture those feelings and moments in my life in an attempt to help you all understand what life was like back in the day. Let us never return there.

Chapter 11

Nige's Story

---------------------------- Nige ----------------------------

This is my story of very proudly joining the Royal Marines, and an incident that would ultimately destroy my world and scar me for the rest of my life

To set the scene, I'm a 61-year-old heterosexual man, happily married with two children.

This year is the first time in over forty-five years that I've shared what happened to me when I joined the Royal Marines in 1977 as a 16-year-old recruit. I've been supported by a veterans' charity called Wintergreen, and also by the team at Fighting With Pride, who've helped me in beginning to tell my story.

Ever since I was a young boy, I'd wanted to become a Royal Marine Commando and wear the coveted green beret. I was even an avid reader of Commando magazines with their daring accounts of war exploits, such as the Cockleshell Heroes. I must also admit that I lied about my age to the local Scout group so that I could join them instead of the Cubs, because the Scouts wore green berets! I did get caught out, though, when the cub master went out with my sister and discovered my real age! Even then, I had my career mapped out and used to discuss it often with my mum. Firstly, I'd join the Royal Marines and learn how to fly helicopters. Then, if selected, I'd become part of the SBS. After serving my time, I'd then join the Civil Service and become a foreign diplomat, travelling the world. It was all sorted!

When I hit the ripe old age of 15, in 1977, I could finally apply to join the Royal Marines. I sat my entrance exam and interview in Wrexham, and after having my medical in Liverpool, which I passed with flying colours, a letter soon dropped on the doormat giving me a start date for Lympstone later that year.

My mum and dad came to wave me goodbye at the railway station, and two stops later, I met a school friend who was off to join the Navy which meant I had some company all the way down to Exeter. Once there, I met several other new recruits and together we caught a minibus to the Commando Training Centre Royal Marines at Lympstone.

It was like nothing I'd ever experienced in my short life before, but along with my fellow recruits, we were all in the same boat. The course is world renowned and inevitably we lost some people within days after they'd decided it wasn't for them. It was tough and many of us had similar thoughts, but I'd prepared well, was determined and I stuck with it. The recruits in my room seemed ok: a young guy from Newcastle in the bed opposite, and another recruit from Northern Ireland in the other corner.

There was quite a bit of classroom work to start with, which I wasn't overly fond of, but I knew it was a necessary part of the training. I didn't quite understand all the slang, but we were given little booklets to help us remember. I look back now and wonder why, as part of the slang in the booklet, homosexuals were given their own title of 'brown hatter'. Looking back, you can see how homophobia was a 'normal' part of military life, especially if it was printed in the training literature you were issued with!

There was, of course, a lot of physical activity, which I really enjoyed. I struck up a friendship with a recruit from Liverpool. We were both very proficient in martial arts, so once the official working day was done, we used to get access to the gym to train and practice our skills

The drill work was a little bit alien to me to start with, but it made me feel so proud: there's nothing better than marching to the beat of a military band – especially the band of the Royal Marines at an adjutants' parade.

I remember once when one of our troop was really struggling after a wet night's bivvy in the forest, so I emptied his Burgan and shared the load between my fellow recruits to make it lighter and more manageable for him to complete the march back to the vehicles. I did get a bit of a telling off for this, whilst at the same time being commended for my actions in supporting a team member. I was even asked why I was going through the ranks in this way, when with my school qualifications I could've gone down the Young Officer Training route, which was also conducted at Lympstone. My answer was a simple one: respect. By starting on the first rung of the ladder and working your way up the ranks, I hoped to gain the respect of the troops I'd be leading.

As we headed towards Christmas 1977, we proudly represented the Royal Marines in the Exeter Cathedral Christmas mass. It was a chance to show off our best uniforms to the people of the city and was a really proud moment for us all. However, we were all looking forward to going home for some Christmas leave, and the camp had organised some live music in the NAAFI for the recruits on that last and fateful weekend before we broke up.

We were young 16-year-old recruits, pumped up with adrenaline, surrounded by mates with access to lots of cheap booze. Before long, my night had become a complete blur, and then a total blank. The next thing I remember was being shouted at and woken up by some of the regular Marines. The young Geordie recruit from the bed opposite mine was in the same bed as me, and I'd no idea why or how, as he wasn't there on my request or invitation. He'd either come back to the room drunk and got into the wrong bed, or someone was having a laugh and thought it was funny to steer him to where I was comatose after my drunken night out.

We were immediately hauled off to a medical room under guard. The doctors were called and I was forced to endure an internal examination, without consent, where nothing untoward was discovered. Following this, I was taken away, still in a state of shock, half dazed, and probably under the influence, and locked up in a cell for the rest of the night, not really understanding what was going on.

During the following day, I had a visit from the camp Methodist minister. I wasn't at all religious but had to put something down when I joined. My dad was Methodist, and I'd been to a Methodist Sunday school once. I tried to plead my case to the minister that I'd done nothing wrong except go for a night out and wake up as I did. I was a heavy sleeper, but combined with the alcohol, there could've been an earthquake and I'd have slept right through it. Nowadays, I could possibly be classed as a victim: an individual had entered my bed, without my permission, whilst I was unconscious. Ever since that day I've had difficulty sleeping and still suffer with a medical condition called sleep apnea.

The following day, I had a meeting with the commanding officer, who told me I was going to be discharged and that a letter was to be sent to my parents explaining what'd happened. I felt such shame, as well as anger: I hadn't done anything wrong. How would my parents feel? My dad, who was a serving policeman, an ex-soldier, and in those days what you'd call a typical 'man's man': a drinker, smoker, fighter and flirt! My mother, meanwhile, was a very quiet church goer. They were both very Welsh and came from small towns in North Wales. How could I explain to them what'd happened? What would they think?

The commanding officer actually went on to say that he didn't think anything had happened but couldn't guarantee my safety from other people on the camp. He also told me the training team had great expectations of me and were looking to make me troop leader following the Christmas break.

I don't actually recall if he told me the specific reason for my dismissal, but I can only presume it was in relation to the ban, as I do recall having to explain my actions. However, all I could say was that I didn't remember how this other recruit had ended up where he did and reiterated that I wasn't gay but a heterosexual male who'd several girlfriends prior to joining the Royal Marines. To be honest, at that time I wasn't even aware of the ban or knew much about homosexuals – I don't think I'd even met one.

I then had to pack up my belongings and return my kit. I was left with nothing to remind me of what was to be, in my mind, the start of an illustrious career, in a role I'd always dreamed of. Not even a beret or a cap badge, and certainly not the green beret I'd spent my days and nights aspiring to wear once my training was complete.

I was then returned to my cell for the duration of my stay at Lympstone. Before going home, I was allowed to join my troop for breakfast to say my goodbyes, which I think added insult to injury. I was discharged the day before Christmas Eve 1977. I caught the same train as everyone else heading home on their Christmas leave, still in a state of disbelief and shock, thinking about what I was going to say to my mum and dad. I was still only 16, not six months out of school. I was also in a state of despair and even considered not going home at all but getting off at a stop along the way and ending my life, so deep was the hurt. But I wasn't a coward and argued with myself that suicide would've been the easy way out. So I went home to a hero's welcome and then had to tell my mum and dad what'd happened. Thankfully, they believed and supported me.

I've no idea if they received a letter, and if they did, they never spoke to me of its contents. However, even though I'd been discharged, I still kept receiving copies of the *Globe & Laurel* through the post, which was agonising, bearing in mind what'd happened to me and that I was now no longer part of the corp.

I am now in my sixties and in all my years, there' never been one single day where I haven't relived those final moments in the Marines. My experiences drove me down many deep and dark paths, and over the years I ended up mixing with the wrong crowds, and I suppose at one point I actually became the wrong crowd. I took to drink and drugs, but thankfully never got into trouble with the police as I was always too quick for them. I contemplated suicide on many occasions and was very close a number of times, but luckily my friends were nearby to talk me round.

I've lived with constant guilt about what occurred, and when campaigns such as the Falklands, Iraq and Afghanistan happened, I felt a guilt and emptiness, believing I should've been there. What made it harder was being with friends who were in the Navy when the Falklands erupted, and them receiving the call to return to base to be shipped out – that should've been me, too! I also had friends in the Welsh Guards who went off to war, and when some returned seriously injured, I struggled to deal with the fact that I wasn't there. Yes, I could've been hurt or even killed, but I didn't get that chance to serve Queen and country as I'd always wanted to. It'd all been taken away from me.

Remembrance Sunday is bittersweet for me, as I so would've loved to march proudly wearing my green beret, but sadly that was not to be. What happened to me should never have happened to anyone, especially someone so young and naïve.

As a straight male I was unsure about whether or not my story would be relevant to the enquiry. However, I've lived through the same or similar experiences to some of the people from the LGBT+ community and now, following the support of both Wintergreen and Fighting With Pride, I've begun to find comfort sharing my story of this dreadful policy and the damage it has inflicted.

It's not easy to tell this sorry tale. I received counselling through Wintergreen, who were the first people I shared my story with. I sobbed through the whole episode as I spoke for the first time about those fateful weeks at CTCRM.

Over the years I've become more and more aware of the struggles people from the gay community have faced, because I, as a heterosexual male, faced those same discriminations, too, all those years ago as a young, naïve, 16-year-old recruit. In more recent years I've become an LGBT+ ally and even organised an event locally to raise awareness of the difficulties and discrimination faced by people from this community. My experiences have indeed strengthened my resolve to ensure fairness and equality for everyone. I was prepared to find courage on the battlefield, but my opportunity for courage has been with a pen rather than a sword.

If you ask me what I want from reparations, I remain unsure, but there is honour in the apology which has been made. At the very least, people know of the ban and of its impact upon those who were hounded out and those, like me, who became collateral damage. Sadly, there is no reparation that will truly make up for all the years of my life that have been affected by what happened to me, and every day I feel a nagging sense of loss.

Chapter 12

I Never Did Make Friends with the Drill Square

——————— Gwen Pettigrew ———————

It's often said that joining the Army makes a man of you.

On the evening of 6 April 1989, I was involved in a road traffic accident (RTA) near my home in York. The civil police attended. As part of the process, they asked to see my driving licence. At that time, my licence was still registered to the barracks in York where I was stationed with the Royal Corps of Signals as a sergeant terminal equipment technician. I was asked for my ID card. I had temporary one, with no picture, and one of the police officers said he would have to go to my base on the other side of York to confirm I was who I said I was.

The next day, I was preparing my Ptarmigan repair node that I commanded as a sergeant for deployment on the Sunday to an annual R Sigs exercise in Germany known as Flying Falcon (also known by the rank and file of the Signals as 'Flying Fuckup'). Working in the back of the ERV, I was repairing a faulty piece of equipment when a corporal from my troop workshop arrived to tell me I was wanted in the Foreman of Signal's (FOS) office. When I got to the office, the FOS was there, as well as the acting troop staff sergeant and two men in civilian suits, who were introduced to me as members of the Royal Military Police Special Investigation Branch. They wanted to talk to me regarding the accident and that I needed to accompany them to their detachment office across the road from the barracks. I was expecting to walk to the Special Investigation Branch (SIB) detachment, but instead they put me in the back of their Ford Escort estate car.

In the car they turned to me saying, 'We don't give a fuck about the RTA. We're more interested in the way you were dressed. What have you got to say?' I'd been expecting to be asked questions about the accident as the military police were interested whenever the civil police were involved with a member of the Army. It hadn't crossed my mind that the civil police officer would've done anything more than confirm my identity. Naïve, I know. My world imploded. Do I make up a story about going to a fancy-dress party or do I come clean? I came clean. 'I'm transexual,' I said. 'I handed my notice in last month and after I get out, I'm intending to undergo the sex change process.' From the looks on their faces, they weren't expecting that answer, and it was a few seconds before they replied. 'Well, you're under arrest pending investigation into homosexual behaviour.' With that, we drove off to the SIB detachment.

I'd joined the Army three weeks after my eighteenth birthday and had served just under thirteen years and nine months at the time of my arrest. I'd grown up in a small, former mining village in North Lanarkshire, although now most of the population was employed in the large heavy industry and steelwork firms in the nearby town of Motherwell, or in some of the big American companies. My family consisted of my dad, mum, younger sister and me. We lived in a housing association scheme. My dad worked for Honeywell's as an engineer and would later work in the Glasgow shipyards. Dad had served in the Royal Signals during the war. He had a terrible temper at times and from what I know now, I suspect he had PTSD. Mum stayed at home looking after us all although she did occasionally get part time jobs. She was a good cook and a skilled needlewoman; often making our school clothes, as well as shirts for Dad and lots of knitting.

As a pre-school primary kid, I was quite happy. It was during the early days of primary school when I asked my mum, 'When did I become a girl?' Her reply was, 'Don't be silly and go outside and play'. I tried not to be silly for the next twenty-odd years.

Primary school was awful. Physical punishment in the form of the Lochgelly tawse or "the belt" was a daily occurrence in all the classes. I was immensely jealous of the girls playing skipping ropes, hopscotch or playing with dolls. I so wanted to join them, but quickly realised that doing so would get me bullied and beaten up, so I joined in the boys' games. I still got bullied and was seen as bit of a 'wee jessie'. The bullying stopped when I splatted my main antagonist's nose into a bloody mess. After that, any time there was remote chance of bullying, I'd strike first.

Secondary school was much better; I loved it. By now I'd hit puberty and hated all the changes that were happening to my body. I remember pushing the now-descended testes back up into the inguinal canals and hoping they stayed there, but they didn't. Body hair was also starting to appear. I'd rip out with tweezers so that it wouldn't grow back; it did. Still, I kept trying. For a very many years to come.

In my second year my parents had become fed up with me moping around the house and so my dad convinced me to join the Army Cadets. I found I really enjoyed it, and it even turned out I was a really good shot, so I ended up in various shooting competitions and winning some prizes. After a couple of years, I was made a cadet sergeant.

When I was nearly 15 my mum found some make-up, a skirt and a blouse in my room. A big confrontation with my parents ensued. I can't really remember what I said, but I told them I liked wearing the clothes and make-up as it made me feel happier. My mum talked to our GP, who suggested I see a psychiatrist.

A few weeks later my father and I took the bus (we didn't have a car) to Hamilton for an appointment with a psychiatrist. The journey was completed in silence. I was totally terrified as to what might happen. I thought I might be sent to the local mental hospital and locked away. After all, that's what psychiatrists did, wasn't it?

The psychiatrist did ask me lots of questions, many of which I was unable to answer as I didn't know how to respond. He asked if I liked boys or girls. I told him I didn't know. How did I feel when I wore the skirt and blouse? I told him I felt better; that I didn't feel I belonged as a boy. How long the appointment lasted, I don't know. I do know I just wanted to get away from all those awkward questions. Next, he spoke to my dad. I've no idea what was said, other than my dad being told it was a "phase" and that I'd grow out of it.

About six weeks later I went for a further appointment with the psychiatrist. Once again, he asked if I wanted to dress in girls' clothes. I told him I didn't. At that moment I didn't, the fear of what'd happen if I did was overwhelming. That was the last appointment I had with him.

A few months later a friend and I were doing a team project for science. I went round to his house a few times to work on our report. One evening, I've no idea how, but we started kissing. After a bit I stopped it, telling him I didn't want to. I was so confused. Yes, it was nice, but it also felt that it wasn't me, I felt out of place.

I was also in the school's dramatics society, not as one of the actors, but instead helping with the lighting and making scenery. I became friendly with one of the girls who was working on the set. We'd just finished some scenery when the teacher who ran the club told us that what we'd made looked really good. My friend gave me a big hug and we started kissing. Again, I got the out-of-place feeling. Now I really was confused. Did I like both boys and girls? I didn't know that bisexuals even existed back then. What was I?

For English we were studying Shakespeare's *Twelfth Night*. We were discussing how the Elizabethan audience would've found Viola's cross dressing as Cesario funny because at the time, Viola would've been played by a male. The teacher made a throw away comment that there were people in the world who did change their sex. It was like being hit with a brick. Was this me? I convinced myself that it couldn't be.

By now the teachers at school were asking what we all intended to do when we finished school. What I really wanted was to be away from my parents and school. I knew I enjoyed the Cadets and so with a bit of research, I settled on REME (Royal Electrical and Mechanical Engineers) or the Royal Signals, where I could indulge my passion for electronics.

So, on 8 July 1975, I found myself at the gates of Helles barracks, home of 11th Signal Regiment, which was the then Royal Signals recruit training regiment. I wasn't given a warm welcome. On arrival I was met by a regimental police sergeant in full apoplectic mode. Apparently, no new recruits should've arrived that day as the Queen was paying a visit. I was rapidly run down to the accommodation block and shoved out of the way.

Basic training was hard, both mentally and physically, but I did enjoy it. Well maybe not the drill (I was later to get a confidential report that said 'Corporal Pettigrew and the drill square will never be friends'). I passed off in December 1975, my dad came to the parade and it was the first time ever he told me he was proud of me.

My first working posting was to 233 Signal Squadron Northern Ireland for three years. I arrived in Lisburn at 08:00 on a cold, wet November Saturday morning. I worked in the Tech Troop workshop and on my first day was given a teleprinter to service. I started stripping the printer and carefully cleaned it. The workshop sergeant laughed at me, took over, and dumped the various modules in a big bath of paraffin. I said in my best Scot's voice, 'Yeh cannae dunk yon bits in there they won't work!' I was wrong. After this, 'Dunks' became my nickname, which I didn't mind because, well, I didn't like or want my own name.

Three weeks in, the reality of being in Northern Ireland hit terrifyingly home when I was attached to 2 Para for twenty-four hours of patrol training in the Falls Road area. The Paras were amazing and watching them made me realise that I would've been a crap infantry soldier.

In the squadron bar I'd made friends with one of the WRACs called J. One night I walked with her back to the block. At the door I said good night. 'You not going to kiss me then?' she asked. I gave her a brief peck on the cheek. 'Not like that you divvy. A proper one!' Next day at work, one of the tech sergeants asked me, 'Young Dunks, were you with J last night?' I told him I was. 'Watch that one. She's dangerous, she'll chew you up and spit you out. She's using you. She's a lezzie and takes sproglets and uses them for cover.' I didn't see J for a few days and when I asked her if she was a lesbian, she denied it.

Women weren't allowed in the men's accommodation, but the rule was regularly flouted. One weekend I'd gone to the washroom and found J kissing my roommate's girlfriend. When I got back, I said I'd just seen his girlfriend in the washroom. He erupted. 'Fucking dykes!' he said and stormed out of the room. He came back a few minutes later, his hand covered in blood, and he necked half a bottle of vodka from his locker. He'd punched a mirror in the washroom. I applied first aid and tried my best to stop the bleeding. He passed out, so his friend and I took turns checking he was ok. Later I'd find out that J was sent back to the WRAC training depot for discharge because she was either thought to be or was a lesbian, but not before she experienced a harrowing SIB investigation. Little was I to know that I, too, would experience the SIB.

Soon I was working a lot in civvies and we were allowed to grow our hair longer, but after a while I was sent on a ten-week course with the RAF and told I'd have to get my hair cut. I was heartbroken, but I didn't know why.

Returning from the RAF course, I'd decided I'd like to become a foreman of Signals. Foreman of Signals are the highest qualified non-commissioned technical people in the signals. I took and passed my Class I technician's entrance exam and had been promoted to corporal. I was also moved to the cryptographic equipment workshop and took to repairing crypto gear like a duck to water.

My tour in Northern Ireland ended in 1979 and I was posted back to 8 Signal Regiment. I settled in well and could also go home to my parents more often. On one trip home I had to buy some new clothes as my traditional attire of jeans, desert wellies and sweatshirt were looking decidedly scruffy. Then something broke and I ended up buying a skirt, blouse and make-up. Over the next few months, I acquired more female clothing, which I'd wear in my bedroom when on leave. I'd lock them away in a cupboard that only I had a key to. The feeling of calm I felt was indescribable, but then my brain would castigate me with thoughts of 'You're not like this, stop it!' and I'd feel like crap again.

Back at the base, I started to feel like I was an alien on a strange planet. I found it very difficult to relate to what they were talking about and their attitudes. I did wonder if I was gay, but I didn't feel attracted to men, or even women come to that. So I tried to push the feeling back in the deep recesses of my mind, concentrating on work, running, and, of course, that good old Army fallback of lots of alcohol. It worked for a bit. One day, I saw an advert for a 'gay switchboard helpline'. I was getting worried about the feeling I was having about my body, and who I was. I didn't think I could talk to my course mates, or anyone come to that. The old fear of being locked away in a psychiatric ward came back. After some considerable procrastination, I eventually phoned the helpline and explained as best I could how I felt. Bless them, they tried their hardest to understand. At the end of the call, they mentioned a monthly meeting for transvestites and that maybe talking to them could help.

Some months later, I plucked up the courage to go to one of those meetings in Newcastle. I got some of my clothes from home and brought them down one weekend, stashing them in the panniers of my motorbike.

At the meeting there were a couple of gay guys and a transvestite. They told me there was a little room where I could get changed if I wanted to. For a while, I just talked to them. Eventually I thought I'd come this far, why not get changed? I did, even though my heartrate was through the roof and I felt sick. After a while there was little knock at the door and a voice asking, 'Are you ok?' No, I wasn't, what the hell was I doing? Was I insane? Was I the only person who felt like this? Above all, I felt alone and frightened. The voice at the door continued. 'It's ok, no one will hurt you or judge you.'

When I came out of the room, the two gay guys said I looked nice. I felt strangely relieved. We had quite a long chat about how I felt and how the other people there felt. I realised I didn't feel the same way as the two gay guys, and after talking to the transvestite, I discovered he had no antipathy toward his body, but just liked wearing female clothing. On the way back to Catterick, I dumped the clothes in a bin. I was still none the wiser as to what the hell was going on with me, but whatever it was, I wish it would bloody stop.

My time at Catterick was coming to an end and I was posted to 2 Armoured Division Signal Regiment (2ADSR) in a place called Lübbecke.

Sometime in 1981, the happily now defunct *News of the World* ran a story on the actress/model, Caroline Cossey, who'd appeared in the Bond film *For Your Eyes Only*. The headline was 'James Bond Girl Was a Boy'. It was the first time I'd heard the word transexual. As I read the story, I remember thinking it was amazing. Part of me thought, 'Is that what I am?' and the other part of me was 'No, you can't be!'

After this, I set off on my 500cc motorbike bound for my new posting in Germany. Lübbecke was a lovely little German town on the north side of the Minden ridge. We called it Sleepy Hollow. There was lot to learn and for the first few months it was intense. I had to learn how to camouflage trucks and get used to the exercise routine of move, set up, boredom if everything worked, followed by take down, move and repeat. One thing sitting on shift in front of the printer console waiting for something to happen or go wrong gave you was time to think. I started to do a lot of uncomfortable thinking. What the fuck was I?

In 1984 I was made a sergeant. Living in the WO and sergeants' mess meant there were often trips out, although they were more like organised piss ups. One of these trips was to Hamburg. After bumbling around a few of the less salubrious places of the city's red-light district, someone, I think he was warrant officer who'd been in the Army since the late 1960s, suggested we move on to another bar. We did, but it didn't take long to realise it wasn't your usual bar. The person who suggested we went there must've seen the expression on my face. He laughed, 'What this, Dunks? Never seen a kai tai before? Lady boys.' Another warrant officer called him a twat, saying we should get out of there. After all, if there were monkeys (RMP) around, we'd be in the shit. The elderly WO continued to take the piss out of me, trying regale me with tales of Singapore and Bugis Street. Eventually, a few of us had had enough and went back to Verden. A month later, I went back on my own to this bar and got talking to some of the girls there. Two of them spoke really good English. They were the first transexuals I met, but after talking to them I began to realise we had a lot in common. It was like someone finally understood how I felt. I was terrified this was true. It mustn't be true. I went back a few times, but stopped when I realised I was putting myself at risk from the RMP.

My head was a mess: so many conflicting thoughts. I tried hard to subdue and obliterate them, but to no avail. It all came to a head on one exercise. The QM had asked me to take a safe with live ammo and store it on my vehicle. I got to thinking that instead of dealing with the crap going on my head, I'd just load the SMG and blow my head off. I opened the safe, looked at the ammo in its loaded magazines, and took one out. The magazine sat by the SMG and for what seemed like ages, I stared at it, tears falling down my face. Suddenly there was a knock at the door. I put the magazine in the safe and shut it. The SMG went in the rack at the back of the truck. I opened the door and a couple of soldiers from a highland regiment came in with some faulty kit for repair. Hiding my tears, I made them some egg banjoes, filled them full of tea and fixed their kit.

I realised then I had to do something and that I couldn't do it there in Germany; I had to get back to UK. Once there, I'd have to find somewhere to live, someone who could help me. So, in mid-March 1986, I loaded my trusty motorbike with all the gear I'd need (the rest having been packed in a couple of shipping boxes), and said goodbye to Germany, pushing my bike to the barrack gate over the ice strewn cobbles bound for my new posting in York.

York was a shock: the mess was in upheaval as it was being renovated, so three of us were told to move into an empty married quarter. At the weekend, it would just be me there as one of my housemates would go off to his girlfriend's and the other home to his wife. Realising that there'd be no one in the house, I brought clothes from home and would dress up. Eventually, I plucked up the courage to park my car outside the front of the quarters and go into town. I also started to look for a house to buy.

I found out about a trans group that met in Leeds. It took a while but after a few failed attempts, I went to one of the meetings. There were about twenty or so there. After a few times, I became friendly with two other people: one was in her late twenties while the other was much older. They both were transexuals and stood out from the from the rest of the group, who classed themselves as straight transvestites. They listened carefully to what I said about how I felt, as well as asking me lots of searching questions. I told them I'd maybe transition sometime in the future, and the younger of my friends left me in no doubt of what the cost of transitioning could be. The older one told me it was something I'd need to decide for myself. There was no rush and if I did and realised that it wasn't the right thing, then it was ok to do a U turn.

By July 1987 I'd found a house and had got a mortgage. I asked for permission as a single person to live out, which the regimental CO agreed to. Living out took some getting used to; I now had to feed myself, pay bills and run a household budget. I'd get home from work and would get changed into the clothing I felt comfortable with. By now, I'd chosen the name Gwen.

When regiment got a new RSM, he quickly took a dislike to me. In fact, he seemed to take a dislike to most of his SNCO. Sometime in 1988, I pissed him off big time and received six months of day-on day-off orderly sergeant duties, which gave me a lot of time to think. One of the female mess staff made friends with me, telling me I looked as if I could do with a friend. She was easy to talk to. One day, I told her what I was feeling and about Gwen. She did seem a little surprised but told me what I'd said was safe with her. Towards the end of 1988, we met up for coffee on a Saturday: I went as Gwen. 'I didn't think you'd look like that!' was her first comment, but after a while she said I looked happy and comfortable. When I asked what she meant, she told me that until that day, she'd seen me as quite an unhappy and uncomfortable person. I didn't know what to say but she was right. It was then I realised that I had to get out the army ASAP and sort my life out. I started looking into resettlement courses and what I had to do to leave.

In the beginning of March 1989, I handed in my twelve-month notice. I was happy I'd made my decision I now just had to bide my time. Sadly, with no thanks to the police, that didn't happen and I quickly found myself in the SIB interrogation room with two SIB sergeants who were about to rip my life to pieces, with no legal representation.

The first round of interrogation was about how I was dressed, so I explained I was not a gay male but a male to female transexual. This session was quite short, maybe about half an hour. The SIB then told me they wanted to search my house and if I didn't give my permission, they'd get a warrant and turn up mob handed with the civil police to search my house. This would be noticed by my neighbours (who I was on good terms with) and would cause all sorts of gossip. I acquiesced and they searched my house. They found diaries, address books, photographs, letters, as well as books and some VHS tapes of documentary programmes with transsexual people. It was more than enough evidence. When they searched my kitchen, they opened the fridge and found half an OXO cube wrapped in foil. They immediately accused me of having cannabis resin. I told them they were wrong, but it took a good while to convince them that it was, indeed, just half an OXO cube.

Back in the interrogation room, the questioning began again. They went through the 'evidence' they'd gathered and asked about each item. Soon they started looking closer at the address books. Who was this? How did I know them? They did the same for the diaries and photographs. One of them took the books, magazines and VHS tapes away to another room in the building. The questioning soon became more aggressive, asking who the people in the photographs were, where they worked, their address etc. I told them the best I could. They started going over the photographs again, but this time asking if I'd had sex with the people in question. This included family members. Next, they did the same with the address books. In one book, I had names and address of companies I'd bought parts for my motorbikes from, as well as other things such as plumbers, etc. They asked if I'd had sex with any of those. I told them no. But there were two photographs they pounced on. They were of me and another transexual friend and were compromising. They questioned me over and over about these, but I wouldn't tell them my friend's name or where they lived.

Finally, at about 22.30, they told me they'd finished for the time being. They were going to take me to the Green Howards' barracks at Strensall, which was about 15 minutes away. When we arrived at the guard room, the orderly officer, a WO2, was waiting. The SIB told him they wanted to put me in a cell, but he said that as I was a sergeant, the correct procedure was to detain me in the WO and sergeants' mess, which deflated the SIB a bit. They then informed the orderly officer that I must be escorted to the toilet and watched with the door open. However, he told them I was now his prisoner and that they could leave. With the SIB gone, the officer asked me if I was ok, and I told him I was. Next, he asked if I was going to do a 'runner' or 'top myself' (meaning commit suicide). I told him no. His next question surprised me: he asked when I'd last eaten. When I told him, he asked the guard commander to phone the duty cook, who then made me steak and chips. After that meal, I went to one of the guest rooms in the mess and went to bed. I don't recall if I slept well, probably not.

The SIB arrived a little after 08.30 the next morning and took me back to York, where they started questioning me again. At first it was the same questions and accusation as the Friday. I gave the same answers. Then they asked a few questions about transsexuality, which I answered as best I could. Around 10.00, they said I was being taken to the medical centre for an exam. The medical officer, who was a local GP and a reservist, was waiting for us when we arrived. She told me she'd been asked to carry out a digital examination of my rectum to see if there was a relaxation of the sphincter, which would show I'd had anal penetration (which I had not). By the end of exam I was in floods of tears. I felt totally humiliated and dirty. The medical officer was also crying, and even asked if I minded telling her what was going on. I started to tell her, but halfway through the SIB knocked at the door, demanding to know if she'd finished. She told them she hadn't and was calming me down. When I'd finished my story, she told me that if I still was in York when this was all over, I should register with her practice and she'd get me the help I needed. Eventually, the SIB let me go home and I was told that until there was an outcome from the investigation, I'd need to commute from York to work at Catterick.

Tidying up after the SIB search took two days. I was crying a lot. On the Saturday, I started the painful process of electrolysis and as a big 'fuck you' to the Army, I got my ears pierced.

And so I went to 11 Sigs depot troop for my work at Catterick. By now my regiment had returned from exercise, and I heard from various sources that they'd a lot of grief on the ferry. They'd been told I'd been arrested for firearms offences, which was believable as I was heavily involved in target shooting. The orderly sergeant who was on duty the night of the RTA had told a lot of people. He'd also started a rumour that I'd been involved in child abuse, which was a complete lie. My troop had defended me on the trip over to Germany, so I felt I had to tell them what was happening. I wrote them a letter and gave it to the troop staffie to read. He later told me that while they didn't really understand, they had a lot of sympathy for me and wished me well. I also asked the RSM to quash the rumours and to get the staff sergeant who'd spread them to apologise. He did put a stop to them, but I never received an apology.

Towards the end of May I was ordered to a psychiatrist appointment at the military hospital in Catterick. The psychiatrist was an RAMC captain. He asked me lots of questions about my childhood, why I thought I was transexual and lots more. At the end of the interview, he told me he didn't think I could possibly be transsexual as I didn't fit the profile: I wasn't effeminate in manner nor did I look at all feminine. I was probably just a gay male in denial, or I was just trying to get out of the Army early (this bit has never made sense to me as I'd already given my notice in March). This was horrendous. I admit I wasn't effeminate, hell, I'd spent the best part of twenty-five years trying to suppress anything that would even suggest I was. Of course I didn't look feminine: I had a military haircut and was in a male uniform. I was a short, stocky Scots person with a heavy accent, not some willowy tall showgirl!

In July I was told that I wouldn't be court martialled, which was a relief (although I was to find out later that they'd known this for over a month before telling me). They then told me I wouldn't get my pension or resettlement privileges. This was devastating; part of resettlement was a lump sum of about two and a half months' salary. I was very upset when I returned to the depot troop. The OC, seeing I was distraught, asked me what was going on. After I told him, he said as I wasn't being court martialled, my pension and resettlement shouldn't be forfeit. He advised I write to the then Secretary of State for Defence, Tom King. He also talked to the 11 Sigs resettlement officer, who confirmed that I was entitled to resettlement. A few weeks later, my place was confirmed on a six-week microelectronics course at Plymouth College of Further Education, starting that September.

Soon after that, I had my CO's interview and reported to the RSM in my No 2 uniform. It was a very loose fit: I'd lost over 2.5 stone since April and now weighed less than 10 stone. The RSM tried his best by pulling my jacket in to make it fit, but he still said I looked like a half empty bag of spuds tied in the middle. The CO's interview was horrible. He gave me the most disgusted of looks. I don't know if that was because he thought I was gay, or that I'd taught his sons how to shoot small bore rifles at his request (I'd run the regimental small bore shooting team until I was arrested). My discharge date was set for 23 October.

After the interview, the RSM told me to wait in his office. I stood at attention for what seemed years but was probably only a minute. He told me to sit and asked if I'd like a coffee. 'I don't know what the full story is, sergeant,' he said. 'I haven't been told much by the CO but would like to know.' I told him what was going on and what I intended to do. After I'd finished, he looked at me and said, 'Bloody hell. You've got balls, I'll give you that.'

'Not if I have anything to do with it,' I replied. He sat for a minute, mystified, then laughed. With that, he called me by my first name and wished me all the best for the future.

On the Thursday before I went on my resettlement course, my troop, with great kindness, held my leaving do in a well-known York pub. All but three of troop turned up. My troop OC (the FOS) was on his resettlement course, another member was also on a course and the third member (a staunch catholic) didn't want to attend. Some other people from the regiment came, as did two WRAC sergeants I knew from living in the mess. They'd had a collection for a going away present: a very nice fountain pen which, according to the troop staffie's speech, I'd need as I'd be writing a lot of job applications. I still use that pen today. They also gave me the remainder of the collection (£30) as they weren't sure what else to get me. We all departed fairly drunk, but on amicable terms.

When I went to my course in Plymouth, the accommodation was in the naval dockyard, HMS Drake. Unbeknown to me, my troop OC was also on his resettlement course and I met him one night in the bar. He was a bit standoffish, which was unusual as he was normally very pleasant to talk to. It turned out he hadn't been informed what was going on with me and the SIB, so I told him what'd happened and what my intentions were. At the end of the conversation, he looked quite perplexed and told me he couldn't get his head around what I was doing, but that he wished me well for the future.

On 23 October 1989, I was discharged after fourteen years and 108 days of service under QR 1975 para 9.414: 'Services no longer required'. As I signed various forms, the orderly room sergeant, either maliciously or by misinterpreting the regulations, falsely informed me that my discharge came under the 'Rehabilitations of Offender Act', which carried a seven-year tariff. It meant I had to declare this to any employer who requested this information, a fact that was to bite me many times in future job interviews.

On the Tuesday, I signed on the dole and registered with the practice of the GP who'd examined me. I was given an appointment to see her on the Friday and when she asked me how I was and if I felt the same way as before, I told her I did and that I wanted to be referred to the GIC at Charing Cross hospital. After pulling out a letter for her desk, she told me she'd already looked into it and had written a referral letter for me. Giving me the letter, she told me to take it away and think on it. I was to come back with a decision, but I had to take at least three weeks or longer to decide if this was what I really wanted to do. Three weeks later, I went back and told her to send it. This was the last time I saw her: she died four months later of a massive heart attack. I never got to thank her. I transitioned in August 1992 and have no regrets, other than I wish I'd done it sooner.

Somehow, with a lot of luck and lots of lovely caring people, I've survived. I often wonder how that lonely soul I was back in Army would've reacted if I was to travel back in time and tell them it was going to be ok. I probably would've told myself to fuck off!

It's often said that joining the Army makes a man of you. In my case, it failed.

Chapter 13

Web of Vice

Steve Thomas

I was born in Bristol and attended the local comprehensive school. Although I wasn't the brightest of pupils, I had a passion for music and started having flute lessons from the age of 12, even playing in the school orchestra. One of my friends was in the local cadet force and so I also joined. We used to go every week and during the summer would go away on a two-week camp, staying in tents and going to firing ranges, getting a feel for what Army life could be like. I grew up in the south of the city, with easy access to countryside and open fields where we'd often have pretend 'battles' and stay out for hours. The days always seemed longer then and on hotter days, we used to swim in the local river, usually in our pants, and boys being boys mean these would occasionally be pulled down. Sometimes we'd swim naked, and I used to look at the other boys and them at me, too. Was this just adolescent fun or was it a sign I was going to grow up different to the other boys – or were they also different? This was during the early 1970s so being gay wasn't a subject that was talked about. I'd gone out with girls, as did the other boys, so who knew whether any of us would be gay or if it was just part of growing up.

When I reached 16, I decided to stay on in the sixth form and continue to study music. We had a new music teacher who decided to break tradition and set up a swing band rather than an orchestra, and I had the opportunity to learn to play the saxophone. As I was one of the older boys, I was given a baritone sax to play due to its large size, and also doubled up on the flute. We gave regular concerts and performances and although I was normally quite quiet, I almost had an alter ego when we were playing and always got a buzz from being on stage.

I never had an idea of what career path I'd take in life. I could read and write music better than I could English, so an office job was probably not the right choice for me. The wife of my head music teacher worked at the local Army careers office and suggested I should talk to her to see if this might suit me. Being a member of the cadets, it seemed a natural choice.

At the age of 17 I enlisted into the Army knowing it would be my duty to defend the Queen and country and help protect the freedoms that being British allowed. My first posting was to Crick Howell in South Wales. (Ironically, the barracks are only 10 miles from where I now live and we occasionally drive past. Although only occupied part time, it still holds memories.) I did my basic training, which involved all the usual infantry duties, before passing out and transferring to the junior band to finish my training. My first posting to the Gloucestershire Regiment was near Blackpool, although we spent a lot of time in London Trooping the Colour on Horse Guard's Parade and marching up The Mall to Buckingham Palace. It was 1977 and I was lucky to take part in the Queen's Silver Jubilee festivities at Wembley Stadium, which included massed bands with nearly 2,000 musicians taking part in the finale: probably the most amazing event of my life.

We returned to Blackpool and for more training in advance of being posted to Northern Ireland, where I was sent at just 18. This was during 1977-78, when Troubles were still at their height. I served there for one year and although we didn't perform street duties, we still had to do armed guard and escort duties. The band performed locally at schools and village halls trying to improve the British Army's public relations. On one occasion, a local pub in Limavady was blown up and people were killed. I can't remember if any soldiers were killed, but they were known to frequent the premises. One night a bomb was thrown into the barracks, damaging the sergeants' mess. We marched through the centre of Belfast, which was a nervous affair and the only time I ever played carrying side arms. During the tour of Ireland, I was given the opportunity to go to the Royal Military School of Music in London, which I accepted as this would save me from serving an additional year in Northern Ireland, as well as improve my skills as a musician.

The atmosphere at the school of music was far more relaxed: no weapons, no running up hills, just music. Certainly not the macho image that was portrayed back at the regiment. I mixed with a lot of other musicians, which was enjoyable, and I think I did well. We all thought one of the student bandmasters was gay and while there was some humour about this, none of it was aggressive, just mildly homophobic, more boys being boys. The bandmaster was also my music theory teacher.

Sadly, while I was there, one of my grandfathers passed away. I was allowed to attend the funeral and wear my uniform with my Northern Ireland medal on show. Although it was a sad occasion, I felt proud wearing it and I think my grandparents and other relatives also felt proud of me.

At the school, I met a guy called Chris. We spent a lot of time together and whenever we were with each other there was what felt like an electric energy. I think we both fancied each other, but the fear of getting caught prevented us from having a relationship. The school broke up for the Easter break and on my return, I was called up to the office, only to be told that Chris had taken his own life. I don't know the exact reason, but I often wonder if it was out of fear of being gay and getting caught. Had we had a relationship, maybe things could've been different. Who knows?

I was then posted to Munster in Germany. When I arrived, the band were on leave. I went to the HQ to let them know I was there and they said I needed to sort out a German bank account etc. One of the junior chefs was there and offered to show me around the local area and where the bank was. After I'd set up an account, we wandered around the town and called into a few bars. By the end of the night, we were quite drunk and after returning to camp, we spent the night together. Everyone had told me that life would be different in Germany, and it looked as if they were right. I saw John later the following day, but he chose to ignore me. I'm not sure if he was embarrassed or didn't want anyone finding out about what'd happened due to the risks involved.

The next eighteen months were spent touring Germany, doing parades, etc. We visited Arnhem on two occasions to do memorials for soldiers who'd fallen. We also went to Denmark and Sweden twice and I was also lucky to go to Berlin to do the Tattoo. We went through Check Point Charlie and stood on the wall looking over to East Germany. Looking at the desperation the other side made me feel proud to be in the Army and enjoy the freedoms of what I thought being British stood for.

Life in the band was going well and I was in line for promotion, but part of my life felt empty. We were lucky to go on a skiing exercise which funnily enough was called Operation Snow Queen. There was a guy called Jim in my skiing class who I got on well with and on the last night before we were due to return, we all got a bit drunk and Jim and I spent an intimate night together. The following day we returned to Munster and Jim went on leave to the UK. I thought nothing more of it until there was a knock on my door and there stood Jim, who'd returned from leave early. The relationship continued and we became quite close. I didn't know when we first met that Jim knew other gay soldiers in Munster so one night, he took me to a gay bar to meet some of his other friends. Some were in the British Army, but there were others in the Germany Army doing national service, as well as some American soldiers. It was a good time; I was happy and work was going well. We all met frequently and went out together. One of the British soldiers was seeing a German soldier who had his own flat, so we often stayed there away from ever-watching eyes. During this period, I went through a process of my own acceptance. I knew my life would be different and not involve what everyone expected, such as getting married, having children, etc.

Jim told me one night that one of the other British soldiers was under investigation for being homosexual. There'd been two occasions when he'd propositioned other soldiers during drinking bouts, and they'd reported him to the military police, meaning he would be court martialled. One of the other British soldiers I knew was also to be court martialled, but only for being homosexual. The court martial took place and one was sentenced to nine months at Colchester Military Prison, while the other was dishonourably discharged. The *News of the World* were at the court martial and the following Sunday, the news hit the front page. The headline read 'Troops are shamed by web of vice' and as was usual with the *News of the World*, the article was over exaggerated, claiming the bar we met at occasionally was also a brothel and that there were up to 1,000 gay British soldiers. The article caused the MOD to initiate investigations into serviceman that might be homosexual and so what can only be described as a witch hunt began.

I don't know who by, but my name was given to the military and I was arrested. My room and locker were searched, including my personal possessions and any personal letters from family and friends were read. I believe this was a removal of any human rights I might've had, but this was just the beginning. Jim was also arrested and had his room and possessions searched.

We were both taken to the military police headquarters where they interviewed us separately. We had no witnesses; it felt more like they were interrogating the enemy, not a British soldier. It was just me and two officers. They went into all aspects of my life, army and private, before I eventually admitted to being homosexual. Following my admission, the interview turned to who I was involved with, when and even what sexual acts were performed. They also did the same to Jim. Statements were taken. We were interviewed on several occasions and they questioned us about what the other had said (I still have the copies of the statements).

The interviews seemed to go on for hours. We were also taken to the medical centre for examination, as if we hadn't already been degraded enough. Following the interviews, we were held in the cells of the guard room at the barracks where we were serving. While we were there, we were subjected to homophobic abuse on numerous occasions by the guards and had to be escorted to the canteen for food. We were marched to the canteen as if on public display. When we got there, the abuse continued – sometimes there were up to 100 other soldiers at the canteen. This happened three times a day.

We then had to go in front of the commanding officer to be told we'd face a court martial and were to remain in the guard room until it took place. A male officer from our regiment was appointed as our defence. At the court martial, the charges (accounts of sexual acts) were read out in open court by a female officer prosecuting and we had to enter pleas against each offence. All ten of them. Two consenting adults in a private relationship were put on public display like we were the scum of the earth. There were approximately thirty people in attendance, as well as reporters from the *News of the World*. I was told that details of the court martial would be in the next edition of the paper. We were both sentenced to six months at the Army Correction Centre in Colchester. The officer in charge of the court martial stated that we'd have normally been discharged, but we were to be sentenced due to our ages: I was 22 and Jim was only 20, which meant what we'd been accused of was still classed as an offence under British law. You could give your life to defend your country at 16, but you couldn't identify as homosexual until you were 21. After the court martial, we were escorted back to the guard room at the barracks. When we were locked in our cells, the full impact of what'd just happened took effect. I'd lost a job I loved. The only thing that kept me going was that Jim and I could be together when it was all over.

The court martial was held on a Thursday and I was told an article would be in the *News of the World* on the Sunday. I hadn't come out to my parents yet and they didn't know about the court martial. I was allowed a phone call and decided to call my parents; I couldn't let them find out by reading the newspaper. My mother was in tears on the phone. On the Sunday, the guards were laughing about the story all over the front page, especially the headline: 'The Gay Glosters'. I found out from my parents that the local paper, the *Evening Post*, had also printed an article and included my parents' address, so all my old school friends now knew, not to mention my parents' friends and neighbours.

After a week in the guard room, we were escorted on a civilian plane by military police. On arrival at Colchester, we were searched and placed in different cells with seven other servicemen. We had to sleep by the window so that we were visible when the guards did their patrols. We were in D Wing with other soldiers waiting for discharge for numerous offences. There was some homophobia, but not as bad as it was when we were back at our regiment. Although Jim and I were in different barrack rooms (old Second World War Nissan huts), we did get some time when we could talk at meals together and we were both in the same German class.

We were allowed to appeal the conviction, which we did, and the appeal was successful on the grounds that my defending officer (male) was having a relationship with the prosecuting officer (female). This meant the court martial process was flawed and the MOD obviously didn't want any further publicity. After serving approximately three months of our sentences, we left Colchester with a few personal possessions, a rail warrant and about £10 to get back to my parents' home. We decided to stop off in London to have some time together, we both just needed some space. I left to travel to my parents' home and Jim was due to follow in a few days.

I arrived home with nothing, no money, no job and no prospects. I'd even lost the right to die for my country. Jim decided not to join me, and I had no way of contacting him, despite my best efforts. I didn't know that our parents had been in contact with each other while we were at Colchester. Jim's father was a bank manager and said that he'd withdrawn money from his account in Brighton but was the last I heard of him.

Although my family were supportive, I was on my own. I applied for unemployment benefit, but this was refused because I'd been dismissed from the Army. I had to give them the full reasons why, which again meant talking about my private life. I was fortunate my sister worked in the job centre and had some contacts. She had previously helped to get a job for the disabled son of the portering manager in the Bristol Royal Infirmary and so he agreed to interview me. She'd told him about my past so the subject wasn't brought up in the interview, and I'd done some first aid training in the Army, as was usual with musicians, so he gave me a job working shifts in the operating theatres.

Living back at home was difficult as I was used to looking after myself and having my independence. My parents were ok with me, but I started going out to gay bars, trying to meet other people and usually finishing up drunk, often staying out all night and sometimes not going home for a few days. I was often asked about my past, but I always put up barriers, even to other gay people. I still felt ashamed and told no one of my dismissal. I did tell some new friends that I'd been in the Army, but that was it. When they asked what I now did for a job, I told them I was a hospital porter, taking people in and out of operating theatres, cleaning up blood off the floors and occasionally taking bodies to the morgue. The pride in myself and what I used to do was gone. The drinking got worse and I started gambling on fruit machines. I didn't want to win money, but it meant that I didn't have to talk to other people.

Sometimes I went to the local pub with my father, where he caught up with his friends. It was difficult for him due to the articles in the *News of the World* and the local paper. He was a quiet man and very placid in nature. One of his friends, who knew me, told him that I was an independent person who could look after himself. He had a son with severe Down's syndrome who'd require care for the rest of his life, and they became good friends.

A family feud developed between my parents and grandparents after the latter said that I'd bought shame on the family. My parents still visited them, but I never saw them again. I also lost contact with my aunts, uncles and cousins. Now my parents have also died, I only have my sister to keep in contact with.

Working shifts at the hospital was tiring and as it was in the centre of town, it was easy to go to the pub after work, and sometimes I'd even call in before starting my shift. On one occasion I turned up over an hour late, completely unfit for work. I had to face a disciplinary interview and luckily, they accepted that I was having difficulty since leaving the Army. My mother was an office manager and had a vacancy in her office, which I took. As I was now working office hours, I started to go to the gym and even started playing music again in a local orchestra for amateur dramatic societies. I was trying to sort my life out, but I'd lost all my confidence and still felt ashamed. I thought I had no future and no prospects. One of my friends who I met occasionally in one of the gay bars introduced me to a friend of his, Simon. We got talking and got on well as we both had an interest in classical music. We began seeing each other regularly and after about a month, he told me that he'd accepted a manager's job in a bingo hall, but that it was in Swansea and was going to move there in a few weeks' time. A week after he started, I went to see him and we had a good time together. I asked if I could also move there as I was frustrated with my life at home. I had no real friends, all my school friends having abandoned me, and I felt the need to break free.

I gave up my job and moved to Swansea to live with Simon. I spent several months just claiming benefits and doing some occasional bar work. It was a hot summer and the beach was just down the road. I needed some space to be me and to try to forget the last few years. We went out socialising a lot and I got to know many other gay people. I also got to know the owners of one of the gay clubs in town. They were looking for a manager and offered me the job, which I accepted. I was finally starting to enjoy life again. When I was working behind the bar, my alter ego took over and I could lock my past away. After working at the club for about six months, I was sacked for a bad stock result, although I later found out that it was a actually a mistake made by the accountant. The club owners apologised, but it was too late by then and I was once again down and angry. We were going out drinking a lot but I found that after a few drinks, my anger would grow and I'd become aggressive. Simon would always make friends easily, whereas I felt I was being ignored and could become quite jealous. Maybe people could tell I was hiding something, or perhaps it was me protecting myself and not wanting to feel the hurt I'd felt in the past.

Simon's job wasn't going so well as he wasn't getting on with his general manager, so he decided to leave and we agreed to move back to Bristol. We managed to rent a house and started looking for work. This was in the mid-eighties and people were starting to get AIDS and HIV – everyone was calling it the 'gay plague' and discrimination was rife. Everyone assumed that if you were gay, you were infected. Some of the people we knew from when we first met in Bristol already had the virus, some were ill, and some had died. Rumours were rife and everyone was frightened. If you went out to a gay pub or club, you had to make sure people weren't watching the door. Gay bashing was quite common, and I guess we were just lucky it didn't happen to us. One night we were in one of the gay pubs and the student bandmaster that was at the school of music while I was there came in. He told me that he'd made it to bandmaster but had been dismissed. Apparently, he'd been investigated, lost his career and his house. I was cold and unwelcoming and didn't want to befriend him. Looking back on it, I think he may have needed help and friendship, but I was still feeling ashamed and if it involved anything to do with the Army then I just didn't want to know. (If ever you read this, Rob, I can only apologise.)

After the review was published, I also read other servicemen's accounts of the treatment they'd received and was appalled that the use of chemical castration was still going on in the 1990s – it sounded more like Russia in the 1950s. I hope the MOD feel shame for what was allowed to happen. I'm sure the people who carried out these barbaric treatments are happily retired and receiving their pensions, while others still suffer. All they wanted to do was to serve their county. Will they ever get justice?

Chapter 14

No PRIDE in Prejudice

—————————— Chris Ferguson ——————————

£250,000 in today's money, that's how much it cost. They wasted course fees, half a lieutenant's and half a petty officer's wage, my measly salary, not to mention basic and medical branch training, before the SIB descended on me and my life fell apart. All because I was a poof, a homosexual, with the nefarious intention of subverting the Navy and causing indiscipline.

The reality was somewhat different. I was a vulnerable, poor, working class 19-year-old kid from an abusive background, who sat in his bedroom scared of more violence, scared of being kicked out onto the streets, and who desperately needed to get away. Anywhere but where I was. I don't remember the bit about plotting how I was going to join the Navy to deliberately bring it down.

I was born in Kenya, in the last vestiges of Empire. My father was in the RAF and stayed on after national service; it gave him more opportunities than the meagre ones he had in civvy life. I've no memory of it. Next was Malta, where I remember the good and the not-so-good. We battered prickly pears with sticks and I remember crossing Valetta's grand harbour on the ferry, losing my 'lumb' (a rather well-loved soft toy lamb) on the bus and being upset, and even seeing the Queen pass by below our apartment when she visited the island. My older sister and I should've gone to the forces' school, but my mother wasn't having that. She was a rabid Catholic and didn't want us tainted by Protestant influences. Malta, such a Catholic island, must've felt like heaven to her.

My sister and I had reached an age when we could be sent to forces' boarding school back in the UK. My mother was having none of it and pressured my father to leave the RAF, where he had a good job and could support his family, for the unknown, where he had no job and no means of supporting us. As long as we could continue with our Catholic indoctrination, that's all that mattered.

Scotland was a cold, grey place after the life of sun. At first, we stayed with my maternal grandparents, since we had no home and my father had no job and no money. My grandfather was a retired miner and of Irish famine descent. He and my grandmother were poor but loving and not quite so evangelical in their faith, simply marking the key moments in life of baptism, first communion, marriage mass on Sunday, and funerals. I've loving memories of them, of lying in front of a roaring coal fire on a Sunday reading the *Broons* or *Oor Willie* in the *Sunday Post*, and of mince and tatties for tea with Bird's Angel Delight, sliced bananas, and evaporated milk for desert. They were poor times, but happy ones.

My parents were given a council flat in a new development in the city and that's when my life started to fall apart. My father wanted to pursue his hobby in the RAF, which was photography. The problem was, he had no contacts, professional training or professional experience. Fine if you're a bachelor, but not when you have kids. My father would come home after having no work, no money and look for a release for his frustration. I was the source of his release, and he dragged and beat the shit out of me with his belt. Those tears are the strongest memory of my childhood. My mother never did anything to stop him from beating me, in fact, she often encouraged it. Wasn't it my father's role to find work and support his family, while my mother's was to love and protect her children? Working-class life can be rough and ready, but it's protective and blunt in its response to what's wrong. Sadly, my grandparents never found out what happened.

I knew on too many occasions the taste of hunger. When we did have food, it was generally fried eggs and chips as they were the cheapest food to buy; there was never any Bird's Angel Delight with sliced banana and evaporated milk.

I remember a recurrent dream of being on a cliff and would jump, spread my wings, and fly away.

School was my real escape in life and I was one of the few kids who didn't want to go home afterwards. I was really precocious and taught myself enough Russian to read Gorky's *My Childhood*. The main character, Alexie, was a poor young boy who gets beaten by his Uncle Vanya. I felt such solidarity with him, but reading Russian books wasn't exactly what every working-class school kid was doing in their bedroom alone.

I stayed on as long as possible at school and had dreams of being able to go to university. I loved to study and it was an escape from my hell. Some of my grades were good, but I didn't earn enough qualifications to go further.

I'd reached an age when the other guys wanted to start hanging out with girls, but I almost felt betrayed because I didn't want to. In the school showers I'd notice the other guys' bodies. One I particularly remember was like a Greek god to me. His skin was so smooth and perfect, his body so perfectly shaped. I couldn't understand what was happening, so I prayed to God, His son, the Virgin Mary and all the saints for it to stop, but it never did. I was beginning to suspect that I was gay but tried to dismiss the notion.

Home in those years meant violence, poverty and hunger. The monster had tried to 'teach me' to box, which was another excuse for him to be able hit me. However, when I'd grown sufficiently, one day when he punched me, I punched him back straight in the nose, which burst with blood. He never 'taught' me to box again.

Things were getting very tense at home. The message that I should be 'going out into the world' was made clear and I feared I'd be kicked out onto the streets. Surprisingly, one day the monster thrust an advert from the paper in my face. It was for joining the Royal Navy in a medical profession. This was my chance to escape. I filled out the coupon asking for more information, and four days later was invited for an interview – they were desperate!

It all seemed to go well. I don't remember them asking if I was a homosexual, but if they had, I wouldn't have had a clue what they were on about. I also don't remember them asking me if I wanted to join the Navy with the intention of bringing it down! After the interview there was an IQ test, which I enjoyed, as well as a medical, where they found that I had a congenital hearing defect and couldn't hear high pitches; suddenly my difficulties at school all made sense. My hearing was below the level for entry to the Navy, but the recruiting office wrote to the Admiralty for dispensation. A week or so later, I got my letter saying that I'd passed my entrance interview and exam. I was given a travel pass to Plymouth and a date to be at the main city station. I'd escaped, I'd joined the Navy.

I remember very clearly the other teenage lads on the train being excited at joining up, but not one single memory of how I got there or who I travelled with: a self-imposed protective amnesia.

At the end of the long journey to Plymouth, standing there to meet us were the 'reggies' in the white gaiters and white belts that defined then as Royal Navy Police. They ushered us onto buses to HMS Raleigh, where we were separated into divisions, messed in and sent for haircuts – short back and sides of course!

We spent hours marching, at first like a giraffe, but I got the hang of it. There was daily circuit training, swimming in overalls and diving for a heavy rubber brick, and in the time of the Cold War, training in nuclear, biological and chemical defence and damage control. I remember being sent to a small building filled with CS gas, a mock-up ship where, after a big bang, alarms sounded, lights went out and cold water poured in, which we needed to stop. Afterwards, I was complemented on my 'proud shaft'!

It took me years to work out why I didn't find basic training difficult when so many other guys were breaking down, homesick, wanting to get out, wanting to go home, or missing their mums. Later in life I came to realise that basic training was easy when compared to my childhood, with the torture and misery of daily violence and lack of care. It was tough, but it was just like big boys' games, like a tough scout camp. I'd changed for the better and had self-respect, not to mention the respect of others. I was on my way to getting a professional qualification that would set me up for life and I now had a true family. The Navy had become my family and I wanted no other.

My passing out was one of the happiest days of my life. I've a photograph of me taken on that day, wearing a genuine smile of happiness. I had lots to smile about.

My next stage was training as a medic at RN Hospital Haslar in Gosport, which was where patients from the Battle of Trafalgar had been treated in 1805. Naval history was all around me and I was proud to be a part of it. The training was great, much of the training to be a sailor was done and now I was learning how to work as part of the Navy.

My role would be to look after Navy personnel when they were sick and unwell, when they needed treatment. I couldn't have wished to be in another branch.

After Raleigh, most recruits go to their first ship, but I was studying for a medical profession and had another three years of study, which meant going to London to an Army hospital for a joint service course. The Army guys were fun and as mad as me. My oppo and I shared a lot of hangovers. The RAF lot were standoffish and seemed to look down on our plebian ways, but it was great fun being a pleb! I still felt different.

I arrived on the Thursday and having never been to London before, I thought I should see a bit of it, so travelled by myself into the centre. I'd get to see Trafalgar Square, look down Whitehall, see the Cenotaph, all these places I'd heard of. I'd never even been on the Underground before. I walked down the stairs to the ticket both, and that's when I saw them. They looked like haunted ghosts and were all so young, I'm sure some were under 16. I'd heard of rent boys before but never seen any, and they frightened me. Is that what can happen to you if you're gay? I thought. I felt so sorry for them, wondering what awful things must've happened to them in their lives. I got my ticket as quickly as possible and almost ran through the ticket machine. I remember getting on the tube, not knowing where I was going, just wanting to get away.

The experience with the rent boys almost made me not go any further in trying to find out if I was gay, but the feeling of 'who am I?' was still there. One Sunday afternoon, I went to a public telephone outside the hospital and, with a lot of trepidation, phoned the lesbian and gay switchboard. I was told about a teenage group meeting that afternoon, but I was probably too late. I'd not realised just how big London was, but I eventually got there, although I walked up and down outside about twenty times telling myself, 'No I can't be gay!' and 'If I don't go in, I'll never find out.' Eventually, I built up the courage and went in. It was... totally normal, like any other teenage group. It even had a pool table and there were teenagers of the same age holding hands! Guys could hold hands and it was ok! I felt at home, it all felt so right. Afterwards they said they were going to a gay bar, and when we got there there was a drag act on. In one day, I'd made my first ever gay friends and kissed one of them!

For the first time in my life, I understood and felt comfortable in who I was. First, I'd found the Navy, I was part of the Navy and wanted nothing else and now I'd found the gay teenage group and wanted nothing else!

I went to the group a number of times after that. They ran camping trips and other activities, but I could never go or do any of them, it was far too risky and I realised I could never share their freedom.

I couldn't even let them know I was in the Navy. At the Army hospital, I'd listen to the guys going on about the women they fancied, their girlfriends etc. and was unable to join in. I couldn't say anything to anyone and I realised that I was trapped in my own silence, trapped in my own emotion. I had to live two lives. What had been a joy now started to become miserable. I was a teenager, I'd finally found out who I was, and could do nothing about it. I'd gone from my prison of not knowing, to my prison of not being able to tell anyone.

One day in the hospital, I had to work on a patient, another sailor, who looked pretty cute and was very friendly. A while later we bumped into each other and chatted, we got on well, spent time together and eventually came out to each other. There was a small group of us, about five, who were all gay, in the Navy hospital. One of the sailors had a house in Gosport where we used to gather, have fun and party, away from prying eyes. Me and the other sailor went as partners, which the others thought was very sweet. It was my first relationship with another man.

I was in the Navy hospital when the Falklands War was announced and was told I was on forty-eight hours' notice, then twenty-four, then twelve, and I thought, shit, they're going to send me out! but in the end it was their priority for me to complete my training and, with mixed feelings, I was stood down. Still, I would've gone out and done my duty if told to.

One morning, on the way to classes with the other lads, my petty officer stopped me and called me into his room. He told me that the Special Investigation Branch (SIB) had called and were coming up from Portsmouth the next day to interview me. He looked so worried. We were good friends, us Navy lot in the Army hospital, just two students, our petty officer and a lieutenant. It's never good news when the SIB interview you. They deal with serious crimes, like treason, spying, murder and, of course, homosexuality! I knew what it was about. There was only one thing it could be about. I was told the next morning when we all went to class, not to go with the other guys I shared a room with, but to stay and wait beside my bed.

I was terrified and didn't know what to do. That night I phoned the L&G switchboard for advice. They gave me the telephone number of a lawyer and even though it was night, I called, not expecting an answer. He did answer, however, and I explained the situation. He told me to just say, 'On the advice of my lawyer, I refuse to answer that question'. Yes, but this was the SIB and they were coming for me! I put the phone down.

The next morning, I stood by my bed as told, alone in the room and terrified. It was just me and the two regulators. I had no one with me, not my lieutenant or petty officer. I was told to open my locker. My legs were shaking like jelly. One of them stood beside me and the other searched through my locker. I knew there was nothing in it. The one searching would take out letters from my mother, for example, read through them and hand them to the other to read. After that I was bundled into a car and whisked away. There was no chance to say goodbye to anyone; they were out of my life and I out of theirs.

I was driven down to the Navy hospital, where I also had a room, and went through the same process. Then I was taken to the Navy detention centre and stuck in the cells. I was with other guys, maybe about twenty or so. These were the Navy's bad boys, the 'trouble makers', those who'd gone AWOL, punched an officer, got into a bar brawl, things like that. Everyone knew why I was there and I thought I was at least going to be shunned. We were all in a kind of hexagonal caged area with regulators all around, swinging their truncheons, and a table in the middle with the guys playing cards. I thought I was going to be condemned to the no man's land between the regulators and the 'bad boys', the poof shunned and humiliated, on his own, mutually hated by both sides. However, the guys were great and I joined in their card games. I was crap at cards, but they helped me learn. They didn't mind sitting beside 'the poof', and if any regulator came near me, they snarled at them. They may've been bad boys, but they were very protective of me and were my angels. They made me feel wanted, human and safer.

The other guys would be taken for an 'interview' that would maybe last about half an hour. Mine lasted for hours and was more like an interrogation than an interview. They asked deeply personal questions: 'Do you like the taste of cum?' 'What does cum taste like?' 'Do you swallow cum?' Do you like being penetrated?' That last one threw me as I didn't understand what they meant at first, but soon realised. You had no right to any personal privacy. I had no lawyer, I was never offered one, and didn't even have someone else there as an independent witness. Having a lawyer, being offered one, even having someone as an independent witness is a basic part of justice. I felt I'd no right to refuse to answer any of their questions, but I did refuse to answer anything about the other sailor. I knew he'd been arrested too and felt that it was all my fault. I didn't want to say anything that would get him into any more trouble. I think that's why they kept me in for three days. Asking the same questions again and again, wearing me down, telling me I was disgusting and had deliberately joined up to corrupt the Navy, that I'd betrayed my family, my oppos and the Navy itself. They wore me down for days, until I couldn't hold out any longer.

Their methods were all psychological, some I realised at the time, some I've learned of since. The bare room, the regulator with a truncheon, the regulator behind me, the clock on the wall that you couldn't see but could hear going 'tick, tick'. You could hear the tension of that tick. The only escape was through the door, guarded by a reggie with a truncheon. I sat there opposite the regulator trying to look unfazed but my legs were shaking under the table. I'm sure he knew. He picked up one of my letters and read it slowly as if it was the first time.

I've sometimes wondered what the SIB officer would say if I found him now and asked him why he'd ruined the life of a 21-year-old lad? Why did he put him through so much psychological torture? Would he say he was just doing his job?

They treated me exactly like the other guys, except for one thing: I was made to shower separately, with a reggie watching me (swinging the obligatory truncheon). Much later, Fighting With Pride arranged for me to have counselling with Combat Stress, the military mental health charity. When I told the councillor what had happened, she told me it was a common interrogation technique to humiliate the person, to remove their dignity and humanity. Luckily it made no difference: the guys, my guardian angels, didn't give a toss. These bad boys weren't going to allow anything to happen to me.

I remember to this day the last question they asked: 'Do you know or suspect anyone else in Her Majesty's Navy of being homosexual?' Saying no gave me a bitter pleasure as I deprived them of an answer and so the questioning finally stopped.

After they'd finished their torture, I was placed under house arrest for three months at the Navy hospital. Ironically, I was put to work in the regulator's office at the medics' school. It was just me, another guy who was also getting kicked out for being gay, and an 'old salty', a sailor doing an easy job on the threshold of retiring who looked a bit like Captain's Birdseye. The other gay guy was very cute, but we never talked about anything gay or being kicked out. I was worried he'd been put there just to see if I gave any more information away or if I made a move on him.

My job involved getting very friendly with a filing cabinet and its contents for three months. I'd never wanted to be in the supply branch or be a writer. The other guy and I did have a joke, though. The sprog medics had to come in at the end of the week to get their 'weekend pass' stamped, and as far as they were concerned, we were the regulators. We'd make them sweat by waiting and checking they were neatly dressed, before stamping their pass. When they'd gone, we'd give them marks out of 10. I'd say, 'He was an 8', while the other guy would say, 'No way! At best he was a 6. You'd sleep with anything!'

I tried to avoid talking to other people at Haslar, but a few people came up to me and told me they'd heard what'd happened and thought it was disgusting. Mostly, they were complete strangers, even officers! There was absolutely no homophobia at Haslar. This, and my guardian angels in the cells, helped me realise that the real Navy had no problem with homosexuality.

Then one afternoon, the other guy suddenly disappeared. I never found out what'd happened to him. Was he kicked out? Was he a plant who reported that I was giving nothing away, except my scoring of men? This seemed to be a theme: disappearing from other people's lives, other people suddenly disappearing from my life. Again, there was no chance of saying goodbye.

I was told one Friday afternoon that my trial was the following Monday, and that they were taking me to HMS Nelson, so I needed to get packed right away to leave immediately. Again, no chance to say goodbyes.

At Nelson, I was put into a four-bed room. I couldn't understand why they'd given me such a room to myself, although I later found out four decades later, when I got my Navy records, that the room was designated as 'surplus to requirements'. How Ironic.

I was able to go in and out of Nelson before the trial so decided to phone my parents to let them know what was happening. I knew I could get up to three years in military prison, so I went out on the Sunday night and found a phone box nearby. My mother answered and I told her. Her words were, 'What are we going to tell the priest?' I put receiver down and walked out of the phone box. There was a pub nearby so I went in and bought a pint, finding a table in the corner, away from everyone. I put the pint on the table and the tears just ran down my cheeks. My life was finished. I'd been rejected by everyone, wanted by no one. How can I end it? I thought. Not 'should' I end it? but 'how' should I end it? My mind was made up; it was just a matter of deciding how.

Finally, I decided that the best way was to throw myself into Portsmouth harbour, which was only about ten minutes' walk away. It seemed appropriate, too, I was still a sailor and ending up floating in Portsmouth harbour seemed a fitting way for a sailor to end his own life. Getting up on the harbour wall, looking down into the dark, cold water and down to my end, my escape, I sat there and wondered, Why are they doing this to me? Why were they making me want to end my life? I hadn't done anything wrong. I'd never hurt anyone, and had been rejected by everyone, wanted by none. I was only 21.

But I didn't. My mind thew up crazy, absurd ideas they'd find me not guilty, or that they'd say it'd all been a terrible mistake and just to carry on as usual. Rationally, none of this was going to happen, but this wasn't a rational time and so I went back to HMS Nelson to await my trial the next day.

I was told that if I pleaded innocent then it'd go to court martial, and there was a greater chance of going to military prison. If I pleaded guilty, then there was a chance that I'd just be dismissed. Given those options, it seemed better to plead guilty, even if I didn't know what my crime was, but my decision was made with no lawyer or advice. My defence was a lieutenant I knew but hadn't discussed my case with.

I was marched into the room like a startled rabbit in the headlights. The lieutenant and I had about three minutes to discuss things in whispers as we weren't given any time or privacy. It was a total kangaroo court, with my guilt and sentence decided before the trial. The Iranian state would be proud to have such a system. Well, in fact, it does.

While I waited, I was left to wander round Nelson. I can't remember what I did, but there wasn't a lot to do. I know I was on suicide watch as strange things had happened to indicate this was the case. For instance, I'd bought a large tub of paracetamol and codeine as I was getting massive tension headaches. I'd been out of my room in Nelson and when I came back and unlocked my locker to take some, they were gone. They had opened my locker, found them, and taken them away.

On the Friday morning, I was told my 'warrant' (sentence) was through and to be outside the sentencing room at 15.30 in my No. 1s (best uniform).

I was marched in. The officer who had my life in his hands in an envelope said, 'I shall read out the articles of war, off caps'. So, I took off my cap as ordered. He read out the articles of war '…the sentence of mutiny will be life imprisonment, the sentence for murder shall be life imprisonment, the sentence for…'

Jesus, I thought, what am I going to get? He then opened the envelope and announced that I'd be dismissed. I was marched back out. There was relief that there was no prison sentence, but confusion as to where this left me now. It was inconceivable to me that I'd not be in the Navy. It was my life, being a sailor was who I was, I no longer knew anything else. Taking that from me would be taking my life. Outside, I was told I had half an hour to get my stuff together, return all my kit, run around offices to get things stamped, and then leave.

My belongings were meagre and I realised how few clothes I actually had, and nothing really appropriate for the end of November. I was given a dark-blue folder with a my A5 dismissal notice (no need to waste paper here!), a P45, a leaflet about the DSS, a travel warrant to take me back 'home' and a list of places I wasn't allowed to visit: the USSR, China, North Korea. I hardly had enough money to buy a cheap packet of biscuits, never mind travel to a communist-block country!

Now I was out on the streets, marched out into a void, not a new life, a void, and emptiness. I was now a non-person. I no longer existed and therefore no longer mattered. I was welcome to top myself now as I was no longer any business of the Royal Navy.

When I walked out of Nelson's gate, there was a feeling of multiple griefs. In those few steps I lost everything I knew, everyone I knew, everything I hoped for, everything I had. I lost all my friends, some of whom I'd been studying with for almost three years. I lost my home, my only home, I lost my future, I lost the only family I had and only family I wanted. I lost any financial security, I lost a warm bed, shelter over my head, food to eat. I lost everything and had nothing, except a sad little holdall with a few possessions in it. The next step had no purpose, there was nowhere for the next step to take me. There was nowhere for me to go. I was a ghost to reality and existence.

I felt the hardness of the road under my feet. I remember the dappled light as the sun was setting, it being a late Friday afternoon at the end of November. Time had stopped and seemed to have no purpose. Everything stopped.

I had a choice, turn right or turn left. Right took me down to Portsmouth harbour and the end of it all, or I could turn left and walk into a world and future I didn't know. Eventually, I turned left: I thought I'd reached rock bottom and things couldn't get any worse. But they could and they did. If I'd known then the life, the struggle, the pain and suffering that turning left would've taken me into, I know I'd have turned right instead.

I walked north into areas of Portsmouth I'd never been to. I'd never realised how grey and ugly Portsmouth was, the result of bombing during the war. It was getting dark by now and I was getting scared as I didn't know where I was and where I was going. The only choice I had was to return the way I'd come from to somewhere a bit familiar, even if that meant being near Nelson. It was Friday night in Portsmouth, the most naval of towns. There'd be groups of matelots on runs ashore. I couldn't bear to see that. It would've totally broken my heart. I had to get off the street. I had no money for accommodation, knew no one to stay with, nothing. The only choice was to go into a park, which I did. I wandered around trying to find somewhere, but only found a strange hexagonal building with mesh over it and a long building near it, perhaps a greenhouse. There were some bushes in front, so I decided to hide behind one of them. I hid there in the dark, I was very lonely and very scared as the tears ran down my cheeks and thought, Why has this happened to me just because I am gay? All I wanted was an arm around me to comfort me. But there was no arm and no comfort. There was just my loneliness and fear.

I was there for four days. It's strange when you become homeless. You suddenly seem to become invisible. People walk past not even acknowledging your existence. The only ones who acknowledged me were the pigeons. I made friends with them and finally understood why the old, homeless alcoholics I saw in London parks spoke to these birds. They weren't mad, it was because they were the only ones who paid attention to them. The pigeons didn't judge you, but even the pigeons leave you in the evening. Even the pigeons have a home.

I was desperate to try to find out what had happened to the other sailor, my partner who I knew was also being tried. We had a mutual friend, a nurse at Haslar, so on the Monday I managed to contact her. She was one of our 'gay club' and we agreed a meet up the following day. I went back to my bush in the park and waited with hope.

The next day we met and I learnt that after he'd been dismissed, he'd gone over to the Isle of Wight where his mother lived and stayed with her. Warm beds and hot meals for him, not living behind a bush in the park. I didn't get mad at him, living in comfort while I lived homeless and destitute in a park. I felt it had all been my fault and was just glad to have found him when there seemed no chance, and that he'd wanted to be with me. He found us a grotty bedsit in Portsmouth, but we couldn't stay like that. He then managed, somehow, to make friends with a florist in East London, and she allowed us to stay in the cellar under the shop, with nothing but a bare light bulb and a single camp bed.

Life was a struggle, a great struggle. I eventually got a place at a civilian college to finish my course, but because I'd missed so much time, I had to do a final year instead of six months. Unfortunately, they decided to only give me a grant for six months. I've never worked out why. This meant I had no access to finances for six months and because of the nature of my course, I couldn't do any part-time work. I had no money and had to do extreme, soul and dignity sapping things just to survive. I lived off the very cheapest foods and skipped fares on the bus to college, I never ate in the staff canteen with the other students but would take a flask of cheap packet soup and eat it with a slice of bread in the library each lunchtime. I could never afford to socialise with

Claire Ashton

Above left and above right: Roger Garford

Below: Ruth and Ju

Right: Terry Newton Laheney

Below: Vito E. Ward

Simon Wallington, Terry Skitmore, Kalvyn Friend

spare Rib

a women's
liberation
magazine
issue 119
june 1982
50p
$1.50/IR70p inc VAT

Sarah Sloane

Above left: Tremaine A.O. Cornish

Above right: Anne Myles

Left: Michael Pitchford

Lesley Davison

Gwen Pettigrew

Above: Steve Thomas

Left: Chris Ferguson

Trevor Skingle

Pádraigín Ní Rághillíg

Steven Waring

Above left: Emma Riley

Above right: Martin Bell

Rowena Purdy

Maggie Pugh

Andy Cowe

Elaine McCrory

Chris Charlie Brown

Carol Morgan

Jacks Connor Fox

Christopher Voce

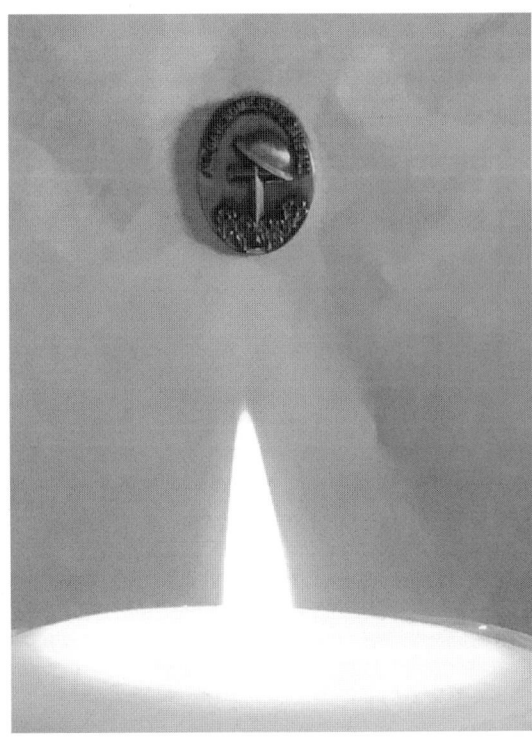

An Airman's Story

the other students, which meant they all thought I was stand-offish and studious. I just wanted to be a normal student.

When I finally qualified, I went to my graduation. Afterwards, as the others went off for their meals, I just went home on the bus, probably trying to skip the fare again. In the end, it was just another day.

I stayed with the other sailor for a couple of years after we left the Navy. I suppose, for my part, both him and our 'relationship' were the last tattered vestiges of my naval life, but I also felt guilty that I'd got him dismissed. I felt I had a duty to him, but sadly we began to drift apart. It must've seemed like we had a lot in common in the Navy, but now I could see that apart from being sailors and being gay, we weren't alike. I tried to share what little I had with him, but he never shared anything and only thought of himself. Even when I had no money and was surviving on cheap packet soup, he had dole money and could buy food, but he'd never share it and never even asked if I wanted some.

I remember having to make a very serious decision one day that would be relevant to our relationship. I came home to find him sitting there on his dole money, doing nothing but exuding the 'I'm alright Jack' attitude. I just looked at him and thought, F***ck it, I'm going to do it, even if it affects our relationship. We had no relationship anymore. We eventually parted waves and never saw each other again. I never grieved that loss.

For forty years I carried the weight of my naval life in silent and painful memories. I'd avoid anything to do with the Navy, turning the television off if anything came on about it. On Remembrance Sunday, if I attended a parade, I'd remain at the back hoping not to be noticed, feeling I didn't have a right to be there as I'd been such a disgrace to the country and to the job I loved. Most often, however, I remembered alone at home. Remembering especially all those from the Falklands, the young lads who lost their lives on both sides. I may have been a disgrace with no place at official Remembrance services, but they deserved my respect in remembering them all. That was the least I could do.

Then Fighting With Pride came into my life. During my first contact by phone, I'd told myself, 'This is military, be formal, keep yourself together', but as soon as I heard the voice on the other end, I realised this was someone military and someone gay, someone who'd understand. It'd been almost four decades, and finally I felt, 'This is someone who cares, someone who understands.' All those years ago on my first night out of the Navy, in that park, behind that bush, the thing I wanted more than any other was an arm around me and to be able to cry into that person. I never had it then. When I got that phone call it was like finally having that arm after four decades, and I burst into tears as the memories and emotions flooded back.

Fighting With Pride have given me so much. They've given me a family where I had none, not to mention my dignity and self-respect back. They arranged counselling for me with Combat Stress, which was the first time I'd had any help with the whole experience and it's helped me to work out and deal with so much. They've put me back in contact with the Navy family. They've fought for my rights and justice, and for others who were treated so cruelly by that vile ban. Most of all, they've been friends and family who've really, really cared. They've listened and cared where before no one listened, and no one cared. And that matters so much.

For over forty years I'd been dragging a heavy weight behind me that always pulled me back. But I was scared to look back in case it was a monster waiting to devour me. Combat Stress gave me the courage to turn and look. When I was finally brave enough to look back, I saw two younger selves: one in Navy No. 8 uniform (the daily uniform, with the beret) and one soon after being dismissed. They looked on me with sad, confused expressions and said, 'Why did you abandon us?' I wept when I realised the heavy weight I'd been dragging for so many years were my younger selves from that time, the ones I'd rejected and tried to forget. But all it did was leave a shattered self. Some may see me talking about them as a metaphor, but I could see them clearly in my mind's eye. Their forlorn, confused looks crushed my heart. I'd rejected and abandoned them. Now, I embrace them and hold them close, like two vulnerable younger brothers. I protect them from harm, from that vulnerability, from loneliness and from pain. I'll never let them go again. I'll never allow anyone to take them from me.

With support from Fighting With Pride, I eventually felt I could face asking for my naval records back. I had to write three times before they responded and eventually received two copies back, or what was left of them as most had been destroyed. They'd destroyed all the records of the investigations, the arrests, the interrogations, the cells, the trials, not just for me, but for all of us, 'for our own good', apparently. One of the documents, though, was a trial sheet from the day of the trial. From that, it became clear that the SIB had got to me because of the other sailor, not the other way around. He'd reported me! I'd never have done that to him. Not only that, but he'd given them the address of the house that belonged to the sailor where us few gay guys would meet. How many other lives did he destroy?

I finally have my family, my Fighting With Pride family. Brothers and sisters in arms; arms that hold each other, arms that've held each other as we cried and laughed and cried again. When we lose one of ours, as we have done, we grieve together. Fighting With Pride has been a parent to all of us, although sometimes I think they must feel like parents to a bunch of wayward kids! They taught me to walk again, where I'd previously feared to tread. Encouraging me to trust again where I'd lost all trust. And when I needed help, they got me that help so that I could face the monsters that'd scarred my soul and memories for so long. I never thought that phone call to Fighting With Pride would change things so completely for me. Things I thought could never be changed.

No one has won: the Navy never won, losing a medical professional it desperately needed. The country never won, losing a lot of money it needed. I never won, losing my life, soul, self-respect, all those friends, the Navy I loved, my future, my hopes my dreams. No one won except prejudice.

Four decades later, when the memories come back, when the emotions return, the tears still run.

Why could I not just be allowed to be myself? That's all I wanted.

'Those who inflict the wounds forget.

Those who receive the wounds remember.'

Chapter 15

The Best and Worst of Days

——— Trevor Skingle ———

I'm from a working-class family and was living at home in Fulham, London. I'd had quite a serious relationship with a local girl but had always known that I preferred blokes. We had little money and I'd had to leave grammar school and go to work in the family green grocery business, owned and managed by a tyrannical uncle, because my mum had left my dad for someone else and my dad had been left with four kids and all the bills the pay. Customers and family told me that I was far too intelligent to continue what I was doing, under the eye of my abusive uncle, which was becoming intolerable. I didn't have the benefit of O-levels and I knew I needed to get on some sort of apprenticeship. I came from a family with a tradition of serving in the military as far back as the Second South Africa Campaign and thought what better way to get a trade than to join the Army.

So, at the age of 17 I went to the Army recruitment office and joined up. At first, attracted by the glamour, I wanted to join one of the Guards' regiments as what at the time was called a 'mounted dutyman', but the recruiting sergeant said I was intelligent enough to go into a branch of the Army which would offer me an opportunity to put my intelligence to good use. So, I joined the Royal Corps of Signals, one of the Combat Support Arms of the British Army, as a combat lineman working in telecommunications. I knew at that time being gay was illegal in the Armed Forces, but it was the job and life for me and I felt I could get through without any sort of gay relationship for the nine years I would sign up for. I wanted to do my bit to defend our democratic principles, not realising then how ironic that was. Little did I know how badly this was going to affect me in the years to come.

The undercurrent of sex started almost straight away at the processing centre at Sutton Coldfield. On the first evening there in our bunks, a couple of guys started jerking off without any apparent reticence, one even describing to the rest of the room what he was doing while he was doing it. Then I was sent to do basic training at Catterick, which was so full-on I didn't have time to think about anything else. I excelled to the extent that I was awarded 'Best Recruit' and was sent home for a while prior to trade training to work at the same recruitment office where I'd joined up, as well as the prestigious one in Trafalgar Square. I was even featured in an article in the *Fulham Chronicle* about my experience and my placement at the recruitment offices. I'd made it!

My next stage was trade training at Catterick, which was slightly less full-on as basic training. Enough so that I had time to form a relationship with a woman who was training there as part of the Women's Royal Army Training Corps (WRAC). I recall us getting caught at night banging up against one of the buildings on the base by one of the patrolling duty guards, but contrary to what it would've been like if it'd been two guys, there was no comeback other than being told to 'go and do it somewhere private'. It got quite serious with the woman to the extent that we went back to where her family lived and I was introduced to her dad, who asked me all sorts of the traditional 'dad giving his blessing' questions I would expect. You know: are your intensions honourable? Do you intend to marry my daughter, etc.? Just before our first Christmas together, we got the details of our postings to our separate working units. I was at home on leave and called her, only to find out from her mum that she'd established a relationship with another bloke in the Army and that they were getting married and she didn't want anything more to do with me. I broke down and wept. It was the only time and the closest I ever got to falling in love with a woman. Perhaps it had been an omen?

At the end of my stay at Catterick, I left for my first posting in Germany. It was pretty full-on, but I was ready for it. Getting settled was quite challenging as the troop I was posted with, Line Troop, had a pretty dire reputation, as did all 'Lineys' (as combat linemen were known in the Royal Corps of Signals), for being hard-working, hard-playing, hard-drinking, and out and out bad boys. There were a couple fairly effete guys in the troop who got a hard time for being perceived as gay. Whether they were or not wasn't explicit. They could just as well have been effete, straight men. Nonetheless, they got it in the neck in spades, as they say. I watched and took it all in and thought it was just as well they couldn't read my mind. I did try to tag along with the rest of the troop and get into the same frame of mind as them, joining in their off-duty activities. It was quite something to see how sexually disinhibited things could get when everyone was steaming drunk in the name of 'beasting', which was fully accepted. There wasn't a woman in sight, and yet the rest of the time they were out and out straight men without a shred of evidence of any leanings towards male-to-male attraction.

To say this added to the issues running round in my head and making me more and more confused was to put it mildly. We had much more time on our hands than had been the case at Catterick, and as they say 'the devil males work for idle hands'. Time went by and I was increasingly thinking about how I was unable to have an emotionally and sexually fulfilling relationship with another guy at my working unit. Yet I was approached for sexual favours by a few single 'living in' mates, and a married colleague whom I did get it on with in private at a drunken party in the pads' quarters, but this had to remain a secret. With the few single 'living in' mates it was usual to have sex with them and a female prostitute. As prostitution was legal in West Germany, it somehow made the tryst 'legit'. There were also what the Yanks called 'having a game of grab ass', which occasionally became quite intense. It involved no holds barred fumbling without penetration or oral in the backs of cars or at parties, but which were followed the morning after by the usual 'I was so drunk last night I can't remember a thing that happened'.

As a result of this, what I can only call a misleading hive of drunken activity, I became very depressed and sought solace in more and more alcohol. My alcohol consumption, spurred on by the hard-drinking hard-partying troop I was with, became very problematic. On one evening, I was so drunk I rampaged around the camp in nothing but my underpants and wrecked the front entrance porch to the sergeants' mess, eventually getting tackled by a guard patrol on the parade ground. The next day I was marched, on orders, in front of the squadron OC and sentenced to go on a run with a physical training instructor (PTI) through the sand dunes in the local woods. They considered this to be punishment, but because I was so fit, it didn't really phase me. Unbeknownst to me, the

PTI on the run had noted how fit I was, which would work in my favour and in the recovery of my mental health later on.

After this, and as a result of the continuing alcohol abuse, my depression deepened and I attempted suicide. I was found by my bunk mates and carried by half a dozen of them at the run to the medical centre on camp and rushed to the Military Hospital in Hanover, where I had my stomach pumped. When I woke up a day or so later, my hair had turned white and I discovered I was in a hospital bed recovering from what I'd done. While I was there, I was interviewed for quite some time by an Army psychologist investigating my sexual habits. As it was illegal to be gay, I told him that I was in a relationship with a local German woman which, though it had been very brief, was true at the time.

The powers that be at my unit must've reviewed my situation because when I got back to my regiment, I had a long interview with the officer commanding Linc Troop. Apart from the hidden physical and mental alcohol damage, I was very fit and as this had been noted by the PTI on my punishment run, I was offered a place in the gym as a trainee PTI. In the gym, away from the heavy drinking and in a fairly tee-total environment, with the comradeship of other PTIs as well as more sober guys from other troops in the squadron, I flourished like I never had before. I absolutely loved the work as a PTI and took to it like a fish to water. With encouragement and help from a senior Army Physical Training Corps (APTC) instructor, I set up a judo club, a sport at which, after going into the gym, I'd taken up and excelled at. I was awarded my judo colours and went on to be part of the winning team at the Inter Formation Judo Championships held at the PT School at Sennelager in 1978. I also took to boxing and as my eyesight wasn't good enough for me to box, I instead managed and coached the regimental boxing team, who I took to Berlin to fight against the team from the Paras stationed there in the old pre-Second World War boxing auditorium, which was attached to the old Olympic Stadium made famous by the 1936 Summer Olympics.

After promotion to full corporal, I was posted to work in the gym at Blandford Camp in Dorset, where I continued my passion for judo by setting up a senior and junior judo club, the members of which went on to meet the Princess Royal on one of her trips to inspect the Royal Signals at Blandford in her role as Colonel-in-Chief. However, the distraction wasn't great enough and I was still thinking a lot about how isolated I was as a gay soldier. Apart from the occasional heterosexual fling, I might have been regarded as a 'confirmed bachelor', but my yearning for a boyfriend was continuing to grow and increase in intensity. I knew at that time that if I were to make the commitment to staying in and serving for the long term, I needed to know which was more important to me; continuing to serve as a 'confirmed bachelor' or leaving so I could have a gay relationship. I made contact with another, gay, judo player in Bournemouth through the personal ads. Though he was a relatively inexperienced judo player, he was a confident and attentive lover. Thankfully, on base, I managed to keep this casual relationship under wraps and away from the eagle eyes of the RMP. It was around this time that one of my best mates at Blandford dropped a none too subtle hint to me that he thought I might be gay. Knowing how abysmal the treatment was meted out to others whose sexuality had been discovered was, I vividly recall the chill I felt run through me when he dropped that 'bomb' into my otherwise stable military life.

To make matters worse, the married colleague from Germany had also been posted to the same unit as me at Blandford Camp, and though I was again approached for sexual favours, this time he wasn't 'entertained'. So, while on an advanced PTI's course at the APTC HQ at Aldershot in 1979, I finally came to realise that twenty-two years' service as a confirmed bachelor was not something I could do. Even though I'd only served five years of my nine-year contract, I requested the option to 'buy myself out', which was granted. I left the Armed Forces on what I considered to be the equivalent of 'constructive dismissal' and was given an exemplary discharge certification. As I walked through the gates at Blandford, I was saddened to my core at the waste the Army had made of the career of an extremely committed and very skilled soldier.

If I'd been able to have a gay relationship, I would've stayed the course for the whole nine years, thrived and with little doubt signed on again, but that could not be. As I left the Army, I lost whatever pension I'd accumulated because I didn't have five years of service beyond my 18th birthday. I was 17 when I joined and the qualifying start date was my 18th birthday on 7 February 1975: I'd missed the minimal five year pension by fifty-five days!

On returning home there were important conversations to have with my parents, family and friends about why I'd left the Army. My dad was ok but curious, asking questions mainly about how I would socialise. My mum and stepdad had a falling out over it, with my mum hitting my stepfather over something homophobic he'd said. I was later ostracised for discriminative religious reasons by my two sisters after they both became Jehovah's Witnesses. My brother was absolutely fine; he'd also come out as gay. My straight civvy mates were nonplussed at first but came to accept it. The biggest problem was when I met up with the straight mates of my friends. I'd chat to them without revealing anything about myself, until they started using homophobic terms and exhibiting homophobic attitudes. At this point I'd tell them I was gay and watch their manner change to 'Oh sorry, I didn't mean to offend you. I do have gay mates.' Yeah, right.

Anyway, after I left I was still in the Reserve and took six months out from Reserve duty to take a backpacking tour of the USA (permission for which I had to apply to the Ministry of Defence) during which I came out as gay whilst staying in San Francisco and had a fling with a United States Marine Corps PT instructor I met in Honolulu, Hawaii. Even though this was before the 1993 Clinton 'don't ask don't tell' policy in the US Military was issued, his other mates in the Marine Corps who shared the house with him were completely ok about it, which for me was a huge breath of fresh air and was made even better when I ended up sharing an apartment in San Francisco with, amongst others, another gay Marine who worked on Treasure Island in the Bay Area.

After I returned to England, I was still required to serve in the Reserve for two weeks every year, undertaking drill instruction, fitness and weapons firing tests and going on a mock battle exercise. I wondered very strongly as an out gay man why in the hell I should commit myself to the Reserve and potentially fight for a country and a 'democracy' that criminalised me for my sexuality whilst serving, yet still continued to expect me to lay down my life in its defence. So, two years into my Reserve service, and emboldened by the attitude I'd seen in the US Marines, I asked a clinical psychologist I knew to write a letter to the MOD, which first declared the psychologist's qualifications and experience and then went on to say that 'Trevor Skingle is a well-adjusted 23-year-old male homosexual who is attracted to men of his own age'. I was sent a single sentence letter from the MOD saying, 'Your service has been terminated as per the date of this letter' (SIC). I was absolutely livid, so went to Chelsea Barracks and stood at the gate and ripped up the letter, throwing it on the ground. Signing up as part of the military contract ultimately means, if necessary, relinquishing one's life and laying it down on the field of battle for society. There's nothing greater that a soldier can offer and I felt, justifiably I think, absolutely outraged.

My experiences during my time in the Army and the Reserve weren't without consequences, as a storm gathered in my head for many years. I'd been forced to end my military career for the irrelevance of being gay and that had left mental scars: feelings of guilt, a lack of self-worth and at times suicidal ideation. I'd been cast out and abandoned by an organisation to which I'd pledged my life. I was sectioned in around 1988 at Homerton Hospital, amidst a boiling anger at the treatment gay men and lesbians had received whilst serving. Not least, the institutional violence, harassment, intimidation, beatings, invasive medical procedures, and imprisonments.

Following treatment and a period of recovery, I settled into a stable relationship with an ex-Army officer from the Worcester Regiment, which gave me some much-needed breathing space, stability and the sort of masculine relationship I'd desired for such a long, long, time. To lift my morale, he introduced me to two people who later became firm friends of mine. They were both gay, both Saville Row couturiers who had both distinguished themselves serving in the Army during the Second World War. One was his boss, the late Sir Hardy Amies, who'd completed one of the hardest training courses in the British Army, P Company, and had served in the Special Operations Executive training Belgian refugees and parachuting them back into Belgium to work as Fifth Columnists. The other was the late Neil 'Bunny' Roger, who as a commissioned officer in the Rifle Brigade had fought at Monte Casino wearing a chiffon scarf and carrying a copy of *Vogue* in his pocket. During the battle, he'd thrown himself down behind a log before being joined by one of his colleagues who asked him, 'How do you do it, Bunny?'

'I just powder up, dearie,' he replied.

I carried on my interest in judo and boxing after I left the Army. Ironically, some of the guys from the Territorial Army Paras and SAS based at the old Chelsea Barracks near Sloane Square used to go to the same judo club as me, which I'd joined before I went backpacking around the USA. We used to 'talk shop' and that felt great, a bit of the old Army camaraderie again. I maintained my connection to boxing as a judge and timekeeper for the Amateur Boxing Association up to and including at international level. The last tournament I officiated at was England vs Kenya at the Café Royal on the Strand.

Then, in the early 90s, I joined a group of people who were setting up Rank Outsiders, a group of ex-service personnel who were lobbying and pressuring the government to rescind the then ban on being gay or lesbian in the Armed Forces. In 1991 I appeared on Ch4's *Comment* as a representative of Rank Outsiders, my first time involved with the media and on national TV, to talk about my experience and why the ban should be lifted. I subsequently lost touch with Rank Outsiders after I moved into the charity sector to work supporting people with HIV, having lost many friends, and three boyfriends, Tony, Graeme and John, in quick succession.

I was still occasionally in touch with ex-Army mates. Though the ban had been lifted in 2000, I was aware that some of the 'old guard' from the military still expressed oft-times quite virulent homophobia (some still do), so to err on the side of caution as far as my old Army mates were concerned, I made no mention of my sexuality. Then, in early 2020, I saw the LGBT+ branch of the Royal British Legion (RBL) advertised online, so I joined. Prior to this I'd not been aware of any veterans' services, let alone those for LGBT+ veterans. As a member of Rank Outsiders in the early 90s, it was the only time I felt supported as a veteran after I'd left the Armed Forces, and that was only by the other members of the group, and my friends and family. Since joining the RBL and then subsequently Fighting With Pride, I've felt that pride return and felt much more supported. I'm really, really, thankful for my engagement with the Royal British Legion's LGBT+ Branch and Fighting With Pride. Through them, in later life my appreciation of the comradeship offered by and engagement with the military has become so much more positive than it was when I served and after I left the Army and the Reserve. I can once again march under a military banner alongside my compatriots and feel that same pride I lost so long ago, supported by my long-term partner, and now husband.

Chapter 16

Out of the Hangar: Crash Landing in Civvy Street, Without a Parachute

Pádraigín Ní Rághillíg

I grew up in a military family. My father was a regular soldier in the British Army before, during and after the Second World War, leaving the service in 1960 after twenty-two years, when I was 4 years old. I can still remember him in his uniform and he always instilled in me a sense of pride, the wherewithal to know the difference between right and wrong, the belief in being honest and truthful at all times, always to live with integrity and to respect authority.

My father was delighted when, in 1976, I decided to join the WRAF, and it gave me immense pleasure to see how proud it made him. He died in 1978 and I'm glad he didn't live to see what became of me.

In 1986 I was dismissed from the WRAF for being a lesbian. I'd joined on 21 June 1976 and quickly knew that it was my career for life.

I signed on initially for nine years and subsequently extended this to twelve. As my career progressed, I requested to sign on until I was 55, but it wasn't to be and the devastation has now lasted for almost forty years and, indeed, will continue for the rest of my life.

In 1976 I'd not admitted to myself that I was a lesbian; I'd never had a relationship with another woman, but had had feelings as a prepubescent girl, which I suppressed.

Following training as a telegraphist and a posting to WRAF Stanbridge near Leighton Buzzard, I received my first overseas posting, in 1978, to RAF Germany, serving at 11 Signals Unit, RAF Rheindahlen. It was there I met my husband, whom I married in 1979. On my return to the UK in 1981, again to RAF Stanbridge, I left my physically abusive husband and met a fellow WRAF with whom I had my first lesbian relationship; it was at this point that I knew I'd always been a lesbian.

In 1982 I was on track to re-trade to flight sergeant air load master, a significant change in trade and rank. I was formally interviewed and was certainly on the brink of being approved when the Argentinians invaded the Falkland Islands, and it was put on hold. I don't recall why the transfer didn't occur, although I believe it was I who didn't pursue it, I include it here to demonstrate that I was considered a valuable member of the RAF at that time.

In 1983, after a short secondment to RAF Brampton, I was posted to RAF Gibraltar. I had an exemplary record and was on track for promotion to corporal. I found the posting to be extremely difficult; this was as a direct consequence of the 'Gay Ban'. Having to hide the fact that I was a lesbian and effectively living a double life meant that on such a small station, and indeed with limited avenues to be myself off duty, the ban made the posting very claustrophobic. When in the UK I did visit gay venues and had met other women, but, when asked about my work, although I'd say I was in the RAF, I never gave my true job as I knew it might be regarded as highly attractive to blackmailers since I did occasionally have access to Top Secret information.

Whilst in Gibraltar, the culture was very heavily dependent on drinking, even more so than at other postings. As a consequence of the claustrophobic and mentally challenging situation I found myself in, I developed a 'severe drinking problem', although I wouldn't classify myself as alcoholic. I was still fully able to do my job and take part in station sports, etc., but on evenings and weekends I was drinking increasing amounts of hard alcohol. I'd usually start drinking in the NAAFI bar and then walk or cycle into town to frequent the bars there, often drinking alone. It was through this that I met a woman from the WRNS serving at HMS Rooke and we began a relationship based, I would say, on mutual loneliness and stress from the constant battle to remain hidden.

On 7 September 1985 I was returning to my quarters when I was accosted by a WRAF policewoman, who informed me I was to accompany her to the guardroom for questioning, and so it began.

At the guardroom I was met by an RAF police officer and another WRAF policewoman corporal, who proceeded to interrogate me with regards to my sexuality, the reason for the failure of my marriage and whether I'd had any relationships with women, specifically in the WRAF. They also informed me that I'd been named by another woman (a Wren), who was being questioned by the Royal Naval Police. I continued to deny that I was a lesbian and refuted all allegations to the contrary.

After a time, the police officer left the room and upon his return he told me that the Wren had admitted to having a lesbian relationship with me, which I strenuously denied. After several hours and under intense pressure, I suddenly admitted everything (looking back now, I know that, had I maintained my silence, I'd have avoided all the trauma that followed). I felt completely worn down and traumatised by the whole process and the constant daily strain of living a double life. I was then formally charged and told I'd be interviewed under caution by the RAF Special Investigations Branch (SIB). I'd been interrogated for a total of seven hours; had been offered no support or advised that I had a right to have someone present with me, nor was I given anything to eat or drink during the questioning.

I was escorted back to my quarters by two WRAF policewomen, who ordered me to stand outside my room while they searched my property. They then proceeded to search the room, going through all my personal belongings, searching my mattress and even tipping out records from their sleeves! They left the room in a complete mess and removed several items, including my passport, letters, greetings cards, address books and other personal effects. I was told that as I was under arrest, I was to remain in my quarters until further notice and not to go to the Commcen (my workplace), or leave the camp.

Clearly, I was now in a complete state of terror, high anxiety and wretchedness; I felt totally numb and unable to fully function, having been taken so unawares and absolutely devastated by the whole proceedings.

The next day I was again ordered to return to the guardroom and the interrogation continued. The SIB advised me that I was entitled to have someone of superior rank present whilst they interviewed me. I asked for the senior WRAF officer, but apparently, she refused (I was not told why), so I then asked for my sergeant to come and he did. I was allowed to have a private consultation with him so that I could inform him of my situation and why he had been called to the guardroom. To say he was completely out of his depth is an understatement; his only comment was that I'd ruined my career and more so as he knew I was about to be promoted to corporal. However, he was very kind and spoke to me with respect, for which I'll always be grateful. I recently learned that he passed away some years ago, I wish now I was able to see him again and thank him for his kindness.

I was then returned to the interview room for further questioning, which consisted of humiliating questions regarding my relationship, asking for details of sexual acts; when, where with whom and exactly what took place; requesting extremely explicit and intimate details. All of this was conducted in front of my sergeant and two WRAF policewomen, one of whom took contemporaneous notes. They also went through all the names in my address book, asking who they were and whether they were also lesbians; this included both serving and civilian friends and family. Some were obviously lesbians, but I denied it all. I was informed that they would be contacting everyone in my address book and interviewing them too. Meanwhile, I was not to contact anyone and they would be retaining my personal papers and my passport. I was not to attempt to leave the 'Rock', although I was now permitted to leave camp.

I was told that they would be recommending my dismissal from the RAF and that my security clearance was revoked so I was not to return to working in the Commcen and instead would be placed in the MT (Mechanical Transport) Section until further notice. This second interrogation again lasted approximately seven hours.

As soon as I could I met up with the Wren with whom I was having a relationship and discovered that she'd not 'given me up', but that they'd told her I'd been the one to admit the relationship first, meaning the police had used deception in order to trap us into confessing. This added another layer of devastation and led to almost forty years of self-hatred, having realised that not only was I the agent of the demise of my own beloved career, but that I'd also ruined the life of the Wren and destroyed any friendships I'd made whilst serving, believing they would also be subjected to relentless and incredibly emotionally trying questioning from the SIB. Some days later we discovered that it was another Wren lesbian who'd named us to 'save herself'. These were the lengths some people were forced to go to in order to save their own careers, when none of us were doing anything illegal.

It quickly became apparent that everyone at RAF Gibraltar was aware of my situation. I was universally ostracised and had no one to turn to for emotional support. I did continue the relationship with the Wren, we only had each other after all, and visited her in her quarters at HMS Rooke, where I was arrested by the RN police, frog-marched through the entire facility to their guardroom, placed under arrest and then questioned by them. I insisted I would not answer any questions unless the senior WRAF officer was present. Upon her arrival, I was released and told not to set foot on HMS Rooke again or I'd be locked up. The WRAF officer didn't engage with me at all and disappeared as soon as I was released.

I was seconded into MT and after a couple of months of not really doing any work, I decided to petition my sergeant to allow me to return to my normal duties in the Commcen. This was eventually agreed with the proviso that I wasn't to work in the Crypto room nor have access to any highly classified materials. In actual fact, I did return to normal duties, including working in the Crypto room, which amply demonstrates my being regarded as a highly valued individual with proven expertise and integrity.

It was at this stage, having heard nothing more from the SIB, that I almost convinced myself I wouldn't be dismissed. Consequently, life went back to some semblance of 'normality', except I didn't have any friends now; everyone being too afraid to be associated with me. That feeling of deluded euphoria was soon dispelled when, in January 1986, I was again arrested by the RAF police and marched into the station commander's office. The station commander formally told me that he had reviewed my case and agreed I should be dismissed forthwith. My case had then been forwarded to the air commodore WRAF (the highest ranking WRAF officer), for her review and she'd endorsed termination of my service. He also gave his own opinion of me as a 'dirty deviant' who deserved to be dismissed, telling me I was to pack my belongings immediately ready for repatriation to the UK.

While waiting to be returned home, I can recall the moment when the whole enormity of my situation came crashing down upon me. I'd been drinking in a bar in town and was invited back to someone's married quarters, and suddenly experienced a complete breakdown, crying uncontrollably and indeed hysterically, so much so that the neighbour came to enquire what had happened. I was so incoherent I couldn't even explain.

In February I was returned to the UK and told I'd be given a date to report to RAF Innsworth, where I would be dismissed from the service. I arrived there on 1 April 1986, returned all my kit and was marched into a room with a squadron leader, who proceeded to explain that I was being dismissed under QR607(22)b, Services No Longer Required, which in his opinion was letting me off lightly. He further stated that I was a liar who'd lied when being recruited by not admitting I was 'homosexual' when asked. Further to this, he advised that my annual assessment (which was consistently 7-8, 9 being the highest possible rating), had been reduced from 8s to 4s (unsatisfactory), as I clearly wasn't to be trusted and indeed was lucky to have escaped a custodial sentence.

He informed me I wasn't entitled to any resettlement courses or support and I was to be dismissed from that day never to return to any RAF establishment again. My last day of service, therefore, was 1 April 1986 and I left with no job, no home and no friends.

I remained unemployed for two years. I'd applied for any number of jobs but was unsuccessful because I didn't have a positive reference from the RAF. I did, however, apply for the position of shift leader at the Commcen in Whitehall, the main communication centre for the MOD. My application was successful and I was called in to Whitehall for an interview and was subsequently offered the job subject of security clearances, despite being totally honest regarding the reason for my dismissal from the RAF. I was convinced I'd be confirmed in post, but of course I failed to pass the positive vetting process. Clearly, I was extremely competent at my job, and this position included holding the keys to the Commcen, so my integrity was not in question, but still my sexuality made me unemployable.

I then fell into extensive debt and was living in sparsely furnished accommodation. I had no carpets, just some pieces of under-felt on the floor and slept on a mattress. Indeed, I was so poor that one Christmas Day I had nothing to eat except a can of baked beans and no money for the electricity meter so was living by candlelight. I spent all day crying uncontrollably and considering suicide. After this I did manage to pick up some short-term work here and there, where having a good reference wasn't required. I spent a month in a factory packing carrots for Marks and Spencer's, a few days pricking out seedlings in a garden centre, and various other types of 'piecework' until eventually I somehow managed to get work as a self-employed ice cream seller, working with the owner. After a while, I did get onto a Manpower Services Commission six-month short course and trained as a joiner, which at the time was almost unheard of for a woman. I experienced a great deal of discrimination and sexual harassment on building sites, which was at odds with the codes of behaviour and camaraderie that I'd become used to in the RAF. It was usual for an 'improver' joiner to work with another more experienced person, but no one wanted to work with me, so I made mistakes and was dismissed on several occasions, which further compounded my grief and PTSD driving me into an ever deeper depression.

I received no support from the RAF and didn't feel able nor welcome to contact any of the forces' charities, such as SSAFA or the Royal British Legion. I'd been paying into the RAF Benevolent Fund during my service but didn't even have the courage to contact them. I had no help with finding a job, a home or indeed how to navigate civilian life. I'd joined as a very young, quite naive 20-year-old straight from my parents' home, so had no experience of life or managing my own home, etc.

I was extremely lonely for a long time and have experienced PTSD since my dismissal. Until very recently, I'd never contacted any of my friends from my former life, always believing I would be shunned after having put them through that terrible inquisition.

One thing that has become apparent to me is that no matter the length of time that's lapsed since this trauma, I can never truly expect anyone, other than those similarly affected, to understand the utter devastation I experienced. I'm now in contact with one or two ex-WRAF friends and when I try to talk to them about what happened, they don't want to really engage, simply saying that was then, time to put it behind me; for them it's in the past, but for me it's there in the background every day and I know it's affected my mental health. On reflection, I do see how before I was forced to live a double life, I wasn't an angry person, but certainly that changed and especially so after my dismissal. I'm not in any way violent, but I do have times when I just feel angry for no particular reason. I can be aggressive and verbally unpleasant and when asked why, I really don't know. It's only now that I'm talking about my experiences and writing this that I can see the direct correlation between my experiences and my altered mental health.

I've also come to realise that even before I was 'discovered' and dismissed, the ban had already affected my personality. I've always been quite a reserved somewhat 'buttoned up' type of person, although reasonably gregarious when I get to know someone or if I'd had a few drinks. However, during my time in the RAF, after coming out to myself as lesbian, I became even more wary of developing close relationships, ever anxious of being caught and, when drinking heavily, would often wake up dreading what had happened the previous evening; had I given myself away or told someone my secret? In fact, one of the direct consequences of my traumatic dismissal is that even now I find it difficult to engage with people; I'm often alone in a crowd and keep most people at arm's length. I guess I've created a wall around me to protect me from experiencing that profound sense of loss, abandonment and betrayal; to keep me safe from any further pain.

The ending of a career, way of life and home that I loved resulted in shame, distress and guilt that I still carry to this day, and no matter what I've achieved it will always be with me. The recent realisation that the negative effect it's had on my personality is also something that I'd never dealt with, and now I know I must look for some support in order to try to reverse that.

All of this, I believe, has been slightly ameliorated by my relatively recent engagement with Fighting With Pride, who've truly enabled me to regain some of my pride in having served and I'm certainly very grateful to have found them.

Having said all of the above, I've survived and gone on to have an extremely successful second career. Through personal relationships I learnt British Sign Language (BSL), and then trained as a BSL/English interpreter, successfully completing the examination to become a registered interpreter in 1994. I then went on to gain a Master's degree in BSL/English Interpreting from the University of Durham in 2000. I'm a former chair of the Association of Sign Language Interpreters and instigated the foundation of a regulatory body, the RBSLI. I've interpreted at the highest level, for instance at the United Nations in Geneva and at the Council of Europe in Strasbourg on many occasions and in numerous countries around the world.

On a personal note, I'm very happy to say I've been in a relationship with my partner Gloria for twenty-four years, living in London with our two Pugs. Gloria has two children, who now have their own children, so I'm a grandparent, too.

I've also been a biker for more than thirty years, riding predominantly Harley Davidson motorcycles. I generally tour alone, have crossed the USA three times and ridden in most countries of western Europe. I'm also a member of Dykes on Bikes® the world-famous lesbian biker club, established in San Francisco in 1976, when a group of lesbian bikers rode at the front of San Francisco Pride and still do today, almost fifty years to the day since I joined the RAF. We lead off Prides around the world, the most famous being Sydney Mardi Gras, which most years will have over 200 bikes. I was one of the founders of Dykes on Bikes® London and was instrumental in the negotiations to allow us to lead off London Pride 2019; the very first time this had happened in London. Further to this, I, as president of the London club, had the immense honour to be the lead-off bike in 2022, the fiftieth anniversary of London Pride. I'm now emeritus secretary of Dykes on Bikes® Rhine-Weser in Germany and ride with them in front of Prides in Germany every year.

In 2014, I returned to Gibraltar for the first time since my dismissal. Despite it being a very traumatic experience, it was also cathartic and resulted in us purchasing a holiday property there, which we visit at least two or three times a year, so it's interesting how life can square the circle sometimes.

Chapter 17

A Dream Shattered in 51 Days

————————— Steven Waring —————————

My dad served in the Royal Engineers and was away a lot, but his homecoming brought stability, and I enjoyed our growing bond as father and son. In 1978 I started my second year of secondary school and was beginning to make friendships that lasted beyond a school year. I loved the 'lads and dads' stuff and when we could, we went to football matches and spent hours talking about the teams and players. When the conversation strayed into Dad's army career, I was in awe; it sounded ace. The stories he told felt like they'd come straight from the pages of an action comic and, month by month, I began to see glimpses of what my future might be like. I'd never been one of those lads who liked to hang out on the streets and so took on a paper round in the morning and after school to pay for my passion of buying records. I liked to listen to the punk rock of the day, but I was never rebellious; the seed of a military career had already been planted by my father.

Consequently, I joined TS Mohawk, the Sea Cadet unit in Blackburn. The unit had a marching band, and I wanted to learn to play the drums, just like my dad did in the regimental band of the Royal Engineers. My dad was proud that I was bringing purpose to my teenage life beyond school, and I started to make new friends from different areas of the town and from different schools, but we all had one common thread: the Sea Cadets. I was hooked and excelled in military customs and discipline and learned everything I could. Day by day it looked more and more likely that, after leaving school, I'd join the Royal Navy.

The cadet band practiced and attended events and competitions at weekends, while on Tuesdays and Fridays during cadet nights we honed our military and seamanship skills. The cadets soaked up every moment of my teenage life and I loved every minute of it. I wanted to excel and worked hard to be a good cadet. In the Easter and summer holidays there were often annual camps at the Royal Navy training bases, such as HMS Raleigh, Devon and RAF Wroughton, Wiltshire, at other times there were camping trips to Wales and Scotland, which were amazing. I felt incredibly privileged, as a teenager from Lancashire, to be traveling all over the UK playing in the band, swimming, sailing or canoeing competitively and generally having the time of my life. My dedication to the cadets didn't go unnoticed and I soon rose up the ranks. There seemed to be no stopping me. Dad and I did laugh about my choice of being in the Royal Navy, but he was proud that I'd set my heart on a career with the military and I felt incredibly encouraged.

The focus and learning of the cadets spilled out into my schooling. My peers looked up to me and I became a popular lad. I had a great set of friends and found time on schooldays to be in the cricket, football and running teams. I'd developed into quite a sporty and likable boy and even girls seemed to be taking notice of me! In my last year at school, my hard work in the cadets was rewarded by a promotion to leading seaman, which brought some responsibility. In summer 1981 I was selected to go to on a training course to qualify as a physical training instructor (PTI) for our detachment. The course was hosted at the Royal Navy Physical Training School at HMS Temeraire, Portsmouth and we were accommodated close by at HMS Nelson. In those four weeks away I lived my dream, immersed in the life of a Royal Navy sailor with other lads from all over the country who felt the same. I excelled in gymnastics, particularly the vault, and gymnastics was quickly added to my life at school and as a cadet. The summer was made even more special by the wedding of Prince Charles and Lady Diana Spencer, I watched the Fleet Air Arm and Royal Navy gun crews train for what would be a spectacular day that I'd never forget. I wanted that life so much. I returned home triumphant, bursting through the door at home telling my parents that I was going to be a Royal Navy PTI as soon as I left school.

There was to be a final accolade at the cadets' annual awards where I was handed the trophy for Cadet of the Year, as well as my final promotion to Cadet petty officer. This came with the opportunity to speak at a regimental dinner where my dad beamed with pride after it was announced that the award came with a trip around the UK on the tribal class frigate, HMS *Mohawk*. In a year that had started so fantastically, it would've been difficult to believe that this would be the year my military career would end prematurely. Twice.

As Christmas of 1981 came and went, it was time to start the selection process for the Royal Navy and I vividly remember seeming to be the only lad at school who knew where their future lay. Around Easter '82 I went through the Royal Navy selection process, passed the initial entrance procedure, and soon after went to Liverpool for a medical. If I passed, I would be in the Royal Navy and could later choose my career path. To my shock, I failed the medical with red/green colour deficiency. I was colour blind. It hit me like my first punch in a street fight: all those years of focus and preparation, lost in one fateful day. There was no Plan B and I walked away from the careers centre after a shake of hands, barely hearing the wishes of 'good luck'. My world had end abruptly and dark clouds filled my sky.

I fell back into my routine at home but felt like a rudderless ship. One evening, Dad picked me up from the bus station in Blackburn after cadets, he dropped into our conversation whilst driving home that I might want to try the Army instead, where the colours of red for port and green for starboard might be less of a problem. Suddenly, the sky was blue again!

It was just after the Easter holidays when Dad and I went to the Army career's office for the first time. We went thought the process of application and I remember Dad guiding me to choose a trade first. I had to be careful what choice of trade, however, as my colour blindness barred me from certain regiments, such as the Royal Signals. Just a few weeks later, I passed the first medical test and was incredibly overjoyed. After that there was a selection process and another medical, this time in Sutton Coldfield, over two days. If I passed day one, I could progress to the second day. At the end of the first day, I was still there and remember lying in bed thinking, 'I'm one day away from joining the British Army.' But I still didn't know what regiment to join. I lay awake reading pamphlets on different regiments and corps until well into the early hours. I had to put four choices down and with my dad's advice in mind, I made the Army Catering Corps my first choice. I was only 16 at the time and needed to be 18 to join up as a PTI, so that would need to come later. My second choice was a Guards Regiment. I was good at marching and the ceremonial duties I'd seen the guards at Buckingham Palace perform had made them seem quite appealing. Perhaps I could play the drums? The last two choices were specialist roles and a bit of 'pie in the sky', but I thought that might make it more likely I'd achieve one of my first two choices. At the end of the second day, after various physical and educational tests, the results were read out and I was finally told that I'd passed. My dreams had come true: I was joining the Army Catering Corps.

Dad had told me to get a trade and now I was to be an Army chef! I remember my welcome home was mostly a family celebration, but I couldn't wait to get back to school and the cadets to tell everyone I was joining the Army. The last term at school was going to be a breeze.

In my remaining months at school, I focused on trying to achieve good results, but I was also relaxed knowing that I knew what I was going to do when my exams were over. At the time, a sixth form education was an easy option, stretching school to the age of 18. The alternatives were Youth Opportunities Programmes, which offered a mix of work and training for what was then a very meagre £25 a week. Joining the Army seemed a great option, but I was a bit mystified why I was the only recruit from my school year. I remember going to see the career teacher, who asked what my plans were after school. It was a very short meeting!

However, I had little experience of kitchen environments and with twelve weeks after my exams before getting on the train to Aldershot, I had to make best use of my time. So, I got on my bike and asked around a few of the local hotels and thankfully, one took me on as a kitchen porter. I finished school one Friday and walked into employment on the Monday. I loved doing the washing up, basic food preparation and learning to cook. Unfortunately, that summer my parents decided to separate. It was sad, but I'd come to the end of my life at home, and knowing I was moving away and joining the Army, I buried my head in my work. During the final few weeks, I had to go and live with Mum, who'd moved to another town. August and Aldershot couldn't come quickly enough.

On the glorious 12 August 1982, I remember saying my goodbyes to my family at the train station in Blackburn as I set off on my own to Aldershot. My journey to Portsmouth the year before had taken a similar route into London, which had given me a bit of experience of navigating the London Underground to Waterloo. There, I boarded the train for the Army Garrison at Aldershot that would begin the career I'd longed for. There were lots of other lads just like me at Waterloo who were heading for the same train, and when I alighted in Aldershot, a tall Army NCO with a clip board was checking off the new recruits. I told him my name and he pointed to a bus, which I loaded my case onto. Inside the case were some civilian clothes to get me by whilst in basic training, along with a brand-new iron, which I anticipated might see some action! The bus was full of nervously chattering new recruits and I found myself sat next to a lad from Padiham, were my grandparents lived. Charlie Webster was the grandson of the local butcher and son of my mother's best friend from her school days, and his presence seemed reassuring. When we arrived at St Omer Barracks, Aldershot, we all lined up as No 3 intake of 1982. We were divided into three companies, but sadly Charlie didn't follow me. I was in C Company and as a junior craft apprentice, my accommodation was on the third floor of a concrete block.

Day one was a whirlwind of administration, medicals and collecting kit and uniforms. There were bewildering camp rules, and we were told that for the first four weeks, we were not to go beyond the wire fences that either kept others out or kept us in! We learned where the cook house was, the NAAFI and the gym, and I discovered the swimming pool where I'd go most nights in my free time. The first four weeks of basic training were full on, but I was well prepared. I enjoyed it and settled into Army life quickly. We could call home daily and as I'd had met a girl and formed a relationship over the summer, I loved calling her and my mum to tell them what I'd been up to. My girlfriend was so proud of me being in the Army and encouraged me to write whenever I could. I'd love to find those letters, which for a moment in time were the accounts of a very happy young soldier.

Our days were a mix of classroom training, PE, swimming, square bashing and time in the accommodation block to tend to our kit. In the cookhouse there were three square meals a day. It was an intense routine that began at 6 am and by lights out at 9 pm we were all exhausted. In our final week of basic training we were told that if we put in some hard graft and received a good inspection, we'd be given weekend leave.

With everything polished to a dazzling shine, the inspection came and was passed with flying colours. It was 1982 and the terrorist risk in the UK was high, so we were to travel home in civvies. In the 1980s the Troubles in Northern Ireland made us targets for the IRA and we were briefed about this before our foray back into the world beyond the fence. We left the camp that Friday morning and were told to be back by 8 pm on Sunday. I stepped in an Army land rover and headed to Aldershot train station, homeward bound. I loved returning home and immediately sensed the pride my family felt in my achievements, after following my father and grandfather and being the third generation in my family to join the Army.

However, on my return on the Sunday the air in the accommodation block had changed, and the body blow that was to come would take me eight years to recover from, with lifetime damage that could not be undone.

Some lads in my accommodation block didn't go home and I started to feel jealousy brewing between us. I was friendly with everyone in my block, including a Junior NCO whom I would go running around the camp go to the gym with. But there was one tall lad from the north-east who seemed to take a sudden dislike to me. He bristled when I spoke and I sensed trouble, but nevertheless laughed it off for a few days. On Thursday evening, I went for a run with the JNCO. He was a local lad, and we stopped off at his parents' home on the way back. On our return to the mess things became difficult. The tall lad had become so intensely jealous about my friendship with the JNCO that he'd broken into my wardrobe and thrown my kit out of the window. He'd even pissed on my bed. However, he'd picked on the wrong soldier: I'm a northern lad and could hold a fight back then, so the mess was transformed into the scene of a wild west brawl. I gave him a good hiding but was eventually dragged off him and put into the JNCOs bedroom. I thought this had been done to cool off but in time, the MPs came, and I was escorted to the camp jail for questioning about what'd happened. I spent the next two nights in jail until, on the Saturday morning, I was brought in front of the camp commandment, who was flanked by a group of senior NCOs. I was brought to attention, standing there as a 16-year-old boy, unable to have my say or reply, as I listened to the false allegations of my friendship with the JNCO and was accused of having a gay relationship. They told me I was a poof and that poofs weren't allowed to serve in the British Army. It was frightening and confusing. I didn't know what he meant: remember, I was 16-year-old northern lad from a family with a long history of service in the Army. All I wanted to do was serve.

The commandant told me he'd spoken to my parents and under the circumstances had no alternative but to dismiss me. He told me there were two ways to go, the easy option being that I quietly accepted the outcome. I was 16 years old, alone and being told I was to be dismissed from the Army for being a poof (whatever that was). It was incomprehensible.

The leaving part was horrific. I remember crying whilst quickly signing forms, wondering what'd happen when I got home, but I did what I was told to do. I attended a discharge medical, handed my kit back at the QM Stores, all whilst no one was around. I felt numb. It was killing me. What was I going to do now? I was allowed a phone call to speak to my mum, but she couldn't believe what she was hearing, and the call became heated. She said I'd let the family down, but all I could say was that I was protecting myself.

My fifty-one days in the British Army ended in an accommodation block fight at the hands of a jealous kid, who was the same age as me, telling officers that I was a 'poof'. I'll never know if he knew what would happen to me or the impact it would have upon my life. As my parents had split up, I went to my mum's new house, but there was no room for me there and terrible rows followed with both parents, so my stay was short lived. With no job to go to, my world had collapsed.

Life was a struggle for the several years and there was also an attempt to end my own life as it took years for me to find my feet again. At the age of 24, I went to college and then university. Thinking back, it took me eight years of bumming around all over the UK before I started to rebuild my life. My dad never spoke to me properly until about a year before his death in 2006. I never went back home to live as I never felt welcome there. In my dad's words, I'd let them all down.

Those fifty-one days and the consequences of what happened to me have been parked in my head for decades. The impact has been shocking and I've struggled to hold down relationships and have children from two different mothers.

The saddest part of the damage done is that never in my life have I had a homosexual thought. The JNCO was simply a good, friendly kid, who, just like me, wanted to serve in the military and do a good job. Purely on the arbitrary judgment of unreliable whispers I'd been deemed what they called a 'poof', and as a result lost a career and life that I'd always longed for. What's more, I'd seemingly let my parents down. How could I possibly have been discharged from the Army for being homosexual? If nothing else, it shows the hate and contempt in those times for LGBT members of our armed forces and the prejudice of those who upheld military law.

Without any shadow of doubt, the judgement stopped me from honoring my commitment to serve my adult life in the British Army. In recent years I've suffered from 'what if' syndrome. My depression, anxiety and anger are so apparent these days, fixing upon everything I've lost. The only salvageable thing from this sorry tale is that I'm beginning to recognize that I can serve the military family as a veteran and can educate and support the lads and lasses who serve our country today.

The Prime Minister's apology on behalf the British people, made in the House of Commons in July 2023, was important me. I'm just sad my parents weren't alive to hear it or read this chapter. I'm also enduringly sad knowing that I was always truthful, but way back in 1982, that frightened 16-year-old boy was alone, in a land of prejudice and hate, where nobody cared enough about the evidence being beyond reasonable doubt.

Chapter 18

Hiraeth

—————————————— James Carter ——————————————

There is a short word in the Welsh language that encapsulates an idea for which I can find no equivalent in English, but this small Welsh word sums up my story.

Hiraeth: a deep, nostalgic, bittersweet wistfulness, or an intense longing to return to something – or someone, somewhere, or sometime – that is now long gone, or perhaps never was. In the sense of a longing for something now gone, *hiraeth* is also entwined with feelings of grief, loss, and remorse. (Paul Anthony Jones, 12 September 2019)

I grew up in a very conservative house in the northwest of England, a home where emotions weren't talked of. Life was about facts and, most important of all, what other people thought of you. One of my earliest memories was asking one of my parents why they didn't hold my hand anymore, only to be told, 'You're too old for that kind of thing'. By the age of 17, I understood that even though I was capable of going to university, I had to get away and try and live a 'normal' life without being controlled, either emotionally or financially. I was so desperate to become independent that I settled on joining the RAF and shunned all attempts by my teachers to get me to apply for a university place. Many years later, I reconnected with my closest school friend and he still can't believe that the shy, nervous and extremely under-confident lad he'd once known had 'joined up' and literally disappeared from the face of the earth without trace. It was my only option and as I joined the RAF in the late 1980s, I escaped a suffocating and mentally abusive parent who's no longer in my life.

I was just 19 when I attested and had no idea I was gay. In fact, I'd very little idea about what being gay was, except, that is, for the horrific images of the 'Don't Die of Ignorance' AIDS campaign leaflets delivered to homes in the 1980s and watching them being unceremoniously thrown in the bin with the words, 'That's what happens to perverts'. I can therefore say, hand on heart, that I signed 'the document' saying I wasn't homosexual quite honestly when I visited the careers office for one of my interviews.

Had there been the internet, or any positive gay role models in the 1970s or early 1980s, I might've stood a chance, but all I had as a reference were the 'sitcom' stereotypes which I in no way identified with. When I joined the RAF, I had a girlfriend; looking back she was a friend, not a girlfriend in the true sense of the word. I was just a lonely young man who wanted company; someone to care about me and someone who loved me unconditionally. In most respects it was inevitable I'd yearn for the sense of belonging that 'paternalistic' organisations like the military purport to provide.

As my first year of service progressed, I slowly became aware I was feeling attracted to some of the lads I was stationed with. It wasn't just a physical thing, it was a feeling that I understood men far better than women; that in some mysterious way I connected with them on a much deeper level. Quite slowly I began to question whether I was gay. This was a frightening experience because at that time the RAF Police were known to actively pursue homosexuals and I was afraid I'd somehow be caught, even though I wasn't acting on my feelings. I was also vaguely aware that someone at my station had been 'caught' and that he'd been unceremoniously kicked out in disgrace. I became paranoid I'd inadvertently betray myself and that the RAF Police were secretly stalking me, or that they could read my mind.

Just before the fall of the Berlin Wall I was posted to an RAF station in Germany. Apart from the excitement of cheap beer and being in a new country, I sadly became even more isolated. The environment in the barrack block revolved around large amounts of cheap beer, even cheaper cigarettes, and an even larger dose of promiscuity. Inevitably, there was also a lot of homoerotic 'banter' and 'getting naked', and I freely admit to finding this exciting.

Of course, there were also lads who weren't drinking or sleeping around. Those who went to the gym. I would've preferred to associate with those guys, but I was terrified of becoming attracted to one of them or letting my guard slip in the slightest way. Consequently, I avoided gyms, sport or anything where I could be 'caught out'. By this point, even being in a changing room with other men was fraught with difficulty and I avoided them at all costs. In short, I was extremely vulnerable, and I knew it!

A month after arriving in Germany, I actually witnessed what happened to someone who was rumoured to have been 'caught'. He was marched to and from the mess in 'fatigues' by the Royal Military Police and degraded in the most horrible way. I knew then that there was no way I must be found out, particularly because I'd nowhere I could call a 'home' to return to.

In desperation, I sought 'safe' company within the service church community. In many ways this was the biggest mistake I ever made, even though I did meet a few lifelong friends this way. I was lucky enough to be 'adopted' by a civilian German family, which was very unusual for a young airman and set me even further apart. I left camp at every opportunity and was able to experience the 'real' Germany and way of life, with the added advantage of spending as much time away from my peers and 'danger' as possible. My son is now great friends with one of this family's grandchildren and we reciprocate bi-yearly visits. It's the most heartwarming of experiences; watching these two boys grow up and experience significant milestones together in a world very different to the one I grew up in. However, on the negative side, I became even more confused because of the Church's stance on homosexuality. I was part of yet another community that could, or would, reject me if I was truly allowed to be myself.

I was lonely and very frightened by this point; I was drinking heavily and not sleeping. One night I lay in bed listening to a very loud party in the block and just cried. By 03.00 in the morning I was exhausted and, in desperation, knocked on the door of a church friend. I broke down and sobbed; my friend was so concerned he took me to the medical centre and I was eventually admitted to a military hospital due to a 'breakdown'. I was unable to explain or seek help as to why I was so distressed because of the fear of being 'found out' and losing my 'home' career and reputation. In short, I was forced to lie to those who should've helped me with the causes of my depression and sadness.

Following a week in hospital, after which I was medically downgraded, I plucked up the courage to talk to an army padre about my feelings. I still didn't even know if I was actually gay. I had no way of finding out or experimenting; I just knew I was different and that I didn't 'get it' when it came to girls. I needed help. When I 'came out' to him, his response was blunt and frightening: 'If you're telling me you think you're gay, then I'll have to report you and you'll almost certainly go to Colchester [prison] and be discharged.' I rapidly backtracked and made up some story about a girlfriend, and to his credit nothing further was ever said again. Even though I now recognise his 'kindness' in not reporting my 'confession' to the police, I wish he'd done so, because I was left in 'limbo'; a place where I feared the RAF Police knocking at my door at any time.

Eventually, I became so fearful of being discovered that I left the British church community and joined an American service congregation in Monchengladbach, where I felt I could be 'safe'. This congregation was several miles away from my station and was very 'conservative'; it was southern Bible Belt 'territory', but it was also distrustful of the military authorities, so I once again plucked up the courage to talk to someone about my feelings. I was told I was loved, something I'd never felt before, but also that being gay was a sin and a choice. However, I could be healed... On one particular day, I was approached by a young lad who claimed to know I was being prayed for because I was 'family'. I had no idea what he meant until he explained! It was exciting but very scary. He claimed to be a special investigator in the military police. I so desperately wanted to be friends with this man, but I couldn't be because I was so distrustful of anyone who might expose me. I often wonder what happened to him because I eventually felt the need to 'ghost' him; the actions of a cruel coward. I'll never know whether he genuinely wanted to be my friend or whether he was investigating me and waiting for me to trip myself up.

The Church told me all I needed was to have enough faith and that God would take the 'sin' away. Not only that, He would also find me the right girl and I'd be 'delivered' of my burden. In the enforced absence of access to any other advice or help, I willingly took all of this on board and fervently followed their instructions, praying each night that I'd be 'delivered', and that God would send the right girl my way.

The loneliness I experienced at this time is something I'll never forget. It gnawed into my soul; I was empty and absolutely terrified. To this day, I can't understand why it was institutionally right not only to criminalise someone's very nature, but to deny them help, support and information at the same time. Not a day does goes by when at some point I don't re-experience the struggles I felt back then, the feeling of being worthless, un-loveable and an overwhelming terror of losing my work and physical home.

In the autumn of 1990, I was posted to another RAF station in Germany, and it soon became clear my squadron was likely to be sent to Saudi Arabia following the invasion of Iraq. The station medical officer told me it was very unlikely I'd be allowed to deploy with my squadron because of my previous breakdown. I was now faced with a situation where not only did I feel less of a male than my peers, I was also likely to be seen as 'too weak' to do my job. I was determined to deploy and was fortunate, following a lot of begging, that the station medical officer agreed to fly me back to the UK to a place called Kelvin House in London, where a very senior psychiatrist could assess me. Once again, I was unable to explain why I'd suffered from the breakdown and made a whole lot of stuff up. The psychiatrist eventually agreed to upgrade me to A4 G2 Z1, which meant I had a medical marker of past problems. The psychiatrist I saw was very unsympathetic and his parting shot as I left his consulting room was, 'If it happens again, you'll be discharged'. His words rang in my ears for the remainder of my RAF career.

I did deploy to Saudi Arabia in early December 1990, fearful that I'd have another breakdown, that I'd be lost and cut off from the only 'support' I'd ever known; the Church and the friends I'd made in Germany. My one overriding memory during this time was hoping that, during the SCUD missile attacks, a missile would land on our building and once and for all end the emptiness I was feeling. This changed when I returned home to a feeling of failure; failure that I'd been to war and even then been unable to find a way to make it end!

I returned to the UK just after the Gulf War and spent the next four years working hard, surviving, but all the time masking my loneliness by self-medicating with alcohol.

I did eventually meet a girl. She was kind, loving and we were well-matched. We married in the mid-1990s and had our first child. Life was good, we holidayed together, celebrated milestones and anniversaries and just enjoyed the experience of living together.

By the late 1990s there was a lot of discussion surrounding the lifting of the 'ban'. I was working close to policy makers at this time on their personal staff; officers up to four-star level, and the overt homophobia I experienced at this time was horrific. This was an abjectly horrible time for me, but I knuckled down further and was lucky enough to be promoted. When I went on my promotion courses, the lifting of 'the ban' was one of the hottest topics! The ingrained homophobia I had to listen to was vile; it degraded me as a person and I felt like I was 'scum'. Of course, I couldn't talk to anyone because I was married with two young children. This time was, in some ways, worse than trying to live 'below the radar'. Even so, I found myself openly 'defending' those in our services who were gay in a very unforgiving and hostile environment. I felt I was in a minority of one and knew I was beginning the process of finally 'coming out'.

Notwithstanding, all this discussion heightened and reinforced the doubts I still had about my sexuality, and I was again struggling massively with anxiety, panic attacks and 'emptiness'.

When the ban was finally lifted, I remained very fearful because I'd an enhanced security vetting, and I believed I could still lose my career because I hadn't disclosed my doubts about my sexuality during my interviews.

In this respect, the lifting of the ban made things ten times worse for me because suddenly I was 'legal', but I'd also 'lied'. In effect, I was trapped, but from the opposite direction. I decided I'd no choice but to 'plough' the furrow I'd started, but I was desperately unhappy and was now drinking even more heavily to get some peace.

Things finally came to a head in the mid-2000s when, on a detachment, I met a man and 'the lights went on'. I finally realised who I was and that there was nothing I could do to change it. I was now in my late 30s, but I knew that when I got home, I had to tell my wife.

After an eighteen-hour flight, and some tearful 'hellos', I told my wife, best friend and partner that I was gay. I'll never forget the pain and anguish we experienced that night. I also remember the real love and compassion we showed towards each other, because there was no fighting, just sadness and an overwhelming sense of wanting to make things right for each other. It was then I had my second full on 'breakdown' and needed the help of the RAF medical services.

We both struggled to get appropriate help and support, but we muddled through and decided we wanted to stay together because we were best friends and, if it's not too hackneyed a phrase, soul mates. Sadly, due to the nature of military life, including me having to explain myself to my bosses, news leaked out and my wife had to move home under the guise of 'stability for our eldest daughter during her secondary education'.

I did have support at this point from DCMH Brize Norton, which helped somewhat, but at this time there appeared to be very little understanding of the impact the ban had had on people and the families of those who'd not been 'caught'. I also believe I was misdiagnosed with a mood disorder because I was prescribed some medication that ultimately meant that I'd be medically downgraded to a level that meant I could never complete a full-service career.

To add insult to injury, I also tried to get help from people outside the military who knew what it was like to be gay, but one of the people who was meant to be helping me ended up raping me. I couldn't report this to the police because it would've meant going public, and in a mixed orientation marriage, this is something you simply can't do! I lived with the memory of this experience alone, until 2023, after reading Lord Etherton's report. Strangely, even fifteen years later, I still find the experience of being raped as being 'just another thing'. I can rationalise the rape. What I can't do is rationalise the reasons for the ban or the impact it's had on countless lives.

For the next two years I commuted home at weekends whilst our family slowly rebuilt itself. In the end we made the decision that as my career was fatally limited by my medical category, I'd seek premature voluntary release. It was a hard decision; I was leaving an organisation that would've criminalised me simply for being me for over half of my career, but which had also given me a measure of security and a sense of belonging.

I then embarked on a new phase in life, looking after my family and not putting myself in any position where I would EVER be so 'exposed' again. Part of this process involved 'coming out' to my parents, my wife's parents and my close friends. It was hard, but I was lucky in that in general we were supported. My wife's parents showed me love and support I didn't deserve; my parents were just glad I was doing my 'duty'. I wouldn't have survived this time without the support of my wife or her family.

The one thing I was unable to do was to have my 'own' life, and in twelve years I only went out on my own once. I was simply too scared of the consequences of meeting another gay person and having to go through the whole painful process again.

The one thing that kept me going during these years was immersing myself in learning the Welsh language in the hope of reconnecting with my roots. I met some incredible people on my 'Welsh' journey; people who I only knew through the medium of Welsh. I could be a different person and, as I didn't have the 'language' to express my fears or feelings, I was able to be the person I wanted to be for the first time in my life! When you're trying to think and speak in a new language, there simply isn't room for thoughts of self-pity, sadness or regret, just because you don't have the words for them.

I've now come out to two of my children. They're incredible and support me 100%. I can't claim that the way I came out to them was ideal, planned or gentle, but I do know that they understand and love me unconditionally, no matter who I am. Their example has shown me what true unconditional love looks like. I am so proud of my children, and they are the one consistent and positive blessing I have in the sorry mess I find myself in.

There have also been a few positive life changes. I finally plucked up courage to join a gym and am the fittest I've ever been. I spend as much time as possible in Wales kayaking, walking and just breathing in the air and enjoying the sense of space. I've also recently volunteered with an organisation and am enjoying repairing engines and getting my hands dirty. The days when I volunteer make me feel free, and maybe just a little bit like I am becoming the person I should've been.

Whilst sat in work eating my lunch last July, I was reading the BBC News website and came across the Etherton Report. I went cold and felt what must've been all the symptoms of shock. I was sat in an open-plan office and there and then had a full-blown breakdown in front of my colleagues. I'd suddenly understood the enormity of what'd happened to me because it was there, in black and white. I was reading about my life and my story. I didn't know about the campaign and then, unexpectedly, I was connected to people who understood and had felt my experiences. Reading the accounts of those who'd been brave enough to write them was massively humbling, but it did make me realise that all the guilt and shame that had built up inside of me wasn't my fault. I'm now in my mid-50s and have always, everyday, blamed myself: I should've been stronger, I should've had more faith. So many wasted chances and a wasted life.

Lord Etherton's report finally showed me that I'd innocently walked into the hands of an organisation that would perpetuate the emotional abuse I'd already experienced, and leave me and my family with scars that would never fully heal.

The ban stopped me being able to truly understand who I was at exactly the time when I should've been allowed to explore my feelings and sexuality. I was forced to repress the very core of who I am because of the hateful, homophobic and discriminatory nature of the ban and those who were expected to uphold it. A ban that is now firmly recognised as having been illegal.

All that said, the ban also had a wider impact than on just those who served. I must also live with the guilt and shame of marrying someone who ultimately found out that their husband was homosexual, and the ripples continue to this day as, one-by-one, I've had to tell my children my story.

Following the publication of the Etherton Report, and a third breakdown, I was lucky enough to be able to reach out to Fighting With Pride. They've been truly amazing and put me in touch with Op Courage, who accepted me onto their treatment pathway as they believed my mental health difficulties over the past thirty years were directly attributable to my military service and the ban, or at the least that it made things a million times more difficult for me.

My diagnosis is Complex Post Traumatic Stress Disorder. Both CPTSD and PTSD involve symptoms of psychological and behavioural stress responses, such as flashbacks, hyper-vigilance and efforts to avoid distressing reminders of the traumatic event(s). People with CPTSD typically have additional symptoms, including chronic and extensive issues with emotional regulation.

As I said earlier, I'm lucky in that I wasn't 'caught', but the pain, shame and guilt remain. I stood no chance of understanding who I was from the moment I joined the RAF until it was too late. I grieve at least once a day, and at the least expected moments, for a young man, full of hopes and dreams that I'll never know.

Most of my responses to everyday stress, or interactions with people and friends, create crippling anxiety. Friendships are particularly difficult as I fear abandonment when I misread intentions or situations. I must work extremely hard not to medicate myself with alcohol and this will inevitably be a battle I face for the rest of my life.

I know I'll never be able to turn back the clock, but I'm slowly learning that I had very few choices, in some instances no choices at all, but that I made the best of those I was able make.

I wasn't arrested or detained and I wasn't dismissed, but I did lose the person I should've been. I was raped and was grossly let down by those who should've been there to support me, in particular the chaplaincy services and the RAF medical branch.

I now feel that there's a glimmer of hope, that with time, and the support of Op Courage, I'll learn acceptance and be able to 'rest'. I'll forever feel angry, but hopefully less so as time passes. Most of all, I live with an overwhelming sense of grief and the thought that, in the words of Fighting With Pride, I ended up being one of 'those who defended peace and freedoms, I was myself denied'.

The last paragraph of this story is dedicated to my darling wife, and if you ever read this know one thing: I married you because I fell in love with you. You were never a smoke screen. I wouldn't be alive today without your unconditional love and support. I love you to the end of the world and back.

Per Ardua ad Astra.

Chapter 19

Discharged but Not Defeated: My Fight for Inclusion

Emma Riley

'Get up, get dressed, get downstairs – you're under arrest!'

Words that changed my life forever.

Born in 1972, I had wonderful parents and a safe and comfortable place to grow up. School life, however, was another matter! My first primary school memory was of a boy stabbing me in the shoulder with a pencil: I was a red-headed tomboy which made me a target. I had to move secondary schools after a term due to bullying and, though the new one was better, it continued.

As I started 'A' levels, I began questioning my sexuality; I'd had a couple of boyfriends, but had crushes on girls, and Anneka Rice! When I did reach out to my year tutor for support, I don't doubt that he had the strictures of Section 28 in mind as he gave me two telephone numbers; one was the Samaritans to stop me harming myself and the other a helpline run by nuns who were ready to persuade me that being gay wasn't a great life choice!

As I came to the end of my school days, what I wanted was a career where I could belong, be part of a tribe, be useful, not be bullied. When I was about 14 there was a career's fair at my school and the Army had a stand. The idea of serving my country, coupled with the obvious camaraderie such a life would bring, really struck a chord with me, but the Army wasn't right. Instead, as my family had spent every weekend and holiday sailing, I chose the Women's Royal Naval Service (WRNS). I applied, went through all the tests, and was accepted to join on 30 July 1990.

I took the train to Plymouth, full of hope, with all the items on my joining list, now I could put the bullying behind me and belong!

The first day there you're briefed, sign your contract, get your kit, and get settled in your shared room. They give you time to read through the contract before signing and it was then that I discovered homosexuality was explicitly banned in the Armed Forces. I read that bit a few times then decided that I didn't really know what I was (I'd had no experience to confirm if I was gay or not and everyone had crushes on girls at school, right?) and the desire to serve my country and find that camaraderie was so strong that I signed and just buried any thought of being anything other than in the Royal Navy.

Training went well. I was in Sirius 31, the last class of women to be trained separately from the men and had the opportunity at the end of basic training to volunteer for sea, which I instantly did. Doing secondary training to learn about my radio operator specialism, I was class leader of the first mixed-sex class, starting to show that I could become an officer one day.

My first draft was to HMS *Cornwall*, a type 22 batch 3 frigate. It'd just been converted to have women aboard and we were the first to sail on her. It was a very lucky draft as after Basic Operational Sea Training (BOST), we were deployed to the West Indies. Months out in the Caribbean, America and Canada, an incredible trip!

They ask you to give preferences as to where you get sent and I chose areas as far as possible from my hometown, wanting to leave that all behind me. This meant my next drafts were both in Scotland, the first was as guard at a communications centre near Dunfermline and the second was working in the communications centre on HMS Faslane, the nuclear submarine base near Helensburgh. I was good at my job and enjoyed Scotland; black pudding suppers (battered, deep fried black pudding sausage with chips) are a delight that everyone should try!

In the year that followed the feeling that I wasn't 'straight' became stronger and I felt I had to somehow test myself to be sure. With the ban in place, I had no one I could talk it through with, so instead I took myself off to London, completely away from the Navy, checked *Time Out* to find out where gay people met just to see how I'd feel, and had an evening out – I kissed a girl and I liked it! I had my answer and it was great to finally feel surer of myself, even though it meant

I had a terrible burden and secret to hide. If anyone found out, I'd be in serious trouble.

That year, my father had been incredibly unwell with heart problems and blackouts, resulting in a quadruple bypass operation. This family stress and worry, coupled with the strain of hiding my true self, meant that I was in a hugely fragile mental state. I lived in shared accommodation and one evening I went for a few drinks out with my roommate, someone I felt was my friend. That night, I confessed to her that I thought I was gay and she seemed supportive and OK with it. I had a kind of euphoria now that I'd spoken my terrible secret and it was going to be OK!

'Get up, get dressed, get downstairs – you're under arrest!'

That morning, my world started to fall apart. Far from being supportive, my supposed friend had reported me to the Military Police. I was led away by two Special Investigation Branch (SIB) officers for a recorded interrogation which went on for hours. I had a chief petty officer with me for support, however, and when I got too upset to continue and they turned off the tape for a fifteen-minute break, she spoke to me. I think I said something about my evening in London, but whatever it was it must've been incriminating in her view because when the SIB turned the tape back on, she told the officers what I'd said. At that moment, I knew I was completely alone.

They took me back to the accommodation block to search my room for evidence. Before entering, one of them asked, 'Do you have any electrical equipment?' clearly asking if I had any sex toys to humiliate me further. Considering we were in a women's accommodation block, I fail to see what relevance that question had; I'm sure there was an abundance of 'electrical equipment'! I said, 'If you mean dildos or vibrators, I don't!' and they proceeded to search.

They went through everything I had, every drawer, bag and piece of clothing looking for evidence of my lesbianism. They confiscated the first Suede album, the one with two androgynous people kissing on the front, and a Julian Clary video, since everyone who watches Julian Clary must be gay! They also confiscated letters I'd written to a pen pal who wasn't in the Navy, in which I'd mentioned I thought I was gay. This was the only piece of physical evidence they had. What they were really looking for, though, in addition to evidence against me, were names. They would've hunted down anyone with whom it looked like

I may have had a relationship and arrested them, it was a real witch hunt era. I was completely celibate, however, so they had no luck in that direction!

They moved me out of the room I shared with my accuser, but I was still in the same block. They shifted where I worked so I wasn't in direct contact with her, but I still ate in the same mess. Everyone knew what was happening to me and why, I was a total pariah. There were a couple of supportive people, but most didn't want anything to do with me so as to not be tarred with the same brush. I was numb and isolated.

They sent me home to tell my parents. I had to tell them that not only was I likely to be thrown out of the Navy, but that the reason for this was because I was gay, it was a forced coming out. I can recall the exact room I was in when I spoke to them, it's a visceral memory that's burned on my brain. I'm eternally thankful that my parents were completely supportive of me and that I had a home to return to. Years later, my mum told me that I cried for about five hours before I could tell them what was wrong.

Weeks went by as the military police machinery ground slowly on, but eventually I was brought up to captain's table and told my services were no longer required: Discharge Shore. I had to sign a paper to say I wouldn't challenge the decision and I did so, but wrote on it that the only reason I wasn't challenging it now was because my father was so ill. My parents collected me from the gates of the base, cold-shouldered by all the guards.

So, then what?!

I had to redraw my entire map of the world and start from scratch to build a career and life after my vocation had been ripped away from me.

I spent perhaps five or six weeks in my old room at home with no clue what to do before deciding I had to put one foot in front of the other and find work. I could touch type so applied to a temp agency for office work and started with filing jobs. One role led to another, and I gradually worked my way up. At the end of 1997, I had got to a place where I had permanent work, a settled home and for the first time, a girlfriend. I needed to go back to the promise I'd made when I was thrown out and somehow challenge it, but where to start?

I phoned Stonewall, the only place I could think of to ask, and am forever grateful to whomever I spoke to that day as they gave me the name of a solicitor at Bindman & Partners, Stephen Grosz, who they understood had a similar case to mine. I made an appointment and the challenge began. I was interviewed by him and the first thing was to take the MOD to court in the UK. I was unlikely to succeed, but due process had to be followed. The day of the public hearing, I was there with my barrister and against us were three QCs - it didn't look good. Exiting the courts it became clear very quickly that one of the journalists in attendance had called the story in, as a camera was in my face the moment we came outside, the one and only time I've felt like a harassed celebrity! My barrister was excellent at protecting me from them and the *Daily Telegraph* didn't get the photo they wanted, although it ran a short piece anyway.

The outcome from that challenge was failure. Another case created a precedent that meant there was no possibility we could win in the UK. There was only one option left and that was to take my case to the European Court of Human Rights (ECHR) and prove that dismissal on the grounds of sexuality was an infringement of my human rights. I agreed, but decided that to protect my family and girlfriend, I'd be anonymous – R vs the United Kingdom.

There were four headline test cases put forward by the organisation Rank Outsiders, who'd been campaigning for years against the ban and all the damage it'd done. My individual case helped support those, lending weight to the call for a change in the law. By late 1999 it looked increasingly possible that the court could rule in our favour, and on 27 September, the ban was ruled an infringement of Article 8, the right to a private life. In the UK there were scores of Armed Forces officers lining up to state that 'homosexuality was incompatible with service life' and that any consideration of allowing such people to serve openly would bring the services to their knees. Such people were a security risk, would be at risk of blackmail, and would corrupt young people under their command, forcing them to accept unwanted attention. The government and MOD put money into teams to survey forces to prove that serving personnel didn't want gays and lesbians serving in their ranks. The reality was that a core of senior officers had lost sight of the values of our Armed Forces.

On 12 January 2000, the Labour government was forced to lift the ban on homosexuals serving in the military. I wholeheartedly believe that without the ECHR ruling, the ban would've continued to be in place for decades, destroying patriotic, brilliant people wanting to serve, whose only crime was to not want to sleep with the opposite sex.

It took a further two years to complete my case. The Royal Navy, unsurprisingly, had 'lost' or more likely deliberately deleted the tapes and transcripts of my interrogation. They tried to argue that as I'd done so well outside of the military, I didn't deserve or need anything further from them. In 2002 everything was complete; I was vindicated and the law was changed. I packed the letters away in the loft and didn't speak of it again for about fifteen years.

It's difficult to describe the impact of what happened. Truly it's only now, almost thirty years since they destroyed my life, that I'm beginning to understand it.

For years I built my ramshackle career and then found a hobby I could be passionate about, singing acapella, barbershop style. Singing as part of a women's chorus started to heal me. I spent years totally terrified I'd look at a woman the wrong way, afraid to touch people in case I was accused of being some kind of predatory lesbian. When changing for a performance, I'd try to make sure I was facing a corner so no one would think I was looking at them the wrong way. A shut down and terrified existence. Gradually, I became more comfortable. I started taking on leadership roles in the chorus and then in the UK region as a gay woman, I was no longer hiding. People accepted me for my strengths, although I still lived in fear of being expelled. Although at a casual glance I might have seemed content, behind the scenes I was far from settled and a series of events in 2014 precipitated a breakdown for me and my relationship. However, as I closed doors on some of my past, there were new beginnings and I started to become me. I had six months of counselling at the beginning of 2015 and agreed to divorce my then partner mid-year. By the end of 2015 I had begun a relationship with the love of my life and the person I credit with waking me from a self-imposed closed off stupor – she brought me alive. Fran made me feel safe, loved, and supported in a way no one had ever done before. She gave me confidence and strength to begin opening up, to begin to heal.

In 2015 Professor Paul Johnson, a professor of law at Leeds University at the time, contacted me. He was collating oral histories for a book about sex, gender and sexual orientation cases which had been taken to the ECHR. Whilst researching the section on military cases, he'd come across my case but, of course, it was anonymous. He had a huge ethical crisis as he'd seen my real name in solicitor correspondence and desperately wanted to include my case in his book, but I'd chosen anonymity. He spoke to his university ethics committee and a friend who worked for an NHS ethics committee, but only made his decision to reach out after dreaming that the only regret I had about the case was that my name was not against it – completely true!

That was the first time I'd properly gone back to those memories and spoken of it. He came to my work after hours and recorded me telling the story, treating me with great compassion. The recording was transcribed and appeared, almost verbatim, in the book *Going to Strasbourg*, which was published at the end of 2016. This was the beginning of opening up about what had happened to me.

In 2017 Fran and I had volunteered to help run the volunteer area at Brighton Pride for a few years and I found the Royal Navy had a stand there, recruiting! I spoke to a Chief Wren, who rather blithely said that her and her female partner were living in married quarters. Mind blown! A marine overheard me speaking to her, followed as we left and stopped me – he thanked me for taking the UK to court to change the law as it'd given him the opportunity to serve. I sobbed to hear that.

I went to London at that marine's invitation to meet other serving and veteran gay people one evening, a very weird experience. Aside from the fact we shared military background, I didn't have any connection with them. It was profoundly odd listening to the usual military banter that I hadn't heard for years, interspersed with one chap talking about his plans to marry his partner in dress uniform with full crossed swords and military honours. I was somehow of that world but forever separated by an invisible barrier, blocked from it. I felt incredibly uncomfortable. On the one hand, intellectually, I was thrilled that these people were openly serving, but emotionally I felt mostly bitterness and shame.

Outside the Navy, I decided never to hide my sexuality at work (one small stubbornness!) and have been lucky enough to work for companies who were LBGT supportive. In 2018, twenty-five years after I'd been thrown out of the Royal Navy for being gay, I marched in London Pride with my company. We gathered in our Strand headquarters after the parade and I gave an impromptu speech, marking how incredible it was to me to have LBGTQIA+ identities celebrated. As I had begun talking, I also started finding out about other LBGT veterans with similar stories. I helped crowd fund a book, *This Queer Angel* by Elaine Chambers, which is her story of being forced out of the military because of her sexuality and her journey to founding Rank Outsiders and fighting the ban. In 2019 the Royal British Legion officially recognised its LBGTQ+ and Allies branch, of which I was a founding member. Through this, I was part of a very small number of serving personnel and veterans who attended the Palace of Westminster on 9 January to hear the Veterans MP, Johnny Mercer, mark the twentieth anniversary of the lifting of the ban by apologising on behalf of the Ministry of Defence. 'As the minister for defence, people and veterans, I wanted to personally apologise to you today for those experiences', Mercer said. It was a surreal and emotional experience hearing that first apology. Twenty years had gone by since the change in law and over twenty-six since I'd been thrown out, but suddenly, I was surrounded by people in uniform.

I had never called myself a veteran. I hadn't felt I deserved that label as there was too much shame and pain. However, it was probably around this time I started feeling that perhaps I could be allowed to use the term to describe myself and applied for a veteran's badge and railcard.

I was also invited that week to be on the red sofa of BBC Breakfast and speak about the lifting of the ban on its anniversary, 12 January. Whilst there I met Craig Jones MBE, the CEO of Fighting with Pride, a new military charity specifically focussed on LGBT veterans like me. Craig had curated and published the book *Fighting With Pride* and the charity has been instrumental in driving public awareness and governmental change for us. Speaking in the green room before the interview, we discovered that we'd served on the same ship together!

Through covid, I followed Fighting With Pride and their progress with campaigning, generating awareness and beginning to reach out to find affected veterans to understand their stories and support them. 2021 was the first year a cohort of LBGT veterans were included in the Cenotaph Remembrance parade, for example, but the biggest step forward came in January 2022, twenty-two years after the ban was lifted. Thanks to their efforts, the government announced they had initiated an independent review of the service and experience of LGBT veterans who'd served between 1967 and 2000. Lord Etherton PC Kt QC, a crossbench member of the House of Lords and the first openly gay judge of the senior courts, was appointed as chair of the review.

In March 2022 I was contacted via Vocal Dimension Chorus (I'm their assistant director), by a producer making a documentary for ITV that featured the LBGT military ban. She'd seen some of the interviews I'd given in the past and wanted to speak to me about my experience and ask for my participation. The programme was *Kelly Holmes: Being Me*, when Dame Kelly Holmes came out after over thirty-two years of hiding her sexuality from the public. Meeting and speaking with Dame Kelly, her story could so easily have ended the same way mine had done. She served around the same time I did, the witch hunt era, and was lucky not to be caught. The damage the ban did to her was huge; she spent all that time living in fear that if it became known she was gay whilst serving, the Army would still prosecute her. A terrible burden to shoulder.

In June, the day before the documentary was released, my wife and I were invited by Dame Kelly to a private screening of the documentary. It's very disconcerting to watch yourself on a cinema screen, especially when discussing something as painful as we did. However, the moment that shocked me the most and released the tears was towards the end, where Dame Kelly spoke to two Olympic medal-winning boxers, partners Karriss Artingstall and Lauren Price. Karriss had served in the Army but had never known about the LGBT ban. She was shocked to learn about it as her experience had been completely accepting. It blew my mind that she had no idea being gay was illegal before.

There was a great deal of press attention after the documentary's release and I was interviewed on BBC Radio Four's Women's Hour with Fighting With Pride and also on Talk TV, trying to raise the profile of the ban and the LBGT Veterans Independent Review.

The review issued a call for evidence in July 2022, asking for LBGT veterans to submit testimonials to understand how we were treated, the impact of the ban at the time and later in our lives, how being dismissed affected us, our careers and our families, etc. Fighting With Pride, Dame Kelly, the RBL LGBT+ and Allies branch and others vigorously promoted the review to reach as many affected veterans as possible, including some who are in their 70s and 80s. Social media, print, TV, attendance at the many Pride marches, all were used to try to reach out to people.

When I submitted my evidence, I wrote, 'I'm a damaged person'. I'm only just starting to understand how much damage those events thirty years ago truly had on me, despite being a resilient and reasonably functional person. Had I had less strength or less support, who knows what might've been. The questions asked you to describe, in as much detail as you could manage, the impact of the ban. I scanned and submitted almost 300 pages of letters and documents pertaining to my cases against the MOD and the UK; I'd kept everything.

For me, living under the ban meant a life of constant fear. Always worried that looking at or touching another woman in the wrong way, or at least in a perceived wrong way, would result in some kind of investigation. I spent a lot of time crying alone because I couldn't articulate the fear. A constant sense of othering, of not fitting in, I couldn't be myself. The experience of dismissal was horrific, shaming, degrading, humiliating. The world was ripped from beneath my feet. The career and vocation I chose was instantly gone and I had no future. The fear, shame and humiliation have been carried for decades – all this I told to the Independent Review.

I've taken career opportunities as they have come to me beyond the career taken from me, although I never feel wholly confident at work. There's always the feeling of being an imposter, of not being safe in a role, that I'll be discovered and exposed.

I had, and still have, a huge problem with those who lie, betray, bully or are unfair. I detest such behaviour and it's caused many issues. I can't watch a TV programme, film, or play that features bullying/discrimination without feeling upset or uncomfortable. I've been a very closed person, only really learning in the last few years to be vulnerable and to trust people.

Coming into contact with more military people and veterans has brought up other feelings, some good, some more difficult. In 2022 I walked with the RBL in Brighton Pride. It was the first time that the Royal Marines Band was there playing along with serving personnel marching. They did a fantastic job and were a great hit. For me, walking with serving personnel was hard enough, but doing so behind the band was very difficult. They played pop songs and things to play up to the occasion ('In the Navy' and 'YMCA', for example), but they also played marching standards. I'd not heard that brass band music since I was learning to march to it in 1990. I spent the first forty-five minutes to an hour trying, and failing, not to cry.

The government needed us to go through the difficulty of picking at those wounds to gain understanding of the terrible damage done and begin reparations. At online community meetings run by FWP and when I met veterans later that year, it was clear that my story, hard as it was for me, was one of the milder experiences. Imprisonment, beating, electric shock therapy, psychoanalysis and psychoactive drugs, manipulative interrogation, unnecessary and humiliating medical examinations, sexual abuse and rape; all these things we experienced as we were being discarded. For many, these calls were the first time they'd ever spoken about what'd happened, as this was a safe space with people of similar experience. Many have struggled with mental health problems, housing and financial issues, relationships and trust. It was harrowing to listen to, but it made me more determined to support where I could.

It also made me incredibly thankful to work for RX and the RELX Group. In every position they've been welcoming and supportive. They really walk the walk for diversity and inclusion. I've never felt excluded or judged because of my sexuality, quite the opposite, and never more so than this year, when the LBGT Veterans Independent Review was published and its first actions taken.

The Final Report was submitted at the end of May 2023, but we had to wait a further two tense months for the government to publish it and begin to take action. I met with my local MP to ask him to help push for its publication, as did many others, along with a lot of correspondence, social media, print and broadcasting to keep pressure on. Finally, I received a text to say that Fighting With Pride expected it to be announced on the last day of parliament before the summer recess and could I make it to London? My manager and RX were incredible in allowing me to adjust my diary and work to enable me to be part of that day.

So, on 19 July I met with Dame Kelly Holmes, Craig Jones and Caroline Paige of Fighting With Pride and about fifteen of the LBGT veterans I'd come to know over the last couple of years, representatives of all the services. We met at the Cabinet Office in a Cobra room with Lord Etherton, the Rt Hon Dr Andrew Murrison (Parliamentary Under-Secretary of State for Defence People, Veterans and Service Families) and the Rt Hon Johnny Mercer (Minister of State for Veterans' Affairs). Being handed a copy of the report and listening to these three people offer words of personal apology and acknowledgement, it began to feel like maybe the right thing was going to happen.

One other veteran and I were asked to accompany Johnny Mercer into the House of Commons. They were only able to take two and it wasn't guaranteed that we'd make it past all the security and regulations. We walked from the Cabinet Office to the Houses of Parliament, an experience in itself given all the attention and harassment Johnny was subjected to on the way, but we made it through to the inner workings of government and were sat in the Members' Gallery above the opposition party, looking down on the government's despatch box.

The house was packed and Prime Minister Rishi Sunak readied himself for Prime Minister's Questions. I sat, white-knuckled, squeezed in between Johnny Mercer and an unknown man, totally unsure how I would react or feel. Would I sit silent? Cry? Shout 'At bloody last!'?

'The ban on LGBT people serving in our military until the year 2000 was an appalling failure of the British State, decades behind the law of this land. As today's report makes clear, in that period many endured the most horrific sexual abuse and violence, homophobic bullying and harassment all while bravely serving this country.

Today, on behalf of the British State, I apologise.'

Sir Kier Starmer echoed this in his first statements, saying that Labour was 'proud to lift the ban against LGBT+ people serving in our armed forces and today we strongly welcome this apology from the Prime Minister'.

After over twenty-three years, we had our apology.

I sat stony faced as the apologies were read and the rest descended into the parody of politics that is PMQs. The prime minister was unemotional, the opposition leader trying to place Labour as the heroes lifting the ban when, in fact, all parties vociferously fought to keep it in place and it was only us taking cases to the European Court that forced the change. The one human moment was around twenty-nine minutes in, when Alicia

Kearns MP was asking her question regarding the government having not yet banned conversion therapies. She acknowledged the apology and, crucially, made eye contact with me in the gallery, reminding everyone in that room that the ban, and the prime minister's apology, affected real people.

We stayed to watch the Rt Hon Ben Wallace, Secretary of State for Defence, read his own statement, being joined by the rest of the veterans in the opposite gallery, and this is when the emotion hit. The report's forty-nine recommendations for reparation were accepted in principle and he committed the government to action all of them, though acknowledged some may 'be delivered by different means'.

'I am pleased that this review has shone a much-needed light on a shameful and unacceptable historical chapter in our Armed Forces history. It is heart breaking that the very tolerance and values that we expected our soldiers, sailors and aviators to fight for, were denied to many of them. I am pleased we now have the opportunity to right those historic wrongs so that LGBT Veterans can once again take pride in their service.'

Crucially, his statement included a personal apology from his perspective of having been an Army officer whilst the ban was in place and that he had enforced it. He acknowledged that the ban was written into military law the same year after the Sexual Offences Act 1967 decriminalised same-sex sexual acts in private between consenting adults. At one point, he described his personal journey from voting against gay marriage to then meeting and getting to know people from the gay community, and becoming friends with the Rt Hon Crispin Blunt, who came out in 2010. As an Army veteran Crispin spoke very emotionally as part of this debate: 'I found a way of accommodating myself, the laws at the time and the rules of society of the time. I then overtly followed a successful journey through my life and career. This report – an outstanding piece of work – is causing me to re-evaluate the damage done to me, the price paid by those closest to me of making that accommodation.'

I wept through that whole debate.

As the LGBT veterans community nears the end of a thirty-five-year campaign for justice, I find myself someone who I'm beginning to be proud of. I'm resilient, determined, maybe a little stubborn, but my strength is built from my wife, family, friends, work colleagues, and the wonderful company for which I work. With all their support, I'll do all I can to help hold the government accountable for implementing the report's recommendations.

The day after the prime minister's apology, one of my fellow veterans hit the nail on the head when they said, 'To quote Churchill, "Now this is not the end. It is not even the beginning of the end. But it is, perhaps, the end of the beginning."'

Chapter 20

Per Ardua Ad Astra

—————————— Roger Garford ——————————

My RAF career began with an initial posting to RAF Leeming, where pilots learning their trade underwent advanced pilot training in the Jet Provost. It was 1963 and I had just completed my training as a junior technician, which offered the chance to be a substantive corporal in a little over two years. My career had begun!

In my first real job in the RAF, I worked in the armament bays servicing ejector seats. The aircrew hoped they'd never have to use them, but if they did, it was my job to help make sure the seats were life savers. Although the rookie in the unit, I quickly made good friends with the safety equipment guys, and all of us were part of the armament warrant officer's team. Each day it was my task to get him a bottle of curdled sour milk for his early morning drink, which eventually would bring forth an early morning 'belch'. The warrant officer was as round as the bottle he drank from and played as a back in the hockey team, where he regularly used his rotund stomach to knock or bounce the opposition to the ground. I played hockey for the station and invariably against Army teams across Yorkshire and other parts of the north. Their pitches were often way out in the bundoo, with no showers, or on the rare occasions there were, they were cold for building fitness.

In my work breaktimes, the guys played five-card brag and when I joined them, I tacitly accepted a rollercoaster journey of cheating and wars of alienation. I was a young man and there was a lot to learn. I never played cards again after my RAF days!

The RAF was somewhere I felt able to thrive. Occasional flights in the Jet Provost observing brake maintenance checks had kindled a yearning in me to get off the ground and so I applied to be aircrew, as a non-commissioned officer, but much to my disappointment, I wasn't selected. My role at Leeming had become a little humdrum and I felt deflated, little did I know that life was about to be shaken up.

Just a few days later, on a halftime break in a hockey match, I was called to the sideline and directed to report to the general office after tea. This I dutifully did, from where I was sent to the photographic centre for a passport photograph for an urgent deployment. I was told to catch the 08.30 train the following morning with a few others to RAF Innsworth, before being detached to Borneo. I had just one question: where the hell was that? I soon found out. After arriving at RAF Innsworth, we met up with other 96 Armourers, destined for the same place. In the dash to deploy, I'd left my fairly knackered but much loved 1946 Morris Eight e-type at Leeming. During my absence, it was picked up and transported on the back of a wagon to my home.

Life was about to be far from humdrum, and I felt excitement as well as a little trepidation for what the future held for us. At Innsworth we were kitted out with khaki uniforms, deep sea bag, and cooking utensils before being flown out to Singapore in a Britannia passenger jet via Cyprus and El Adam (where I spent the whole time in the loos), then across the Indian Ocean to RAF Changi in Singapore. Here I had permission to go to married quarters, where I called on my auntie, who asked if my mum knew where I was. She advised me to put my civvy clothes in a sealed bag as they would go mouldy in a short while.

Within twenty-four hours we were sent to various parts of Borneo. I ended up on a 'rattling' Hastings, whose part of the propellor dropped off on the tarmac, meaning we were transferred to the next one on standby. We flew to RAF Labuan, a small island off the Borneo coast. It was about 8 x 12 miles in size with a mixture of around 1,000 troops, mostly Army and RAF. Some of the 96 Armourers also followed, like Johnny Irish, Chas Marshall and Andy Hanks, and we were to act as a supply base for lads in the jungle. We also had two Javelin surface-to-air missile systems on quick release standby at all times. We built a bomb dump and when the monsoon rains came, they buried the first layer of bombs, which then had to be dug out and the traverses shorn up with sandbags.

Most of the guys were then sent to RAF Seleta, leaving just the three of us to maintain the dump. We also serviced the ack-ack guns, which were on either side of the runway and at either end. We guarded the quick reaction aircraft with a No 4 rifle and ten rounds of live ammunition and the regular challenge of 'Halt or I fire', was barked three times to those unknown. It was scary at night and in the early hours of the morning it pissed with rain. One November morning, the engineering officer came down to congratulate me on my promotion to corporal and told me that Hitler had started out as a corporal and look where it got him. 'Thanks, boss', I laughed!

My two mates were doing their National Service and were keen to get back home. We were given the opportunity to stay but decided to come back with them to Blighty and were home for Christmas.

I returned to RAF Leeming until I was posted to RAF Gatow, Berlin in May 1965. This was 0.7 of a man posting and each time I had leave, a guy come over from West Germany RAF HQ to take over.

In Berlin I ran the armoury and helped the servicing crews with the Troopers (BAC 111) that came in and out with personnel. I was skilled with personal firearms and trained the Special Investigations Branch RAF Police on the range for pistol accuracy for the Queen's visit. While I was there, I also had the honour to fly in the back seat of a Chipmunk with Group Captain Oxspring, a Battle of Britain pilot who wanted a last look at Berlin, but this time with the lights on.

At Easter 1966, when my parents visited, a Russian aircraft (Firebar Yak 28) crashed into Lake Harvel, in the British sector of Berlin. I was just about to leave my room on the base in civvies when there was a knock on the door. It was the engineering officer Flight Lieutenant Pharoh, who said, 'You can take those off and come with me! We have this crashed aircraft and need to make the ejection seats safe." I told him I'd had no training on Russian ejector seats but would do best I could.

We were taken down to the lakeside, where I could see the aircraft's tail sticking out of the water and blue lights flashing. We couldn't get access that night, so we returned back to the base and specialists of each trade were flown in from the UK. On the Sunday, the stricken aircraft was to be hoisted onto an Army pontoon which had been placed near the aircraft with lifting equipment. The Russian contingent were on the bankside floodlighting the scene with searchlights. As darkness descended, the aircraft was lifted out with the dead pilot and co-pilot in tandem, in the cockpit. One seat had partially detonated and risen up the rail a little, but the other hadn't gone off at all. The officer in charge said, 'Well, off you go and get them out.'

'What, me?'

'Yes.'

Firstly, using nails and tools from the pontoon, I was able to make both seats as safe as possible and take the cartridges out. Both seats were based on American-style ejector seats with an arm-handle ejection. The pilots had no 'Bone Domes', but leather headpieces. It took about five hours to cut the bodies out. We were in thick rubber suits and, with the Russian searchlight on us, were steaming from the sweat. It was a ghoulish scene. Two of the ground crew offered their help to get the pilot and navigator out, which was made more difficult because the bodies had been in the water and had become swollen in size. The navigator was cut out reasonably easily, but the pilot was more of a problem because he was heavier. It took us nearly three hours because his head had gone into the consul in the cockpit. The whole operation took about five hours to complete.

Our job done for now, we went with the bodies, draped with the Russian flag, to the riverbank where they were handed over to the Russians with a lone piper playing. The aircraft was new and was taken to an RAF airfield before being eventually handed back to the Russians a month later, after a very detailed inspection. Much was learnt during that month that further assisted in enhancing our defence systems. I received a Commander In Chief's Commendation for my work.

I played hockey for the station and with two others joined the Spandau German Indoor Hockey club. The team went on to win the RAF Germany hockey cup, the same year as England won the football World Cup. We celebrated in the city until the early hours of the morning. Berlin was a city of intrigue and full of nightlife to be enjoyed. Daytime was sometimes spent digging up buried Nazi equipment, even bodies, and sometimes involved getting explosive technicians in to sort things out.

November 1967 saw me posted to RAF Coningsby, this time working with Phantom Aircraft. The TSR2 system had been cancelled by the Labour government and we were working with the Americans to build the Phantom. I was placed on the Phantom training course, but there would be no aircraft until early 1968. In October 1968 I was promoted to sergeant and sent to the Phantom evaluation team at the Naval Air Test Center, Patuxent River, near Chesapeake Bay in Maryland.

We were the poor cousins, having to borrow tools and equipment. My role was to make independent checks on the ejection seats teams and write evaluation reports. While there, I grabbed the chance to hitchhike around a little and at one time visited a mining family in Stotsbury in the Appalachians. There, I tried the local hooch, moonshine. I was also lucky to fly in the backseat in the Phantom a few times, once at TWICE the speed of sound! I still have the certificate I received on my return to the UK. During this time, I met and made friends with a Norwegian Air Force team who were evaluating the Orion, which they were buying. They also had a large liquor allowance and many early mornings were spent in their company. I travelled in the backseat low over the country to deliver the aircraft back to the factory in St Louis.

April 1969 saw me back at Coningsby helping prepare for the first two deliveries of F4Ks for the Royal Navy. These aircraft stayed with us for around a month until the RAF F4Ms arrived. They both had arrester gear, so the stations were equipped to take the aircraft.

During 1970 we detached to RAF Akrotiri for a month for armament practice camp and to RAF Tengah for two months for missile practice camp. On the way out to Tengah, we beat the nonstop flight time to Singapore, doing it in twenty-four hours, helped along by a bit of tanker support. These were all exciting times for me: I was doing something valuable to the nation, I was doing well, loving life and had found my place in the RAF as a respected and valued sergeant.

In the summer we detached to Norway with an American ex-Vietnam squadron. There was some terrific rivalry but they were allies and I fondly remember flying in bacon and eggs because the fresh fish breakfasts weren't appreciated much. We also flew in crates of beer, which were expensive in Norway. At Laarbruch we helped to run the private flying club on the base, but I left after seeing my flying instructor, who was ace of the base in the Canberra aircraft, killed in front of us trying to do a wheel-over in a Dornier aircraft belonging to the club. It was a stark reminder of the importance of our work to keep the aviators safe and I mourned the loss of this immensely talented man.

In 1974 I was promoted to chief technician and my career was going incredibly well. In November 1975 my squadron moved to be based at Leuchars. I travelled ahead with my sergeant to set up and run the flight line. We had a Quick Reaction Aircraft team to look after, at times with eight aircraft and tanker support in the air, monitoring the Russian spring exercise. That summer we kidnapped 43 Squadron's 'Fighting Cocks', which were suitably accommodated and well fed, in our hutch housed on the side of the Tay. There was much controversy and a handover ceremony quickly convened.

While at Leuchars I got married. It was September 1977 and I lived with my wife in a crofter's cottage on the side of the Tay near Dundee. Like so many service families, we moved around, but we had two sons who were born at RAF Wegsberg in September 1978 and June 1980.

My career was still going incredibly well and early in 1983 I applied for a commission, on the advice of my wing commander. I attended the interviews and completed the very detailed assessments. My wing commander felt that all seemed favourable and that I just had to wait for confirmation. In May 1983 I was detached to RAF Coningsby to train RA teams for South Atlantic deployments. It was here my life changed dramatically.

It was 28 March 1983, an otherwise ordinary day, until I was summoned to the guard room. I duly went and was subsequently interrogated for homosexuality. By then I'd seen a great deal of life and readily recognised the good cop/bad cop routine. It lasted a whole day, by which time I was exhausted, frightened and ready to admit to anything. I was able to resist some of the coercion, but in the end admitted to some of them. Three more interviews were carried out throughout the year, after which they told me to forget about my commission.

In the fullness of time, when challenged by my solicitors, they couldn't find one of these interviews. Copies of what was purported to be on these tapes were sent to my solicitor, but they were unreadable so they typed onto forms what should've been there. I challenged it all the way up to the Chief of the Defence Staff, with a little support from my MP, but there was no chance of success in those days.

My immediate commanders supported me, but nevertheless I received notice of my administrative discharge on 23 December 1983, effective February 1984. This meant it was 170 days too early to qualify for my pension and so I lost a career which I loved and a job in which I excelled. I would never again experience the comradeship of the RAF and the names of those who interviewed me are scars in my memory.

I lost so much. My wife and family were gone, my job, employment, income and home were gone. It was a bleak and lonely time for me; there was no support.

In time my life began to recover and in the early 1990s, I had the good fortune to meet with Elaine Chambers, a dismissed nursing officer from Queen Alexandra's Royal Army Nursing Corps, and Robert Ely a warrant officer band master, who'd formed the support group Rank Outsiders. At first there were five of us, all military men and women removed by the 'Gay Ban', but not long later there were 130 of us! I became regional coordinator, with Alan (who later became my partner) as my deputy.

Rank Outsiders became a national movement and would be the catalyst of the challenge that would ultimately lead to the Gay Ban being lifted. Some of our members gave horrific accounts of physical and sexual abuse at the hands of superiors. One poor woman, I remember vividly, was raped by her sergeant to prove she wasn't a lesbian (and had to abort a baby).

Every court in the UK was petitioned, often with the support of MPs who were sympathetic to our cause, but to no avail. With the backing of Stonewall, in October 1998 we began the journey to the European Court, which ruled in September 1999. The Court criticised the MOD's Homosexual Policy Assessment Team reports, which had been used by the MOD to justify keeping this dreadful policy. These were trumped up documents, which guided members of our Armed Forces to offer the opinions the MOD used in justification. The case was won, and the ban was lifted on 12 January 2000. I was present in the House of Commons to hear Geoff Hoon, Secretary of State for Defence, read the statement which lifted the ban. It would take a further ten years of fighting to win meagre recompense, which in no way was compensation for our loss.

In 1990 I became a volunteer in the HIV and AIDS field at a time of crisis in the LGBT+ communities and my work has now spanned three decades. It was around that time when I met my partner Alan, who has supported me throughout the fight to get the ban lifted.

If there's to be any good from all this, it must be that today, LGBT+ personnel serve in our Armed Forces everywhere. They do a brilliant job, as we did before them, but now they're welcomed. In later life, it brings me comfort that this was not all for nought.

My final thought is that with all my heart, I support Fighting With Pride, which has helped bring justice and honour to those who are left, and is helping ensure that we don't forget those we've lost on this long and arduous journey.

Chapter 21

A Trooper's Tale: In Plain Sight
—————— Martin Bell ——————

The day had finally arrived, the day I'd dreamed of since I was 9 during my first riding lesson at the Dortmund Garrison Saddle Club on 5 May 1978. Little did I know how from that lesson, on a black Dartmoor pony with four white socks called Kinky Boots, everything would change, leading me right to this moment, my here and now.

I completed my basic and trade training at Woolwich Garrison, during which I ran up 'Fu*k Off Hill' too many times; was the fastest over the assault course more than once; the first to pass my driving test; and saw my first stripper. I'd cracked it. I felt like a soldier, ready for the next twenty years. I strode through the black iron gates of the King's Troop Royal Horse Artillery, a small high-walled unassuming barracks on Ordnance Hill situated in the middle of the very posh St. John's Wood. My life, as I'd planned it, had finally arrived.

I was 19, single and ready for my commitment to the troop, the army and Her Majesty the Queen. I settled into life well and felt at ease with my fellow troopers, especially around the horses. I was assigned to F Sub Section, where all the horses were black and were used for state and royal funerals when needed. There were six sub sections starting with the light bays in A Sub, with B, C, D and E sub horses becoming darker bays.

The newest recruits got the dirtiest, smelliest, and most difficult of tasks and chores, which I fully expected. The seven years of experience gained while riding horses and ponies won me a certain level of respect from my colleagues and superiors, who saw me as an established and competent rider.

Arriving at the beginning of the show season I wasn't selected to be part of the musical drive team, but I was given the privilege of being a lance marker at the Royal Putney Show. As a lance marker, I was one of eight who'd march into the middle of the arena during the performance and mark a smaller area for the part of the drive where the gun teams performed without the trio of riders following the guns. It was exhilarating, nerve wracking and scary. You weren't allowed to move position other than the arm's length you held the lance, even though there were times those spinning guns and wheels would come a little too close for comfort.

Eventually, when the show season had finished and many county shows and royal salutes had been fired, autumn arrived and I was given the responsible task of moving up to Melton Mowbray for five months, along with five other soldiers, one for each sub section. We took charge of the newest intake of Irish Draught horses, called the Remounts, freshly shipped from Ireland. The morning we travelled up was the very morning after the great storm for which the weather presenter Michael Fish had given the 'all clear', which meant the journey up in the horse box took three hours longer than it should have. Upon arrival, we settled into our accommodation and familiarised ourselves with our new surroundings.

Within a few days I took possession of two 4-year-old black mares and proceeded to tame, back and break them in, as did my five colleagues with their charges. Bones were broken, bruises were blue, and bumps were usually hoof-shaped, but both troopers and horses survived the five months of training to make the journey back to St. John's Wood and welcome the spring. The relaxed and informal time I spent at Melton Mowbray was the longest I'd been away from the troop, and it was there I realised just what an issue my sexuality was going to be and the impact it'd have on my time in the army. The angst started to appear in the pit of my stomach and the ban on gay men and women in the armed forces became very real.

I tried to stem the fear and was thankfully kept busy with introducing my mares to their new way of life. This was my first real taste of how competitive it was to get yourself noticed and to stand out from the crowd, with the aim of becoming part of the musical drive. There had already been mutterings regarding me being given the Remounts' job so early on in my time at the troop, and any gossip of any kind would've been welcomed by some, so I had to keep my wits about me.

Preparations for the new show season were intense and took place regardless of the weather. Twice a week we'd process across West London to a large field right next to HMP Wormwood Scrubs. This is where the teams would practise the routine, giving new team members and horses a flavour of what was to come. It was at one of these practices when a gun and a limber went over and the two-wheel horses attached to them slipped on the wet ground. Luckily, no one was injured other than some scrapes and bruises. However, the rider of the wheel horses was a bit shaken and as a new father, took the decision with his wife to step down from the gun team.

I was called to speak to my sergeant and A Sub's sergeant but wasn't prepared for what they were about to discuss with me. In the week since the accident there'd been discussions among the senior staff regarding my suitability to take the place in the team as wheel driver. This was a huge honour and I couldn't have been prouder to accept. It would mean moving from F Sub to A Sub and working and living with a whole new team of lads – and immediately! This was another achievement that would be met with more mutterings of how I'd leap frogged over others who'd been in the troop longer, but I put that to one side and prepared for my first time in the saddle as a wheel driver.

We had the horses harnessed up on parade ready to set off for the Scrubs. I was legged up into my new wheel driver position, having had a quick tutorial from my predecessor, before the troop captain made his inspection, mounted his 17 hand dark bay charger and signalled us off on our way. It was such a proud moment to be riding out of the barracks into the streets of London, sitting upright with my whip in my right hand and chest puffed out to the max. Suddenly, there was a huge 'DOINK' and my team came to a sudden halt. I'd been peacocking so much I'd forgotten to take into account the extra foot of space needed for the wheels of the gun and limber with the huge brass nuts that held them on tight. Before I'd even broken into a trot, I'd nearly broken the gun and the gate. I could see the look on my sergeant's face, clearly thinking he'd made a huge mistake. From that moment on, however, I was always aware of where my gun and limber were.

It was about this time in my life I started to explore my sexuality. I was young, inquisitive and horny, just like my fellow troopers. Unlike them, who were free to go about their conquests and dalliances openly, I had to creep around and lie about my endeavours for fear of being found out. I was constantly covering up where I'd been and who with. I skulked around and lied to cover my tracks in fear of getting caught, never striking up a relationship for fear of being black mailed or outed. Going out to gay bars around London was like a full-blown military undercover operation, and having to act in such a secretive manner was not a happy time for me.

The show season was upon us and with rehearsals complete, we were ready to hit the road covering county shows across the country. The late 1980s were great for the troop and a good number of sponsorship deals meant we were booked for quite a few shows, from the Royal Windsor Horse Show to the Glasgow Show in the North, as well as regular fixtures such as Royal Windsor and the Royal Tournament.

The Royal Tournament was by far the hardest work of all: two and a half weeks of two shows a day. The best thing about it was the fact we shared the show and the site with other regiments, as well as the RAF and Royal Navy. Each took it in turn to host the event annually in Earl's Court, West London, an area well known for having many gay bars, clubs and restaurants, one of which was a gay leather bar on the Old Brompton Road called The Coleherne. When we'd finished our final performance, we'd ride as a regiment back to St. John's Wood and put the horses to their own beds for the first time in nearly three weeks.

Early on in our journey back to barracks, we'd file past The Coleherne and, as with every other bar and restaurant along our route home, the clientele would come out to clap and cheer. The biggest cheers and whistles definitely came from those guys, and I'd beam with pride and delight while trying not to look at the men too much in case someone noticed.

It just so happened that shortly after this, I nervously took my first step inside a gay establishment. I remember being terrified someone would see me, so I didn't make eye contact with anyone. I had one pint and left, but the deed had been done. To me, that was it. I was now a gay man in the army, the place I'd longed to be in for half of my life, but also the place that considered it illegal and wrong for me to be gay, the place that now filled me with fear.

This was a time when the government of the day scorned homosexuality, and when the national press hunted gay celebrities and others in the public eye in an attempt to 'out' them on their front pages. Imagine the sensation of a member of the King's Troop being outed as gay! The King's Troop was, after all, the Queen and Queen Mother's favourite regiment, having been named by the late King upon his first visit to the barracks in 1947. It was at this visit where the King crossed out the word 'Riding' in the visitors' book and wrote 'King' thereby renaming it from the 'Riding Troop' to the 'King's Troop' we know and love today.

I was now leading two lives and had to be constantly cautious and alert so as not to slip up about where I'd been and with whom. In my day-to-day life I was a member of Her Majesty's Armed Forces, but by night, was exploring all that gay London had to offer. While the others shared the details of their nights out in the city, I never could and began to feel ever more isolated and alone.

Despite these conflicting feelings, the first show season had passed and the troop was now well and truly my home. Even with the challenges of my secret, life was great. I got along with my colleagues, I was part of the event team and head of the second show jumping team, with the regimental sergeant major and a few of my bombardiers under my command, for the show jumping at least. Christmas came and I spent it with my parents in Surrey, joined by two army mates who couldn't get up north for the festivities.

We were now gearing up for my second year as wheel driver for A Sub. Our first show was the Royal Windsor Horse Show, one of our favourites. Not only was it staged in the Queen's back garden, it was framed by the incredible backdrop of Windsor Castle and had the longest gallop out of any arena we performed in. This meant that when we'd finished the drive and turned the final corner with the gun team horses, the limber and the gun were in a straight line. As we'd rehearsed so many times before, at the precise moment, the lead, centre and wheel riders would put whips across our lead horses' shoulders, lean forward and fly like the wind. The hairs across my neck and shoulders would stand on end as we galloped at full pelt with the crowd screaming and cheering with delight.

Unfortunately, on our final performance, and with A Sub being the last gun team out of the arena, tragedy struck. Part of the harness holding the main breast plate across the lead rider's horse snapped and dropped, falling to below the horses' knees and tripping him up. Thomas, one of the lead horses, fell over at full gallop, taking his rider with him, followed by the centre horse and rider, Mouse, and his lead horse, then me and my two horses. Travelling at about 25mph the huge oak pole between me and my lead horse that helped steer the gun and limber stuck fast into the area floor, causing the limber and gun to almost pole vault over on top of us.

Suddenly, the cheering and clapping had turned to screams of horror and disbelief. I was now at the bottom of the pile with horse, harness and gun all around me. Three things stood out to me at this point. Firstly, I thought, that's it, I'm a gonner. Then, I saw my lead horse was looking at me straight in the eye and although I could see she was also panicking and terrified, she was watching out for me and making sure that when she was thrashing around, her feet and legs were well away from me. Finally, I noticed a huge hand reaching into the middle of the carnage, grabbing my uniform by the back of my neck and hauling me out into the freedom of the arena, all to a tumultuously deafening cheer from the crowd.

I quickly jumped into action to pull apart the harness at every point to release my two horses, and the others, and so prevent them from any further harm. My ride horse sustained a horrible gash to both knees and my lead horse had a deep slash to her shoulder. Sadly, Thomas didn't fare as well, and having managed to walk out of the arena, he had to be euthanised just outside, shrouded by a tent. My horses and gun team crew were transported back to Combermere Barracks via horse box, where we were stabled on the parade ground. By the time we'd reached the stables and were tending to our horses, a message of condolence and support had arrived from Her Majesty The Queen, who'd fortunately not witnessed the crash but was truly shocked and saddened by the event. This was my lowest point in the troop and having returned home to St. John's Wood, we mourned the loss of a great and spirited lead horse in Thomas. Meanwhile, I'd managed to walk away from it all with only a slight cut on my knee. I was very lucky.

The rest of the show season went ahead without any problems, other than I managed to flip the gun over at the Royal Tournament. No one was hurt or injured, but my pride most certainly was. It was around this time that I was collected by two Regimental Police and quick-marched to the guard room and put in a cell for questioning. One of the RPs was a mate who'd been to Surrey to celebrate Christmas with my parents. Also quick-marched in for questioning and put into a neighbouring cell was Gasgoine, a lad I'd get together with from time to time. As we chatted quietly through the walls, I could hear he was in a bit of a state.

'Say nothing, admit nothing', I told Gasgoine, and with that I could hear the telltale footprints of the regimental sergeant major approaching the guardroom – you could always hear him before you saw him.

This time his arrival into the building was met by a shudder. I could hear the two accusers state their case to him and a huge bellow from him: 'GAY?! Show me!' A few clattering steps later, my cell door flew open and there he stood, all 6'4" of him, my show jump protégé.

'These two said that you're gay, Bell. Is that true?'

'No, Sir', I replied.

'Good. Fuck Off.'

I didn't need telling twice and marched out quicker than when I marched in.

As I left, I could hear the same being asked of Gasgoine, who made the same reply. He, too, came speeding out of the building, which was now filled to busting with the sergeant major's huge voice tearing into the two 'not-so-full-of-themselves-now' policemen, having unearthed no illegal sex scandals in the barracks. Not only did he rip them to shreds, they were also were given extra duties for their actions. However, the ordeal had done its damage to both myself and Gasgoine and we kept our distance after that, which was a shame as he was a nice guy and we'd a great time together.

The event shook me to the core, but after the shock subsided, I began to wonder how they'd found out about us. Had I not been careful enough or had I slipped up some time? Something must've happened for them to accuse me of being gay, and my head was in turmoil about what'd given it away. The rumour mill was rife and the gossip was plenty. Some gossiped amongst themselves, while others were more vocal about it. When they had an audience, they'd shout things like, 'Oi, Dinger! You and Gascgoine been at it again then?' and 'Who's the post box and who's the postie?'

Eventually it died down, but it never went away completely so we were still subjected to those slurs on a regular basis.

My final season in the troop had arrived and I was moved to D Sub for the next show season as wheel driver. After that year's performance, the plan was not to ride straight back to barracks, but instead ride back in the morning after the end of show party. This was an annual event and the area was turned in to a massive bar, food court and disco. In the Gods, the navy's gun teams each had their own bars, frequented and entertained by their very own drag queen, who'd entertain the navy's best throughout the tournament.

Once the horses were fed and put to bed, me and the guys went to our accommodation and showered, shaved and dressed to impress. We hit the arena, getting stuck into the food and drinks. Performing two shows a day for two and a half weeks, and all with very little sleep, had taken its toll. We had also hadn't had any alcohol during the tournament, so happily took advantage of the free food and drink. At some point towards the end of the night, I left the party and entered the streets of Earl's Court; infamous gay village and playground.

My next recollection was waking up and not being sure where I was. I remember looking out and thinking, thankfully, it was still dark! It was then I heard a voice say, 'Morning, sleepy head. Boy, can you snore! Would you like a coffee?'

'Ah, yeah, I snore a lot apparently and coffee would be great, thanks', I replied, before asking, 'What time is it?

6.30 came the response.

'Shit, I need to be back in work in half an hour', I exclaimed and asked, 'where are we?'

'Near Clapham Junction and its 6.30 at night', he replied.

Those words drained the blood from my body and the very fear that I'd dreaded hit me stark and cold. I should've been back by 7am that morning to lead the regiment back to St. John's Wood. This would've been my first time as lead rider and the lead sub section, not to mention the fact I was being considered for promotion.

It also dawned on me I was AWOL! I jumped out of bed and into this poor guy's kitchen like a man possessed. I rifled through his cupboards, looking for something I could use to inflict wounds to my head. Grabbing a saucepan, I bashed myself several times on the side of my temple, expecting some huge gash to appear and look 'wound-like'. When that didn't work, I took off to the bathroom, found his disposable razor blades and tried to slice myself open with them, but they were cut-safe ones. I tore one apart and removed the blade, determined this would do the trick.

Slash, slash and bingo! I now had blood all over my face from my 'injury'. I threw on my clothes, apologised to the now-traumatised guy and ran out the door, down the stairs, through the entrance door and onto the streets of South London. It was dark and a bit nippy, and all I was wearing was a pair of jeans and my favourite white cotton shirt, now covered in blood on my left side.

I looked for a street sign, I was on Bluebird's Hill near to Clapham Junction Station. I looked up the hill and, in the distance, I could see two police officers heading my way. I sat down in a nearby shop door, with my bloody head down, waiting for their arrival. After what felt like an eternity, they were finally standing in front of me. 'Hello, mate,' said one of them. 'Are you ok?'

'Looks like you've been hurt', he continued, before asking who I was.

I looked up and replied, 'I don't know.'

'Ok, have you got any ID or a wallet or something?'

I reached into my back jeans pocket and held out my wallet, knowing my army ID was in there.

After finding it, they said, 'You're in the army. Let's get you some help.'

They called for an ambulance and when it arrived, the paramedics did their usual checks and asked their usual questions, to which I had no answer. I was taken to St. George's and placed in a room on my own. After a short while, a consultant came bounding in and announced, 'I hear you're saying you don't know who you are? I don't believe you!'

Without flinching, wincing or showing any emotion whatsoever, I replied that I didn't care if he didn't believe me. I was adamant that I didn't know who I was and that I didn't have any idea how I'd come to be injured.

'Ah, that's ok then', he replied. 'I believe you, but just had to check.'

The consultant gave his instructions to the nurses to treat my wound and to find me a bed on a ward. The police told me they'd contacted the troop to make them aware of the situation, and that someone would come to see me in the morning. Although I'd slept for over twelve hours in Clapham, I fell asleep straight away, my mind awash with thoughts about what the morning would bring.

The next morning, having slept well and waking up in a hospital ward, the enormity of what'd taken place started to dawn on me. I knew questions were going to be asked and that I had to be prepared for anything. As I was midway through eating my breakfast, there was a kerfuffle at the end of the ward and three people barrelled into the room. Leading the trio was my mum, followed by my dad and my fiancée.

'I hope you remember who I am or I'm going to kill myself!' was my mother's opening gambit.

'Yes, I remember you, Mum', I replied. I hadn't taken into account what the ramifications of my actions the night before would be and how far reaching they'd go.

I couldn't tell my mum and dad that I didn't recognise them, but unfortunately, I did tell my fiancée that I didn't recognise her. I did say she looked familiar, however, and so the amnesia tale had definitely begun.

To me, she was not a fiancée in the truest sense of the word and I'm sure not what you'd have expected to be reading about now, but I'd done as so many other gay service men and women felt they had to do and entered into a relationship as a cover to deflect suspicion. Some went on to marry their cover person and lead unhappy lives. I chose to end my relationship with Beverly the day after Valentines Day. Although she was devastated at the time, and I was truly guilt ridden, it was the right thing to do. I cared too much for her.

I was discharged from hospital and left in the care of my parents with two weeks' sick leave at home to rest, recuperate and work on finding my memory. Despite the enormity of what'd happened, I used that time to wrack my brains trying to find a way to be my true authentic self and still stay in the troop, all with the threat of being found out constantly hanging over my head.

I was exhausted living this double and dangerous life, and the decision to leave the army, the troop and my childhood dream was the only outcome I could see. I realised I couldn't stay in a place where I wasn't allowed to be my true self and I wasn't going to compromise or lie any further, so I made the hardest decision of my life: I'd leave the King's Troop the following summer.

My decision was not well met at all. Following the news of my imminent departure, all manner of tactics were used to try to get me to stay. There was the promise of a promotion, and my parents were even invited as VIP guests to the firing of a royal salute in Hyde Park, all with the hope of getting me to change my mind.

Once the deed had been done and my resignation tendered, I was immediately taken out of the gun team and the D Sub lines and was given the job of groom to the centre section's troop commander. This was a job I loved as I was looking after three large thoroughbred horses in training for point-to-point and one-day eventing. I was in my element and struck up a great working relationship with my troop captain. After being in the limelight and front and centre all the time, I was now happy to be tucked away and pretty much left to my own devices.

My release date crept ever closer, and I was more than ready to go. In my head and heart, I'd already left. I'd also been seeing a handsome South African chap and was spending most of my evenings and free time with him. He suggested I move in with him rather than go to Surrey to my parents, and the move would prove to be a good decision once I'd left.

On the day before I was due to be released, I got a call from my troop captain, Simon, asking me to meet him in the regimental offices as soon as possible. I said I'd be right up as soon as I'd dealt with the horses, after which I dutifully made my way to his office.

'Sit down', he said, whilst waiving a piece of paper at me. 'Do you know what this is?' he asked.

'Haven't a clue', I replied.

'This is your release form and I'm not going to sign it. I'm going to rip it up unless you tell me why you're really leaving the troop', he demanded.

'Well,' I replied, 'that'll be a waste of paper because I'll be off through those front gates as soon as I can tomorrow morning, ready to start my new life.'

He demanded again that I tell him the real reason.

I'd grown very fond of Simon during the time we'd shared training and exercising the horses. I respected him and thought he deserved to know the real reasons for me leaving.

'I can't discuss it here', I said, looking around at all the other offices with only thin glass walls between them. If I could easily hear the conversations others were having, they'd definitely be able to hear mine.

'Ok, I'm going for a run at lunchtime', Simon declared. I'll be back around 13.15. Come to my room in the officers' mess and we'll discuss it then.'

I agreed and left. It was only a two-hour wait so I kept myself busy around the yard.

At 13.20, I knocked on Simon's room door and entered, once he'd given me permission to do so. As I walked in, Simon was stepping out of the shower following his run, butt naked! Ah bollocks! I thought. I'm just about to tell this straight man, towelling off his nuts, that I was gay. Could the universe honestly take the piss out of me any further?

'So, c'mon then, tell me', said Simon. What's so terrible you couldn't talk about it in my office and is making you feel you have to go? It's not too late, you know.'

I started to bottle it. 'Can't we just let me go tomorrow and that will be that?'

'No!' he said. 'I need to know what the real reason is. I'm sure it's something that can be worked through.'

'It really can't', I said and asked again, 'do you really need to know?' I do', he declared.

'Ok, I'm gay', I announced.

'No, you're not!' he blurted out.

'Yes, I am', I said, 'and I can't live the double life I have been doing so for the last three years with the possibility of being found out always hanging over me.' I also confessed to Simon that I was being emotionally blackmailed by a guy I'd been seeing, who was threatening to expose me to the troop commander and the only way to take away his power was to leave. I told Simon about being taken to the guardroom and questioned about my sexuality, and also how my blackmailer would call the barracks asking for me saying they were Lily Savage and Regina Fong, two famous drag queens at the time.

Simon insisted we could still make it work, reassuring me he wouldn't tell anyone.

I thanked him for his offer but explained I just couldn't do it any longer and he sadly agreed to let me go.

The next day was the end of the King's Troop chapter of my life. I didn't even shed a tear as I walked through the big, heavy iron gates; the same gates I'd smashed into on my first trip through them as A Sub's wheel driver, the gates I'd hauled open and closed when I was on duty protecting the barracks, the gates that'd been so familiar to me at the start of my dream. A dream that was now over.

I moved in with my South African guy and his two flat mates: a lawyer and a journalist. I was welcomed into the household and was made to feel at home. About a week after I'd left, I received a call from the troop adjutant to say he'd sent me a letter informing me that after my departure, it'd become common knowledge that I was gay. He said that because I was on the reservist list for three years, I was technically still in the army and so he was taking steps for me to be called back up in order for me to be properly court martialled for my crime.

I was completely shell shocked and terrified. When my new house mates heard of what'd happened, they were incensed, and the journalist asked for the officer's name. I gave it and he immediately called and demanded to speak to him, declaring that should they continue with this ridiculous course of action, he'd have it posted all over the front page of the *Telegraph* the next day. Little did I know he was a senior journalist with the paper at the time. The action never happened.

I come from an environment where whatever life throws at you, you suck it up and get on with it. That's what I did for thirty years until I heard on the radio that the government were going to commission an independent report into the ban and what effect it'd had on those involved.

That was the start of my unravelling, having to recant my time in the troop and relive the good and bad times, then realising the injustice and the pain it'd caused for the way that we, as gay men and women, were penalised, marginalised and chastised just for being who we were. It was not right, and it was allowed to continue for far too long. I'm still feeling the effects of what happened to me thirty-three years later but am hoping that writing this will be part of my healing.

I've always been extremely proud of my time and achievements in the troop and still am today. I only wish the way it ended had been different and not so traumatic.

I didn't see the troop again until the late Queen's Platinum Jubilee, where, through Fighting With Pride, I was able to get two front-row tickets in the grandstands outside Buckingham Palace. I was so proud to show my husband what I used to do, but it was a bittersweet moment for me. The whole event was overshadowed by the stark reality that I was literally watching the dream that'd been unfairly taken away from me, taking placing right in front of my eyes.

The years following my departure from the troop have certainly been eventful. I established a livery and training yard down in Surrey, after which I stumbled into hospitality working for a golfing group. My career in catering thrived and I was heavily involved in arrangements for the decommissioning of the Royal Yacht *Brittania*.

In 2008 I married my husband and we moved to Dorset, where I opened two start-up restaurants for a world-renowned celebrity chef. With the beach right on my doorstep and the New Forest no more than 10 miles away, we love the time we share together with our Thai Bangkaew rescue dog, Jackson.

I do wonder what I might have achieved had things been different, but I'll never know. I miss having the connections with the horses and am sad that horses are no longer a part of my life. I take comfort in the fact I was privileged to serve the Royal Family and I will always treasure my time being a soldier in the King's Troop Royal Horse Artillery.

Chapter 22

Under the Radar

—————————— Rowena Purdy ——————————

I was 7 years old when I first wore a dress and petticoats. However, when my father saw me so clad, his reaction scarred me for most of my life. 'Boys don't wear dresses', he shouted at me. I enjoyed the sensation of the silk and often fantasised about being a girl and wearing such pretty clothes. But I now need to turn the clock back and look more closely at my past.

When I was 6, my family moved from England to Cyprus, where my father taught Science to Greek and Turkish boys at a school in Nicosia and my sister and I went to the local junior school. After my experience with wearing feminine clothing, I became surreptitiously interested in what my fellow female students and members of staff wore. As this was the early fifties, gender dysphoria was totally unknown, although the newspapers of the time had reported on various men who'd had a 'sex change'. One of these was a wartime Spitfire pilot and amateur racing driver, who became known as Roberta Cowell after she transitioned. Also top on the list of newspaper reporting was April Ashley, who later became a great supporter of transgender ladies. Such articles fascinated me.

After Cyprus, the family moved to Northern Rhodesia (now Zambia), where father taught in government secondary schools and where my sister and I also studied. At 11, I was the youngest in my form and now amongst girls who were older than me and boys who were older and more mature. I became fascinated by several girls who had pierced ears, another facet of being female.

Towards the end of my pre-certificate year, my father decided to send me to a boys' public school in England. It wasn't an option I supported, especially as it meant I went backwards by eighteen months from the end of my third year to the start of the equivalent second year, even though I was in an English third year. Confused? So was I. But I stopped working as I'd already covered most of what was being taught, although I remember a few rather amusing episodes. I'd never studied Geography, so this was a new subject, and we were told to open our textbooks and told we were to study Africa that term. On the page was a map of NR on which was an error which made me exclaim and thus attract the attention of the master, who wanted to know what was causing such mirth. I explained that whoever had drawn the map had misplaced the source of the Zambezi. I was totally unaware that the author of the textbook was standing in front of me!

At the beginning of the third term, I was admitted to hospital where my second hernia, a rugby injury, was operated on. Before the actual operation, I fantasised about a surgical mistake which would cause me to wake up as female, but of course this couldn't happen, and I woke up still fully male.

My family came to England while I was in hospital and visited me before they went north to stay with my grandmother and before I returned to school with a bed in the school sanatorium. During the school holidays, I spent time at the International Scout Jamboree in Sutton Park, working as part of the background staff, but spent much time with a group of local Girl Guides, who were also part of the support staff. We were all hosting French visitors to the camp, so my French improved, as did my feelings of femininity. After the Jamboree, we crossed the channel for a two-week camping holiday travelling round Europe, but as the weather had deteriorated and our equipment had become saturated, we had to return to England. It was also to be my final term at my English school, as my father had accepted a post in Kenya and so I accompanied the family there and attended a boarding school in Nairobi.

School in Kenya was tough. It strengthened my thoughts of femininity and I'd dream of going to bed at night and waking up having miraculously 'changed sex'. My hernia operations kept me off any participation in games, but I eventually convinced the medical staff I should be allowed to start swimming. This was the only sport at which I was any good, having been selected for training with the NR Olympic team before I left. I proved my worth, being one of the fastest swimmers in my House, helping them to gain the House Championship. However, my single game of rugby ended up with me in hospital with a broken wrist, having scored the only try for my House.

My four years at school in Kenya came to an end and I managed to gain a place at university in Londonderry, Northern Ireland where I managed to hide my female feelings as I'd had girlfriends with whom I attended dances and university social events. During the summer vacations spent in Fowey with my parents and sister, I answered an advert for RAF aircrew and applied for pilot training. I'd experienced many civil flights, flying from various colonies back to England, and many years earlier, while in Cyprus, I'd had the opportunity to be shown round the first Comet airliner and had even spent four days flying from NR to England in a Vickers Viking on my way to school. I'd come across both aircraft types, suitably modified, over the next few years.

I attended a four-day selection session at the Officer and Aircrew Selection Centre at RAF Biggin Hill, consisting of leadership exercises, aptitude tests, interviews, and medical assessments. Although I'd done no preparation for the interviews, at the end of the four days I was offered a place at the Initial Officer Training School (ITS), not, sadly, as a pilot, but as an Air Electronics Officer. I'd done very well at the Morse aptitude tests but had managed to make a mess of the pilot aptitude test. I accepted the offer and left university to fly home to newly independent Kenya to join my family for a short holiday, during which I improved my fitness by erecting a volleyball pitch and teaching the boys at my father's school to play volleyball. I also ran a mile every day before breakfast (at 5,000 feet). I still had strong female feelings that I still didn't understand and which I'd always managed to suppress and would keep hidden throughout both regular and reserve service.

Thirteen years after seeing that Comet, I was standing at the gates of No 1 ITS at RAF South Cerney, clad in standard student wear: a well-worn duffel coat and college scarf and feeling very cold, having just flown in from Kenya. I was also four hours late owing to a derailment outside Manchester. For the next four months we cadet officers, divided into flights, were pushed to our limits with physical training exercises, leadership exercises, and daily academic lectures and tests. As part of our leadership training, we spent a week camping in the Brecon

223

Beacons where we carried out all sorts of leadership exercises in all weathers. Our week was extended by a further two days, which were devoted to survival lectures and exercises, which I thoroughly enjoyed. Before we graduated, we were initiated into weapon skills and I gained a marksman's qualification.

After I was commissioned, I had leave before my flying training started and so went back to Fowey, in Cornwall for two weeks of relaxation and dinghy racing. The next phase, my Flying Training, was spent at the Air Electronics School at RAF Topcliffe in Yorkshire. There, I spent the next two years learning electronics, valve theory, maths, radio communications procedures, and Morse code, before I started the flying phase. The training aircraft was the Vickers Varsity, a modified version of the Viking, but now fitted out as a flying classroom. I spent many flying hours training to be an AEO, operating the radios and monitoring the aircraft electrical systems. I enjoyed all the flying, but not so much the ground school. Two students flew a standard four-hour route, up over the north of Scotland, with one student spending two hours as the radio operator and then sitting in the co-pilot's seat communicating with the ground radios to let them know of our position. During one of the regular assessment sessions, I was criticised for not appearing in the bar in the evening as this was actually part of my officer training. I was uncomfortable with this as I'd be surrounded by a totally male crowd, but I did start to attend and even learnt to play liar dice with the station commander and some of my instructors – I could usually lie well enough to win many times. I suppose I'd become adept at living a lie, so this became easy.

After I was awarded my 'Wings', I was posted to join the maritime world as a Shackleton AEO and made my way to RAF St Mawgan and the Maritime Operational Training Unit (MOTU) for the six-month course via RAF Mountbatten, near Plymouth, to learn about sea survival, which included getting thrown into the Solent to be winched up by a Search and Rescue (SAR) helicopter. Ground school at MOTU included lectures on specialised subjects such as underwater detection, radar, more specialist radio procedures, and 'target' recognition skills to enable me to identify both friendly and non-friendly ships, submarines and aircraft. We trained on old, converted Mk 1 Shackletons, known as T4s. Inside, the aircraft was dark, and after many years of training crews being thrown around while flying at low level around a radar buoy simulating the prosecution of a submarine snorkel, rather malodorous. After the course finished, I stayed on at MOTU to learn more transistor theory, a new branch of electronics, supplanting the valve theory already learnt. While I was at St Mawgan, I met the WRAF officer who would eventually become my wife – who'd suspect me of any gender issues now, especially after a son and a daughter appeared?

My first posting was RAF Ballykelly, near Londonderry, where I arrived very early one Saturday morning, a little unkempt from the Stranraer to Larne ferry, before I was due to report to No CCIII (203) Squadron the following Monday. At breakfast on the Monday, I still had no idea where the squadron buildings were and therefore how to get there. Fortunately, I met a young officer who introduced himself as the navigator on the crew I was about to join. On arrival at the squadron, I joined my new colleagues and crew members. At the time, the squadron was converting from the Mark 2 version to the Mark 3 version of the Shackleton, and my crew had been tasked to fly one to the Norwegian Air Force base at Andøya, inside the Arctic Circle, on a NATO surveillance task. This was our first opportunity to fly as a full crew and become an efficient team. For the next two and a half years, I flew from RAF Ballykelly on surveillance sorties searching for the elusive Soviet submarine and monitoring the Soviet Navy when it was conducting its own exercises – something it didn't like and it made sure we knew we weren't welcome. NATO exercises took up some of our flying tasks, both in the North Atlantic and North Sea from RAF Kinloss or RAF Macrihanish, and overseas from Malta or Cyprus. I was once detached to Malta as an operations officer on a large-scale, three-week NATO exercise briefing NATO maritime crews. We also flew anti-submarine training exercises out of the Royal Navy base near Londonderry, which once gave me the opportunity to fly with a US Navy crew in its P3 Orion maritime patrol aircraft and watch how its crew operated – very differently from us. As I was the squadron's sonar specialist, I watched the USN crewmembers using the aircraft's more modern sonar equipment. Other than the important maritime surveillance sorties, I flew several search and rescue sorties, including one when we were diverted off a normal task to look for a yachtsman whose yacht had sunk on a trans-Atlantic race and who was sitting in his dinghy.

We flew many different sortie lengths, from short five-hour training flights to full length twelve to fourteen-hour surveillance sorties, the Long Range Operational Flying Exercise (LROFE). To help break up the length of these sorties, we had rest periods when we could put our feet up on the bunks in the galley; we also carried in the crew 'navigation bag' a selection of *Playboy* or *Penthouse* adult male magazines, with the semi-clad female centre fold 'Bunny (or Pet) of the Month'. I used to read these, but more to wonder what it'd be like to be one of those girls, although, I suspected other crew members may have had different thoughts.

In January 1969 the entire squadron was transferred from Ballykelly to RAF Luqa in Malta and I moved with it. Our four Shackletons made the journey in two phases of two aircraft and I flew on the first pair, which overnighted in Gibraltar to await the arrival of the second pair the following day. The day after their arrival, all four aircraft flew in a very loose formation from Gibraltar to RAF Hal Far in Malta, where we were met by the Air Commander (Malta) and the Station Commander of RAF Luqa.

Until my family arrived, I lived in the officers' mess and had many evenings free, so when I wasn't flying, I joined the station's Amateur Dramatics Society and became its sound technician, operating the professional equipment at the famous Manoel Theatre in Valetta. I also joined the local motor sports club and started to rally my FIAT 125, an interest which continued throughout my service career and afterwards. I was also appointed as officer in charge of the Combined Services Kart Club as part of my motor sports' portfolio.

This was the start of three years of monitoring the East Mediterranean Sea and keeping our eyes on Soviet vessels who were entitled to enter the Mediterranean either through the Straits of Gibraltar, or the Bosphorus. This meant operational deployments to Akrotiri in Cyprus to keep an eye on Soviet submarines operating out of Egypt. We also took part in NATO exercises from Crete and Turkey. The squadron was also involved in SAR and we flew a Royal SAR sortie when Prince Charles and Princess Anne flew to Kenya on a visit. We also flew on an SAR sortie when Prince William of Gloucester was taking part in an Air Race over the Mediterranean. We were twice selected to take part in NATO SAR competitions run out of Antalya in Turkey and won both times, flying out of Cyprus. We frequently flew our aircraft back to the UK for various flight safety modifications and one of my trips to St Mawgan coincided with the delivery of the first Nimrod (a modified version of that Comet I'd been round so many years earlier in Cyprus) to the RAF – we could look, but couldn't touch.

Although I'd volunteered to become a Russian linguist and had achieved top marks in the service language aptitude test, I'd been told to wait until I returned to England for my Nimrod conversion and apply again. Instead, I was suddenly asked if I'd be prepared to learn Chinese; the RAF needed a snap decision over the telephone. I agreed and later spent four hours with a member of the RAF Special Investigations Branch (SIB) to assess me for top level security clearance, way above the level I held as an aircrew officer. It transpired during the interview that the SIB had even interviewed my old school secretary in Nairobi, with whom I had stayed during a band camp. That rather shook me, but as the main thrust was to find out if I was homosexual, which I wasn't, I wasn't duly alarmed.

At the end of 1971, Malta had its elections and the Labour Party, under Mr Mintoff, replaced the Nationalist government. The British government decided to withdraw completely all three services and their equipment from Malta and so the squadron flew its remaining Shackletons back to England. I'd flown one of the squadron's Shackletons to Malta, and now I flew one back to RAF St Mawgan, again via Gibraltar and another night stop to allow the final two to join us. I then flew one of the RAF's last Mark 3 Shackletons to RAF Kemble in Gloucestershire on its final flight. It would be mine as well, but I wasn't to know that at the time.

At RAF North Luffenham, I was soon inducted into the shady world of signals intelligence gathering, hence that long security session in Malta, and three years of language training under the instruction of Chinese teachers. Learning any language means hours of drills and vocabulary work, but Chinese is different – it has no alphabet, just somewhere in the region of 80,000 unique characters, each of which had its own pronunciation and tone, of which there were five for each character. I had to commit to memory only a small portion, 3,000 or thereabouts, and had a calligrapher to teach me how to write each character correctly. Six months after I started the course, I'd progressed well enough that my chief instructor decided I should sit the Chinese 'A' level exam. Having to study for my 'A' levels at the same time as my normal studies provided me with a wider view of Chinese literature and grammar, so after six months of study, I sat and passed my Chinese 'A' level.

Other than my Chinese studies, I was presented to HRH Princess Margaret on her official visit to the station and I continued my rallying and was presented with my Station Colours.

My time at North Luffenham was unexpectedly cut short and I was posted to the Ministry of Defence Chinese Language School (MOD CLS) in Hong Kong for my final year. As there was no family accommodation for me, I was again on my own, now living in an Army officers' mess at Lyemun Barracks. The mess had a library with a selection of Chinese language books, one of which was about an island inhabited only by women and where any man who arrived would be fed with herbs to change him into a woman. Mythical, as the island didn't actually exist, but it did help with my literary Chinese.

MODCLS was run by the Army Educational Corps and staffed by Taiwanese instructors rather than instructors from mainland China. It also used different materials, which I found confusing, so I had to re-learn most of what I'd already learnt in England before I sat, and passed, my Civil Service Linguist examination. I then moved onto the next advanced phase to study for the Civil Service Interpreter Examination, to be held the following year. Another pass.

I returned to the UK on my own for a three-month introductory course at the UK Government's Communications Headquarters (GCHQ) and lived in the officers' mess, surrounded by young RAF female officers, which didn't help those gender issues I was suppressing at the time. After finishing, I returned to Hong Kong, now seconded to the Foreign Office for the next two years as the RAF Linguist Officer in a high security communications centre. Although in a non-uniformed post, I maintained my RAF links and attended many of the formal dinners and family occasions at RAF Kai Tak. I also flew with the resident helicopter squadron; I was aircrew, after all. With my own office, I studied for my promotion exams, which I passed, and then embarked on the RAF's eighteen-month Individual Staff Studies correspondence course. I had continued my motorsport, now as a co-driver for the Honda importer and won the Rothman's National Hong Kong Rally Championship with a friend in his 1200cc Honda Civic, just before I returned to the UK. As the RAF's Officer in charge of Motor Sport, I was responsible for entering four RAF Land Rovers into an Army organised rally – another first for the RAF. I was also asked to become Kong Commercial Radio's motor sport reporter and thus also commentated on the 1976 Macau Grand Prix.

After two years, I was posted to the Vulcan Operational Conversion Unit (OCU) at RAF Scampton. This was definitely not the posting I wanted or expected. As a maritime AEO, I fully expected to return to maritime flying in the Nimrod, but this was not to be. The Commander RAF Hong Kong, my immediate RAF boss, had pulled a few strings to get me back to flying. However, he thought I was a bomber AEO, hence my Vulcan course. I was now subject to another move, another home, another course and another aircraft, but at least I was back flying an aircraft, not a desk. On my return, I did try to change my posting to Nimrods, but was unsuccessful, so I started to learn to fly the Vulcan B2.

First, I had to attend a refresher course to bring me back into the flying mindset, during which time I also sat and passed the Civil Aviation Authority's VHF radio licence; not necessary, but it came in useful later. Once that was over, I started at the Vulcan ground school to learn all the electrical systems which controlled the Vulcan's equipment and flying controls. After the ground school, I started to fly the Vulcan, with an instructor watching over me. I'd never operated a jet-engined aircraft before and was totally unprepared for the speed at which everything happened, but by the end of the conversion course I'd become more used to the aircraft and its operation, even though I was uncomfortable flying it. I also sat and passed my Independent Staff Studies course, much to the amazement of my OCU instructors, who were unaware that I was continuing with the course while learning about the Vulcan. As my crew was yet to start at the OCU, I stayed on as an extra AEO, flying with staff members and some of the training crews as their AEO.

Whilst still at Scampton, I was asked by the Commandant of RAF College, Cranwell to prepare a brief for him, in Chinese, about all the RAF's training aircraft for a visit from senior officers of the People's Liberation Army Air Force's flying training establishment for him to present to the visiting Chinese officers. This all had to be handwritten (no computers then) and then duplicated. It was a long job, but I managed and was later asked to join the Cranwell team to act as the interpreter for the actual visit between the RAF pilots and the Chinese officers when they were looking round all the RAF exhibits.

My crew and I arrived at No IX (B) Squadron to start two and a half years of flying the Vulcan – very different from my maritime days. Before we were classed as operational, we flew many conversion flights with various screens to both instruct and monitor our abilities. These flights concentrated on new tactics using our electronic warfare equipment. This was my department and it was very important to keep us safe should we need to fly in anger. After all, this was the Cold War and we had to be able to defend the UK from any enemy incursion by becoming offensive ourselves and getting airborne within the four minutes we anticipated would be available. Many of our exercises were centred round simulated war sorties over both UK and mainland Europe, practising our tactics whilst evading ground-based radars and practise surface to air missile launches. As the Vulcan had become a low-level aircraft, we frequently flew both Canadian and American low-level routes where we could fly lower than we could in Britain, both night and day. I'd been appointed the squadron's EW officer and spent time at the Air Warfare Centre, learning about electronic warfare equipment theory and tactics; I was also the squadron's Flight Safety Officer.

I was now also very involved in RAF Motor Sport as the Motor Sports Association's Publicity Officer. In this role I accepted a challenge from the Army to form a team to take part in its annual driving tests, which were mainly based on rallies and autocross. Normally the RAF didn't use service vehicles for such events, but with the experience of Hong Kong, I managed to convince the inspector general of the RAF Regiment that this event would be good training for his drivers, and he agreed. Four Land Rovers were prepared, I organised training camps and we entered, and won, a number of cups. This led to the RAFMSA entering a team of Land Rovers on the 1979 International Mintex Rally, competing against a number of top-class civilian works rally teams. I was co-driver on the first of the RAFMSA Land Rovers leaving Harrogate, whilst still carrying out all the publicity and media interest for the RAF. At the end of the rally, my driver and I found we'd won a couple of awards, which were then presented to us at the final celebrations.

Towards the end of my tour, I was offered specialist aircrew terms, which would mean an extension of my service until I was 55. I'd been hoping for this, but my wife was against me extending so I had to retire at my optional retirement date. My last trips in a Vulcan were part of a week-long flight to Cyprus via Italy where, on the way, we flew against the French Air Force and flew Italian low-level routes through the Apennines, and even visited Venice. When we arrived at RAF Akrotiri, I noticed several Nimrods lined up and later joined the crews in the mess bar, even flying on a Nimrod sortie from Akrotiri before my return Vulcan flight home. Eighteen years after I'd walked through those gates at RAF South Cerney, I climbed out of my Vulcan. I'd managed to end my aircrew career flying the Nimrod and the Vulcan on successive days. What a finish.

By then, I'd been head-hunted by Marconi Space and Defence Systems at Stanmore to become the manager in Beijing, a position I accepted, but which changed before I arrived. For the next few years, I flew around the Far East and China as an export manager for a number of electronics companies. By now, I'd separated from my first wife and had weekends free, so I accepted a commission as a maritime operations officer in the Royal Auxiliary Air Force (RAuxAF). At the same time, I was offered a place at Manchester College, Oxford University to read for a BA Honours in Oriental Studies with Chinese, which I accepted just as I was made redundant.

I spent the next four years with much younger colleagues, both male and female, all of whom had just left school with excellent 'A' levels. I added Classical and Literary Chinese to my rusty modern Chinese, but my tutors at the Oriental Institute decided to advance me to the second year for modern Chinese. I wasn't particularly happy with this decision as I knew I needed to start all over again, but I presumed Oxford knew best. At the end of my first year, I sat and passed the 'Preliminary' examination, and at the end of my second year, I spent four months at the Taiwan National Normal University in Taibei. The following year I was awarded a Taiwan government scholarship to return for another four months of immersive Chinese language training. At the end of my fourth year, my final examinations took place: nine three-hour exams between Monday morning and Friday evening, set, as one of my tutors explained, for 20-year-olds – I was 52. Nevertheless, I graduated with my BA (Hons), later to be awarded my MA.

At the same time, I continued with the RAuxAF and took part in many NATO exercises as a maritime aircraft tasker, operating alongside other NATO personnel in a bunker deep below north-west London or with the Royal Navy at Faslane. The extra money came in useful and enabled me to buy a number of Chinese textbooks for my essays.

After graduation, I remarried and spent a year tutoring at the University of Portsmouth and Southampton University's Adult Education department. I was also on the team organising visits to the Farnborough Air Displays from overseas buyers, until I was head hunted for a position as general manager of a Hong Kong electronics company with a factory in China, which I visited frequently. The company was in financial difficulties and my contract was terminated just before the Hong Kong 'handover' in 1997. On the evening of the handover, my wife and I stood by the harbour side and waved goodbye to HMY *Britannia* as the RAF VC 10 flew overhead. A month later, my wife and I were on our way back to England; my company had been taken over by a Chinese business and my contract was terminated.

Once I was back in the UK, I accepted the role of training officer for the Maritime Headquarters Units (MHU) in HQ 11/18 Group, and while there, I taught IGCSE English to service personnel who needed the qualification for promotion. I was also attached for a short time to the Chief of Air Staff's team hosting several very senior PLAAF commanders who were visiting RAF stations around the UK. This gave me the experience of flying in one of its passenger aircraft and chatting to the more junior officers on the delegation about the differences between the RAF and the PLAAF structure. I subsequently became staff officer reserves with more squadrons to look after, now on Full Time Reserve Service terms and responsible to my air commodore for reserve policy matters at the time when reserve squadrons were changing focus from pure maritime tasking to more operational support roles with the RAF Regiment. This restructure meant the re-establishment of some former RAuxAF flying squadrons, one of which was my old unit which had become No 600 Squadron, and I thus had the honour of being presented to HM Queen Elizabeth the Queen Mother. Training became very important to ensure that reservists were fully able to operate beside the regulars, who were not at first accepting of reserves being added to their units – at least until they realised the reserves' training was as good as theirs. This was also a time of change in the RAF and I soon found myself working with the RAF Regiment in HQ 2 Group whilst maintaining my maritime responsibilities in HQ 3 Group. I enjoyed this role, but budgets were tight and the decision was made not to extend my contract when it was due as it was felt that a regular in my post would be cheaper for the RAF. This wasn't a decision with which I, or my commanders, were happy with. Consequently, I was dined out from the RAF in the officers' mess at RAF High Wycombe in 2005, forty-one years after I'd first signed on as a cadet officer.

My wife and I moved to Lincolnshire but because I'd no responsible role to play, I became depressed and suffered some very serious headaches, lasting up to three or four days at a time. Although I'd suffered similar headaches throughout my time in the RAF and university, these were much worse. My GP was unable to find the reason and after finding a psychotherapist in London, I travelled down to see him. Halfway through the appointment, he asked the important question, which I so nearly evaded: 'Do you think you should have been born female?' He then diagnosed my headaches as 'incongruent headaches' with my conscious (male) fighting my sub-conscious (female), the latter being more powerful than the former, and so suggested I may be gender dysphoric. My GP later referred me to the Gender Identity Clinic in Nottingham, where I was medically diagnosed with gender dysphoria.

I now had an even more important, and incredibly difficult, decision to make with my wife: to transition and lose her, or live with constant headaches and stay with her. After much deliberation, she was the one who really made the decision for me to transition. However, we'd have to live apart, while remaining married, so that I could concentrate on my transitioning, medical procedures and hormone treatment to bring my appearance more into line with that of a woman. I also had to learn to dress as a woman (at last) and to try to behave as one as well. To help with the separation, we bought a house in Gloucestershire where my wife could be near her family while I stayed in Lincolnshire. I met Caroline Paige, whose own transition I'd heard about while a staff officer at Northwood, and who told me about Fighting With Pride.

Since my transition, I've found my true self, although this has been more difficult than I thought it would be. I've had a great deal of support from my family, my friends, former RAF colleagues, members of the Porsche Club GB, and the local WI. I was recently elected as the chairman of the Parish Council and I sit on Motorsport UK's LGBT+ expert committee. As a transgender rally driver, I've been featured in a number of magazine and newspaper articles and podcasts, both at home and overseas, and in the local BBC News and newspapers. I still rally, but now in Historic Road Rallies in my 1966 Porsche 912, christened 'Poppy' by one of my earlier rally navigators.

Chapter 23

Playing it Straight – Until the Tide Turned

——————————— Maggie Pugh ———————————

In 1978, when I first joined the WRNS (Women's Royal Naval Service, also known as Wrens), women weren't allowed to go to sea. In fact, the motto of the WRNS was 'Never at Sea', just to ensure there could be no misunderstanding!

There were no frontline roles for women in the service, but Wrens still provided a much valued and necessary support role to the men and ships at sea, something they'd been providing on a permanent basis since the end of the Second World War.

I joined up at the age of 17; the youngest you could join at that time. I joined because I wanted to do something more exciting with my life. I was raised in the Black Country where my family and ancestors had lived for centuries. Black Country people are friendly, funny, loyal, kind and fiercely proud of their industrial working-class history, as was I. Many live all their lives in the same area, within the same community, but as much as I loved my home, this was never going to be enough for me.

I spent most of my early childhood years with my older brother, Bryan, who I adored and followed everywhere. Despite our six-year age difference, I saw his friends as my friends and would gate crash any football games they were playing, turn up unannounced at gatherings and even pinch his clothes to wear on occasions. He was so lovely and accepting of this and it helped me to feel accepted, to feel that I belonged.

During my school days I experienced crushes and infatuations for both female and male friends. I attended an all-girl grammar school in Dudley and while I thoroughly enjoyed my school days, emotionally they proved to be both painful and challenging. In the 60s and 70s no one ever spoke about the feelings I was experiencing and if they did, it was always met with ridicule, disgust or pity. I became an introvert as a child and kept my own council the best way I could. I masked my true self and my true feelings, choosing instead to play a role that was acceptable in society. Indeed, I played that part so well that over time, I began to believe I really was that person.

I entered the WRNS as a photographer, a trade that was small in numbers and therefore quite difficult to get into. New entry training took place at HMS Dauntless in Berkshire. It was an eerie place made up of old wooden Nissan huts, originally built to house munitions workers during the Second World War, standing around a central brick building and parade ground. It was grey and misty most days, with just the sound of cawing crows and the occasional voices bellowing orders on the parade ground to break the silence. I loved it from the moment I stepped off the coach. I joined up with twenty other new recruits on that day and we became Theseus Division 280 – the new intake. The training lasted for five weeks, with an added two-week break for Christmas in the middle. We really bonded as a group, which made the whole experience so much more enjoyable. We rarely left the camp, even in the final week, as we had read on the noticeboard that due to the antics of some previous trainees, we were now barred from any local pubs in the near vicinity! We didn't mind, we had each other and now, forty years on, we're still meeting up and having regular annual reunions together.

After HMS Dauntless, myself and the other five WRNS photographers went on to HMS Excellent for our three months' photographic training, before I was drafted up to Scotland to work as a public relations photographer for Flag Officer Scotland and Northern Ireland (FOSNI) in Rosyth. Naval PR photographers could be called upon to photograph a broad range of events, from local boy stories for press releases, visits to ships by VIPs, awards ceremonies, recording events of historical interest, in fact anything that could be used to raise the profile and visibility of the work of the Royal Navy with the general public. Good publicity was important to keep the work of the Navy in the public eye and, of course, to help drive recruitment.

My next draft took me down to central London to work for the Director of Public Relations Navy (DPRN). During the Falklands War in 1982, the male photographers in my unit were called down to the South Atlantic to keep a photographic record of the war. The girls, of course, could not join them, so we stayed behind and manned a new Muirhead satellite machine that'd been specially shipped in to ensure the MOD had a direct and secure connection with the ships in the fleet. Photographs could be wired through directly to the MOD for clearance before they were then shared with the media. It was a level of control that was unpopular with the press at that time and would eventually lead to a change in policy after the war.

The photographic section in Whitehall was situated in the basement, just off the Admiralty courtyard. The Muirhead machine was a huge beast, as all new technology was in those days, so it could not be sited in the photographic department and instead had to be housed in an unused building up in the courtyard, just to the right as you approached Admiralty Building through the archway from Whitehall. The Muirhead satellite receiver was linked to three of our ships down in the Falklands; HMS *Hermes*, HMS *Invincible* and the cruise ship *Canberra*, and was manned 24/7, mainly by WRNS photographers, some of whom had been drafted in for the purpose.

I celebrated my 21st birthday whilst working shifts on the Muirhead machine in London and it was around this time that I began to think about exploring my sexuality. I'd had a number of painful infatuations with other Wrens, and started to realise that my feelings for women were much stronger than any feelings I'd experienced for the men in my life up until that point. But meeting someone seemed an impossible task. The only 'safe' way seemed to be by responding to newspaper adverts. I was too scared to venture out into gay clubs and meeting places because I felt sure that I'd be seen, so I decided to answer an advert in the *Evening Standard*. I wrote a letter and included a photograph of myself. I remember standing in front of the red post box in Queen's Gate Terrace, Kensington (where the Wrens' quarters were located then), trying to find the courage to post it. I knew that once it was gone, I was potentially crossing a point of no return and could have no idea where this would eventually lead. I agonised over posting that letter, but decided it had to be done, so in it went.

I actually never heard anything back from that letter, which was a huge relief as just a couple of weeks later, I was called to attend a clear lower deck at HMS President in Kensington. A clear lower deck is a military version of a three-line whip, a summons for everyone to gather together for an important briefing with senior officers. Everyone is expected and required to attend.

The meeting started as a pleasant farewell gathering for one of the senior ratings at Furse House who was retiring after a long and distinguished career. But then it became clear there was a second purpose for the meeting. We were told by our senior officers that the Navy had just completed a purge on young men and women in the service who were believed to be homosexual. Several souls across the fleet and shore-based establishments had been arrested in one coordinated swoop and had been expelled from the service as a result. This is how the service operated then: they would gather intelligence on an individual, which may just start with a suspicion or an association with another person who was believed to be homosexual and then, through interviews and observations, the intelligence file on the person would grow. Then when the service had several individuals on its records, they'd conduct a single swoop, arresting all in one go.

The senior officers told us all to be on the lookout for homosexuals in our day-to-day lives and if we suspected anyone or indeed if anyone admitted to us that they were homosexual, then we were to report it straight away to our superiors. I was so shocked and frightened and all I could think about was the letter I'd posted a short time earlier. Had they started a file on me?

As a result of that evening, I went firmly back into the closet and was not to venture out again for another six years.

Over that time I became quite accomplished at playing it straight and focused all my energy into furthering my career. In 1984 I attended the Admiralty Interview Board (AIB) at HMS Sultan for officer selection and to my joy, was accepted for training at BRNC Dartmouth between January and April 1985. Whilst at Dartmouth I met a lovely young sub lieutenant and later that year we got engaged. It seemed as though life was going to take me down a different path, one which I embraced and settled in to. I planned the wedding and imagined a future that would certainly include having children, just the kind of family life that was acceptable and expected by everyone around me. It felt comfortable to conform and I no longer felt scared. My future and my career looked rosy.

After leaving Dartmouth I was sent to join the ship's company of HMS *Birmingham* to take over from the captain's secretary. The ship was moving into its midlife refit, which was to take place at Rosyth Dockyard in Scotland over a two-year period. I joined the ship in Portsmouth and then went on to London to participate in the farewell parties before crew members started to leave and move onto new ships and postings. The captain of HMS *Birmingham*, Martin Ladd, had tried to get permission for myself (as the first ever female member of a Type 42 Destroyer's ship's company) and his niece, a fellow WRNS officer, to sail with the ship from London up to Rosyth in Scotland. Unfortunately, his request was declined by CINC Fleet as women were under no circumstances allowed to sail onboard. The fact I was a WRNS officer, and an actual member of the ship's company, made no difference at all. So, when the ship sailed between ports, I would have to get into my car and drive myself there.

Whilst serving in Scotland on HMS *Birmingham*, I found myself in an all-male environment, both at work and back in my accommodation in HMS Caledonia. I had limited opportunities to meet with other WRNS officers, who were all accommodated in HMS Cochrane and therefore had no female friends at all. I admit that I found this really hard, but as I had a summer holiday in Italy planned with my fiancée coming up, I focused on that to keep me going.

On the flight back up to Scotland after my holiday, something strange came over me. I suddenly felt a deep sinking feeling in my stomach as a black cloud descended on me, I don't know where from, and I fell into a state of depression. Every morning when I woke, I was physically sick and at work I would burst into tears for no reason at all. It was as though I'd no control at all of my emotions, and I really struggled to hold it together. I eventually went to sickbay to seek help and the QARNNS sister, who was really kind in a military no nonsense kind of way, sat me down and listened to my symptoms. There were no drugs dispensed, as there probably would be today, and instead she set about getting me transferred to the wardroom in HMS Cochrane. She was told there were no places left in the WRNS officer wing, but that a cabin could be allocated to me in the male accommodation, located just outside the double doors that led through into the WRNS block. That would work, and I was moved that afternoon.

The sickness in the morning and dark moods started to lift slowly but steadily as I made friends with my fellow WRNS officers, and I made a full recovery thereafter. At the time I'd no idea why the depression had hit me so quickly and so hard, but in hindsight I've since concluded that deep down, I knew the decisions and plans I was making in my personal life were not right for me and the years of pretence and subterfuge were catching up with me.

I called my engagement off later that year and entered a much-needed period of 'me' time without any romantic attachments. A much-needed time to heal and reflect. I'd trained for a new role as a personnel selection officer (PSO) and joined an all-female team of PSOs at the new entry training base, HMS Raleigh in Torpoint, Cornwall. I flourished in that role and found a new state of happiness and confidence, untethered from any personal attachments except for the friendships and camaraderie of my fellow officers. Whilst at HMS Raleigh, I was called away on winter deployment with the Royal Marines in Norway. For three months every year, during the Cold War era, British tri-service arctic warfare training was carried out in Norway, where military personnel would learn to ski and fight in the snowy and icy cold terrain of Scandinavia. Skills that would be vital if we were ever to face a Russian offensive through Finland, as was experienced in the Second World War. Of course, as women were non-combative, my role was to run the tri-service wardroom in Lillehammer and to oversee the welfare of the female recruits supporting the deployment. It was the only foreign travel I experienced during my thirteen years in the service, and I felt really lucky to have travelled at all.

In 1987 I was appointed to be a personnel selection officer at the Admiralty Interview Board in HMS Sultan, a job I thoroughly enjoyed and excelled at. The role involved assessing, interviewing and selecting young men and women to be officers in the Royal Navy, Royal Marines and WRNS. Each board consisted of a senior naval captain, a commander, a head teacher and the PSO. The PSO was a full board member but also had specific responsibilities for invigilating, marking and interpreting the psychometric tests on day one. Then on day two, the PSO would lead a tabletop discussion exercise with candidates, was observed by the other board members, and also carry out a personal one-on-one interview with each candidate to explore their home life, interests, relationships and the dreaded questioning regarding homosexual tendencies. I remembered being asked that question myself when I went through the AIB, but at that time I was dating a male lieutenant and had never had any lesbian encounters at all. I didn't know anyone who was gay and hadn't spoken about possibly being gay myself to anyone.

I always dreaded asking the sexuality question and was always hugely relieved when my question was met with a negative response. In my two years at the AIB, no candidate ever shared that they had any homosexual tendencies, and I was very thankful for it.

Whilst serving at the AIB I spent a great deal of personal time on my own. The weekdays were very full, with boards to complete and write up and the next day's set of candidates to prepare for, which would often require working into the early evening. The weekends, however, were quiet and as I'd no partner in my life, I became quite lonely. My thoughts turned again to trying to find a female partner. I felt braver now, I was more confident and more senior in the service, and I was living on shore in my own house. I was older but not necessarily wiser!

There were still limited 'safe' options for meeting other gay people in those days, going to bars and clubs was still too dangerous but there was a gay pen pal organisation called Gay Pen, which I decided to try. You just paid a subscription, filled in a questionnaire about yourself and sent it off. Then, sometime later, the details of three potential matches were sent through to you. There was no obligation to contact any of them but one of the three looked like a possible match for me, so I contacted her straight away. It was an exciting time. Just being able to talk to another person about being gay for the first time was wonderful and a relationship blossomed from this. She lived on the island of Jersey, and it wasn't long before she came over to the mainland and moved in with me. I felt like a teenager again. All those suppressed feelings I'd quashed and kept hidden in my youth were now let out and embraced and it felt wonderful. Tentatively, we explored the gay scene together and I got bolder and more defiant, angry even that I'd not been able to be myself sooner and I lamented those lost years. I knew now for sure that I was gay and could see no way back into my old life, whatever happened next.

What did happen next was that I was appointed to a new job at HMS Dryad as the commander's assistant. I was sad to leave the AIB but working in the military is like being on a carousel; every two years you have to move on to the next role to give everyone the chance to try new jobs, broaden their skills and have new challenges and experiences. It's the fair and only way to keep the cogs of the military machine working effectively and efficiently.

HMS Dryad was a very busy training establishment nestled in the quiet village of Southwick, just north of Portsmouth. During the Second World war it was the HQ for the main allied commanders General Eisenhower, Admiral Ramsey and General Montgomery during the D-Day landings and the large wall maps they used on the day are still in situ within the wardroom. As the commander's assistant, I wore many hats, PA to the commander, visits officer, PR officer, band officer, schools and charity liaison officer and the management of a small team of three based in the commander's office.

It was during my time at Dryad that I met Kate. She was much younger than me and a WRNS rating, so it was only by chance that our paths crossed. Straight away I felt drawn to her. Initially it was a protective concern for her as her life didn't seem happy. We grew close quite quickly and the attraction between us was mutual from the start. I knew it was going to be a difficult and probably unwise choice, but I decided to let my heart take the lead and see where it would take me. One of my favourite philosophical quotes is 'one often meets one's destiny on the road one takes to avoid it', which basically means you cannot escape what's meant for you in life, so I went with my heart. I was clearly crossing the boundaries set by the military at that time, but for some reason I embraced the risk and stepped over the invisible line anyway. I knew my position as an officer and hers as a WRNS rating made our relationship seem reckless to those around us, but officers dating and marrying ratings had been an accepted practice for years in the heterosexual military world, so the only difference and challenge for us was going to be the fact that we were both women. I knew the risks, but I was in love. So I chose to be true to myself and take a leap of faith.

It didn't take long for other gay personnel on the camp to hear about my relationship with Kate. I actually felt strangely comforted by this at first and less isolated once I was known and accepted into the gay community on the base. They do say that there's a safety in numbers and that's how I'd started to feel.

Living ashore in my own house gave me some added security, too. I could escape the prying eyes and impromptu raids on cabins and personal belongings undertaken by the SIB (Special Investigation Branch), but for those living on the base there was nowhere to hide. I remember one day hearing about a raid on Wrens' quarters that was taking place. Two young Wrens who lived in quarters and who were known to be seeing each other were trying desperately to hide some personal letters, photographs and magazines they knew would incriminate them, if found. They stashed them all in a holdall but didn't have anywhere to hide them.

I think they were very brave and clearly very desperate as they turned to me for help. It was just the kind of compromising situation I'd always feared I might face and that I'd hoped would never arise, but on that day feelings of compassion and solidarity were overwhelming. So, I put their holdall in the boot of my car and took it home with me that evening.

The strain of the situation was starting to build, and it was taking its toll on mine and Kate's relationship. The pressure and stress led to frequent arguments, and it became increasingly difficult for us to maintain the level of discretion needed to stay hidden. I decided it was time to bring the relationship to an end in the hope that we could both weather the storm we both felt was coming and salvage our careers, which we were both desperate to hold on to. I thought this was for the best, for both of us, but in the end, it led to the SIB making their move.

My own day of reckoning came around my 30th birthday in April 1991. I remember there being an eerie quiet around the establishment that day, you could sense that something was going on. Unbeknown to me at the time, Kate had been arrested and other suspected lesbians on the base had been put under a kind of curfew.

I wandered down the corridor between the commander's office and the chief regulator's office, who was a friend of mine and also on their 'suspect' list. We sat and chatted in her office and shared our concerns for what was happening around the base. Then, a knock came at the door and I was told I was required outside by the master at arms, which seemed like a perfectly legitimate request, so I left the office. As I entered the corridor, however, he turned and went back into the office and closed the door behind him. I stood alone in the corridor fearing the worst for my colleague still inside. I returned to my own office but couldn't concentrate on my work so decided to wander over to Southwick House (the wardroom) to see if I had any post.

As I stood chatting with the wardroom manager at the main reception desk, I saw the first lieutenant accompanied by the master at arms walk in through the main door and straight up to me, face on. I attempted a friendly greeting but then heard him launch into the words I knew but had never been directed at me before. 'You have the right to remain silent but anything you do say may be taken down and used as evidence...' The words petered out from that first sentence, I think I was in a state of shock, and I became an observer of the situation playing out in front of me. It was like I was watching it from afar as a third person and not really accepting that this was happening to me.

When the caution ended, I kept asking what I was being arrested for, as he hadn't said that. Doesn't that come at the beginning of the caution? I kept repeating the same thing 'what am I being arrested for?' But there was no answer given.

I was marched off to an unused part of the wardroom and put in one of the empty cabins, where I was told I had to remain for the rest of the day. Food would be brought up for me and an WRNS officer would be placed on guard to watch over me from the cabin next door, although she wouldn't be allowed to talk to me or keep me company.

Several officers came and went during the day, working in shifts and leaving me alone, as instructed. All except my friend, Sue Lloyd. She was like a breath of fresh air that day when she started her watch. Always the voice of reason and compassion, she was appalled at the whole situation and was incredulous that the Navy could be treating people in this way. She sat with me and kept me company and I was thankful for it.

From the cabin where I was kept, I could look down into my office, seeing my team going about their business as normal. I sensed this was the end for me now and thought about what I'd do next and what I'd tell my parents and my family, none of whom knew I was gay. I wondered where Kate was and what was happening to her and how she was coping. Initially I felt defeated and sad about the whole situation, but as time went on, I started to grow angry and defiant.

I was eventually taken to HMS Nelson, the home of the SIB and questioned under caution. I'd decided during my time 'in captivity' that I'd deny everything. I wasn't ready to lose my career and I wasn't ready to come out to my parents and family. In hindsight, I wish I'd had the courage just to admit my sexuality and my relationship with Kate, but I was so frightened and so desperate to try to save the career I loved so much.

I was sent up to London to work for a while with the senior Royal Navy psychologists (with whom I'd trained to be a PSO), away from the people I knew, out of sight and out of mind. It was a lonely period in London as I sensed that the WRNS officers I knew up there weren't keen to engage with me. I remember one day walking down Whitehall and a WRNS officer I'd known well, and thought was my friend, actually crossed over the busy road to avoid meeting me. Well, that's how I saw it anyway. I didn't want to embarrass anyone, so I kept as low a profile as I could for the rest of my time there.

On the evening of Friday, 6 September 1991, I received a phone call from a colleague working in the Department for Public Relations (Navy). She told me that the department had been informed that mine and Kate's story was going to be published in the *News of the World* that coming Sunday and she didn't know if my name was going to be mentioned or not. This was it. There was no burying my head anymore, I had to get to my parents and come out to them before the story broke. I knew they didn't read the *News of The World* newspaper, but I didn't want to take the risk of them hearing about this from anyone else.

The next day was my father's 65th birthday and so I phoned them in South Wales on the Friday and told them I'd be driving up to see them the next day and had something to tell them. I'd no idea what I was going to say or how I was going to say it, but my hand had been forced and it was now or never.

Saturday, 7 September 1991 was not the joyous day of celebration it should've been. My parents were lovely and tried to help me explain what my news was, but I was just sobbing. Their first question was 'is it anything to do with your health?' and when I said that it wasn't, they visibly sighed with relief and reassured me that whatever it was, it would be OK. Interestingly, they went through a number of options to try to help me: was I pregnant? Was I in trouble with the police? Was it drugs? But they didn't think of the answer I so wanted them to offer, so I still had to actually say it out loud. It was the most difficult conversation I've ever been forced to have, and there was no time to think it through. I wasn't ready to come out to them, it'd taken twenty-seven years to admit it to myself, but thankfully my parents rallied and gave me all the support I needed.

The next day we got a copy of the *News of the World on Sunday* and read it together. The story was salacious and, for the most part, untrue and totally fabricated. It talked of lesbian rings, lesbian orgies, offering young girls quick promotions through the ranks and predatory lesbian behaviour being rife throughout the base. It was a devastating and embarrassing read and the shame I felt from that day on took a long time to heal. As we've since learned, practices at the paper were unconventional and often illegal during that period, and when the infamous hacking scandal broke, the *News of The World* was eventually closed down, with its last publication in July 2011.

After the story broke in 1991 it took another four months of waiting until I was finally told I was being administratively discharged from the Royal Navy. I'd offered to resign but was informed that the Admiralty had recently changed their policy on this and had agreed that 'resignation would be reserved for those who voluntarily admitted that they had or may have homosexual or other sexually deviant tendencies'. This was relayed to me in a letter.

During this time, I heard that Kate had already been discharged. I knew this would hit her hard and felt for her; she was at the start of her career and had so much to look forward to, but that had now been cruelly taken away. We didn't see each other again after that. Our paths have crossed occasionally in the last thirty years, and we're now in touch again via social networks, but our lives have remained very separate.

In my final letter from the Navy, I was told that the Admiralty Board of the Defence Council had decided to 'remove me from the active list on account of my unsuitability within my own control and that my commission was to be terminated….and I would no longer be entitled to use my former rank or wear naval uniform.' In other words, it would be as though my thirteen years of service never happened.

On my final day, 5 December 1991, I walked into HMS Dryad main gate and handed in my ID card and gas mask. That was all they wanted back from me and then I left, and the door was shut firmly behind me.

Entering the job market having known nothing but life in the Navy was a shock to the system. We were in the middle of a recession at that time, and it was a recruiter's market. No-one was interested in ex-military personnel, and unless you had the right qualifications for the job, then was impossible to get an interview. I went to live in the Channel Islands for a while as I had friends there and found a job selling financial products on a commission only basis. The job market in Jersey was even worse than on the UK mainland as jobs, quite rightly, were reserved for local residents first and foremost and I couldn't argue with that.

When I returned to the mainland, I settled in Brighton and signed on at the Job Centre. I eventually found a job working for Brighton General Hospital in their sterile services department implementing a quality standard BS5750. The pay was so low, about a third of my salary in the Navy, that the council used to send me a cheque every month to top up my income and I was very grateful for it!

I lived in bedsits and a one-bedroom flat to start off with as that was all I could afford, but I was happy because I was free to be myself at long last. The role at the hospital was actually the start of my second career in quality management which I then pursued for the next twenty-five years.

When the ban was lifted in January 2000, I felt euphoric. It'd come too late for me but to think that gay men and women could now be themselves in the forces without fear of being hunted, arrested and dismissed was a blessing I was still happy to celebrate. I actually wrote to the Royal Navy to ask if I could now rejoin and they wrote back to me to say that, yes, I could re-enter the service at the rank and seniority I had when I was administratively discharged nine years earlier. I'd have to retrain as a seaman officer and be willing to go to sea. I was 40 years old.

I wrote back to the Navy and thanked them for their response, but after due consideration told them that I'd decided I didn't want to re-enlist. In truth, I didn't want to go back as I knew it'd never be the same again after all I'd been through, but what I'd done by asking the question was to take back the power I'd lost when I was dismissed the first time. It hadn't been my choice to leave, but it was my choice not to return.

Who knows where life would've taken me if I hadn't served under the ban. I loved being in the WRNS and I was doing well. I had recommendations for early promotion in my reports and had hopes and plans for a long and successful military career ahead of me. But the ban on homosexuality was always a dark cloud that hung over my time in the service and only by denying myself and my true nature could I have made it work. In the end, it proved to be a price I was unwilling to pay.

Chapter 24

A Submariner's Tale and a Shattered Dream

———————————— Andy Cowe ————————————

I joined HMS Fisgard in January 1983 after a searching interview process and a strange and extensive medical, during which the army doctor made me do the full medical, including press ups and pull ups, naked. I passed, however, and was so excited to begin my career as an artificer apprentice in the Royal Navy. This was an apprenticeship which gave a formal qualification (HND) and a fast track to become a petty officer and beyond. My dream job since childhood was to be a submariner; it's all I'd wanted to do as a child, partly from a fascination with submarines and partly from a wish not to get seasick bobbing around in the surface flotilla!

I was 17 when I joined. I was an innocent, straight, and virgin in life, literally. My only experience was school and I longed to begin my life in a man's world. On the first day of my journey to become a submariner, I was picked up at Plymouth station by the Royal Navy, who were awaiting the train's arrival in dark-blue trucks, and we were driven to Fisgard, an older training establishment of wartime-styled hangers connected by narrow passageways made from old bricks. We'd be the last intake before the unit moved across the road and became part of the vast HMS Raleigh. I was nervous but excited.

I got through basic training and 'passed in' in February 1983. There were days when I wondered if I would break, but I got through it, my resilience building every day. I was so exhausted but knew the pain wouldn't last forever. I was much younger than the other recruits, most being in their late early 20s. I was very slim and weighed very little so was picked on more than most, but that's what it was like in those days. Seeing the pride on my parents' faces as they watched the parade is something I'll never forget.

HMS Fisgard was a training college for artificers. The tutors were officers, but it didn't feel like the real Navy that I'd come to know and, in many ways, it felt more like a boarding school. Most of my time was spent studying for my HND, with a bit of naval training thrown in here and there. We were divided into streams according to our chosen specialism of mechanics, electrics, electronics or, for the very best, the Air Fleet. It was fast-paced and highly technical learning and with the risk of not keeping up the pace, I recatagorised as a marine engineering mechanic and joined HMS Sultan in Portsmouth to learn my trade.

HMS Sultan felt like a proper naval establishment and I was much happier, passing out after a few months as a marine engineering mechanic. Ready to join the fleet, my class were allocated to units. I'd requested submarines and was thrilled to be selected, completing my submariner training at HMS Dolphin in Gosport, which involved a mix of academic training and the 'Tank', which is a simulated underwater escape from the seabed. You never forget the first time you break the surface in the tank and it was a moment of incredible achievement for me. And so, in 1985 I joined the fleet as a nuclear submariner in HMS *Splendid*, based in Devonport.

In a military career, your training never finishes and the coming months were spent learning about every system and switch in my boat. Working on a submarine is dangerous: you're underwater at great depths in a small metal tube. *Splendid* was full of state-of-the-art equipment and electronic systems, as well as high-pressure systems such as air and hydraulics. Anything could happen at any time and every man on board needed to know every system, every valve, every emergency procedure and actions to be carried out. My first three months on board were spent memorising everything because until you pass what's called your 'Part 3 Test', you're simply a passenger and a risk to the boat. I was hugely relieved to pass and receive my 'Dolphins', a small, golden badge with two dolphins either side of the Queen's crown and anchor. Sometimes submariners, who have their own sense of humour, would call them 'kissing kippers' or the 'Queen's legs', but make no mistake, submariners are very proud of their Dolphins because of the work needed to get them. They are a symbol that you can be trusted and are part of the team. You also get paid more as a qualified submariner, and it was quite a lot more than those who skipped around in the waves on surface ships.

For those who've never been on a submarine, I'll try to paint a picture of what it's like to live and work on one. From the outside they look quite small, but that's because you can only see the fin and a small part of what lies beneath the waterline. To board a submarine, always known as a 'boat', you climb down the hatch on a vertical ladder to the top of three decks. As you step off, you're technically underwater. There are no windows, just narrow corridors barely wide enough for one person, and cramped spaces. You can't see much more than 5 metres ahead and when you come back from patrol, you're not allowed to drive for twenty-four hours so that your eyes can adjust to distances again.

Splendid had a 120-man crew and 60 of us were junior ratings. It would be our shared home for two to three months, often spent entirely underwater; as long as you had enough food, you could stay submerged for any length of time. The corridors and spaces were packed with valves, safety and emergency equipment, breathing equipment and all manner of technology. It was cramped. After coming back from patrol, most of us had bumps and bruises where our body connected with an unnoticed hazard. The engine room where some of the pipes were hot was even worse. People joining the submarine service needed to be 5 feet tall and very skinny!

If you were lucky and were qualified, you'd have a bunk and a locker about the size of a very small bedside table, as well as a locker for your boots and shoes. That was all the space you had for all your kit for three months! The bunks were about 7 feet long by about 3 feet wide, in stacks of three. There was space under the bunk to put your uniform (if required for an important visit) or your civies (jeans, t-shirt and trainers). There was no space for anything else. Each bunk had a lamp and a pouch to put your book in and a blackout curtain. That was the only privacy you had. The golden rule was that if someone was in their bunk, you only disturbed them in an emergency or for their watch.

If you hadn't completed your Part 3 training, more than likely you'd be allocated a rack in the torpedo room to sleep, where racks would be set up on the actual torpedoes or rails and you'd sleep on them. I used to think that at least if it goes off, I won't know anything about it. Despite these privations, I loved it. I was so proud.

I was an engine room watch keeper, also known as a 'back afty', and was stationed between the condensers that cooled the steam used by the turbines created by the reactors. I was responsible for the distillation and transfer of water, lubricating oil and the bilges. The engine room was painted mostly white and made everything look more spacious, but in truth, it wasn't and was very much the opposite. As I was so skinny, I was often called upon to get at areas others couldn't. Guys like me who were short or skinny were known as 'bilge rats', a creature with which we shared our ability to access the tightest of spaces. I was always messy but was doing things that needed doing. There was always a feeling of being dirty and you could only shower once every three days. A shower consisted of you getting wet, switching the shower off, soaping yourself and then rinsing. That was it. If you were caught abusing it, then you soon learnt not to. We all smelt the same. There was no deodorants, aftershaves, talc, or shaving foam, which were all banned, so it was 'eau de bloke'.

So there you are in this cramped metal tube with over 100 other men, under water for two to three months at a time. You never know where you're going. There's no sunlight or communication with the rest of the world, and only the captain would receive signals from command. There's no privacy, no indication of what day it is, or if it's even night or day! Were it not for the menu, which featured breakfast lunch and dinner, the days would blend into the longest of days. Fish on Friday, steak on Saturday, roast on Sunday and curry on Monday.

The first few days on patrol were always a bit tense; you just did your job and kept quiet. People were coming to terms with leaving their wives, kids and girlfriends, and many stopped drinking while they were at sea. You could have three cans a night, but if it was your birthday then you got a cake and they'd let you have other people's allowances and someone would do your watches for you.

Time passed, however, and I enjoyed my work and felt that I'd found my place to be. A couple of weeks before coming home or going ashore, everyone would start to cross the days off in their mind, getting excited. It was also a time to keep quiet and keep your head down. On board everyone knows everything about each other. There's no hiding place, but there is that special camaraderie. When you do go ashore, you do it large, with all ranks together. It's a remarkable bond between the submariners in a crew; they're your 'oppos' through thick and thin.

Sadly, during the best times in life, sometimes the worst things happen. In the submarine service, everything was top secret. The tensions at the time with the USSR made our work critically important to the defence of the UK and our allies. Submarines were sent out to find other submarines, record their signature and monitor them, especially the new submarines the Soviets were deploying. So, all submariners had to be 'security vetted'. There was the fear that those with something to hide could be blackmailed and give information to the Soviets which could damage our military capability. I sometimes wondered why the Soviets didn't work as taxi drivers, who always seemed to know which ships and boats were going out or coming in from all the drunken matelots after their nights out.

There were also two other career risks in the Armed Forces which would bring instant dismissal: the use of drugs, which seemed to me entirely understandable, and the less easily fathomed ban on being gay. Anyone who was either caught or even suspected of being gay would be arrested, investigated, charged and removed from the Armed Forces. If someone was caught, then you could be discharged just by connection or assumption. That was how it was in the 1980s, and it was when things started to get really difficult for me.

My time in the Royal Navy before joining HMS *Splendid* had been fast paced and my days exhaustingly full; there had been no time for contemplation. Now the Navy was going to start to vet the whole of my life, everything from bank accounts, family, girlfriends, sex life and anything and everything they could to make sure I wasn't a blackmail risk. I was petrified.

As far as the Royal Navy was concerned, there was another issue I had to hide in order to protect my wish to serve and be a brilliant submariner. It was an issue that had no bearing on my work, an one that never for one day made me anything other than a 'splendid' member of our crew: I'm non-binary.

It dawned upon me that I could lose everything! And even worse, I could be sent to prison. Slowly but surely, everything started to unravel. I couldn't be myself anymore. I was having to cover my secret up and lie all the time. I wasn't deliberately lying, I just wasn't telling the whole truth. Now that all the training had finished, I had time to be myself and was curious to find out more about my sexuality, which had been pushed from view by the world we lived in then and to some extent live in today.

I remember the exact moment when I knew my name should've been Andrea. I can still picture it now. Aged 3, standing on the chair in my parents' bedroom looking out across the street, I knew I should've been a girl, I wanted to be a girl. That moment has been constantly with me ever since. It's the one consistency in my life and is something I'd always hidden and I'd never been caught out. Until now.

I was always playing dress up or borrowing my mum's clothes at every opportunity. I loved it, I had lots of girlfriends, preferring female company. I came from a very sheltered and strict family background. The only thing that mattered was work and you certainly didn't talk about sex or anything like that. I experienced so many negative and confusing messages, especially growing up and going through puberty and adolescence. In fact, puberty was the worst and the best time. I used to love cross dressing, and the only disappointment was that my mum had rubbish clothes and a wig. I wished I had a sister. I came alive when I dressed up, I loved the fabrics, the feel, it was so magical and, yes, there was a sexual excitement, but that's not what it was about. For those short moments, when the house was empty, I could parade around and be me. I had a great figure for it: slim, with great legs and no body hair. However, there was just one thing I couldn't do and that was to look at my face in the mirror when dressed as a boy again. It made me sad.

I tried to stop cross dressing several times, and even prayed, but I couldn't. I knew I wasn't gay, though, as I wasn't attracted to men. I just wanted to be feminine. In my teenage years, when all my friends were going out to the pub and chasing girls, I just wanted to dress up. I was more interested in their clothes, fashion and make-up. I didn't have anyone I could talk to or who would understand. Listening to everyone else, it seemed like people like me or gay people or anyone out of the norm should've been shot or put in prison, and I was now facing that fact. In the 70s and 80s there wasn't the understanding there is now around fluidity, bisexuality, transgenderism, pan-sexuality or just that people could have sex for enjoyment. Yet on the TV there were still stars like Liberace and Freddie Mercury and of course there was no internet back then. I couldn't get a girlfriend as I didn't know what to do as I couldn't take the lead, preferring to take their role instead. Why couldn't I stop and just be normal?

My head was spinning all the time, I was trapped and my thoughts were getting darker as I saw no way out. I couldn't continue. I wasn't sleeping, couldn't talk to anybody and was petrified of prison. The vetting was done in parts: they would send you the questions, you'd answer, then they'd interview you face-to-face and question your answers after they'd done initial investigations. These were all done by officers. It was brutal, they went in to everything especially around relationships, sex, type of sex, partners, when? Who? How many? What did you do? Are they related to anyone you suspect of being connected to USSR? It was just a barrage of questions upon questions. I couldn't take living a lie anymore and admitted that I was confused about my sexuality. I was only 20, with virtually no experience in life. I was petrified and knew I was going to lose everything, maybe even go to prison, but I hoped that I'd get help. The only other option in my head was far worse.

Following my admission, I was isolated from everyone and told not to say anything or I could go to prison. The doctors (all officers) recommended I went for psychiatric evaluation, so I was sent to the Royal Naval hospital at Haslar and spent several weeks in a psychiatric ward being evaluated and, as they called it, treated. I guess it was better than prison. Looking back, the Navy had already decided my fate, but I hoped that I wouldn't lose my job. I was filled with fear and shame. I'd told my secret and now I was having to tell it to everyone.

In the 80s you can't really call what happened to me a 'psychiatric evaluation'. I was put in a ward of people who were mentally ill, and because all the doctors were officers, whatever they said you had no other say or options. You'd have one-to-one sessions with them and communal sessions where everyone would be in a circle and made to talk about why they were there. The doctors would then feed back to you following the reports they received from the nurses and the sessions. Throughout the seven weeks I was there, I was told I could be cured if I listened to the doctors as they were qualified. I was told I wasn't trying hard enough to get better and was strongly advised (more like ordered) to tell my parents why I was in the psychiatric hospital (outed). You must remember that I was a petrified, ashamed 20-year-old who, three years before, had made my parents the proudest people in the world. Now I faced telling them my secret knowing I'd lost everything. I could picture the shame in their eyes and it broke my heart.

What was strange was that the doctors encouraged me to cross dress (in private, of course) and told me to explore myself. There were lots of sexually invasive questioning around masturbation and penetration; you name it, they asked. Again, I was constantly being told I could be cured and they that they knew what they were doing! The truth was they didn't and they weren't even listening to me. I'm just so pleased that they didn't try conversion therapy on me, which was also one of their options. They didn't seem to care and as soon as they had a statement from one of the sessions (I remember this most clearly as they asked for a copy of it), they told me I was going to be recommended for discharge for being 'Temperamentally Unsuitable'. I was escorted to the train, and even when I asked for help was told to 'get on the train otherwise I'd be put on a charge.' They had their statement and didn't care. I was a disgrace to them!

Back at Devonport, I was only allowed to talk to the doctors and my divisional officer; any contact with anyone from my boat or anybody else was forbidden. I don't think they knew what to do with me and were pissed as I'd passed the initial vetting. My engineering officer on my boat wanted me back as I was a good engineer, but I was just told to take leave and start getting ready to be discharged. Then, there was more humiliation as I had to request to be punished at captain's table to be discharged. In full uniform, I was marched like a criminal and charged. Again, there were more discussions about my sexuality and my medical statement, and I was told I was a disgrace to the Navy, my boat, my family, everybody and that it was all my own making. Ironically, both my statement, which they made a copy of, and the testimony at captain's table are NOT in my records. I know because I have them. I was told to hand all my kit over, was given a train ticket and told to leave. My last memory of the Navy was handing over my ID card to the quartermaster at the main gate and having to sign off for it with my papers. He looked at me and the papers and said, 'F*ck me mate, what've you done to deserve this?'

'Sorry, I can't say anything,' I replied. And that was that.

However, there was one final twist where I was told that if I was found to have mentioned to anyone outside about why I was discharged, I could be charged and sent to prison, even though I'd been discharged!

The early years beyond the Royal Navy were horrific. I went back to live with my parents, who told me that I couldn't mention anything to anyone. They lived in a small town up north, close to everyone who'd given me references to get into the Navy, who'd also been vetted too. I could feel and sense everyone's disappointment and shame and had a complete nervous breakdown. I couldn't get references for jobs as the first question they asked was, 'Why did you leave the Navy?' Everyone knew you had to serve four years from the age of 18, and I'd done just over three. With no reference, I had no job. Not that I was really able to work as I was in such a state. The Navy had broken me. The disgrace, being outed and being told it was all my fault. I wanted to die. The doctors prescribed me anti-depressants and put me on a waiting list to see a therapist. Therapy in the 80s around sexuality was like going back to the Dark Ages and I would probably only see someone once every six weeks or so. It was useless. In one session they gave me the book *The Joy of Sex* and told me to read it. That was it! Other times they would do group sessions, not in groups with people who were going through similar circumstances, no, but others who had all sort of mental issues, where they would sit you in a circle and get you to tell your story. Again, the therapist would tell me I wasn't trying hard enough and everything would come spiralling back. My parents would want to know every detail and then ask if they'd done anything wrong. I would hear them arguing about me all the time, until one day my father came and talked to me and told me that he wanted me to leave because I was splitting the family up; I was a complete embarrassment to them and everyone. In later years I did forgive my parents, but I never forgot what they said and never will.

Luckily, at that time, I met a couple of distant relatives who talked to me and advised me to look for work away from home. Little did I know that they'd change my life forever and if it wasn't for them, I wouldn't be writing my story today. They saved my life on numerous occasions and although my journey was a long battle, they gave me support that I'd never had before.

There were several times I felt suicidal. I was trying so hard, doing everything everyone was telling me. One therapist was actually close to signing me off on hormone tablets but then stopped seeing me, so I had to start all over again with a new therapist. Eventually, after years of on and off therapy, I was given a place at a specialist NHS clinic in London and they offered weekly sessions. 'Great,' I thought, 'progress'.

However, I remember one session where I sat down and saw the therapist in a knitted jumper his mum had probably made for him and I thought, 'You're weirder than I am,' and walked out. I never went back.

I tried to find my own way in the 90s and went to a couple of gay bars, but I didnt fit in and was called a 'prick tease'. I didn't fit in with girls and in straight bars, either. Was I gay but just trying to hide it? I knew I didn't fancy men so it was very confusing. I fancied women, but was more interested in what they were wearing and I couldn't take the lead. Everything was a mess and I hated myself. Around this time, while in London, I heard about the bombing of the *Admiral Duncan* pub, which I'd visited a few weeks before. One of my work colleges was killed that night and it was a stark reminder of the hatred for my kind, whoever my kind were. I'd had it with sexuality and emotions and feelings and everything that went with it, so decided I'd just be celibate. It just wasn't meant to be and it wasn't for me. I was so alone.

And that's how it was until 2012. My father was dying of dementia and, ironically, my family now wanted my help, as though nothing had happened. My father died in 2014 and I know he never got over the shame of me as he saw it. He never talked much but when he did, I could see disappointment in his eyes. Although the family asked me to leave, I forgave them many years later. Yes, I spoke to them and saw them on occasions, but my father's dementia brought us a bit closer. We'd never talk about the past, though. I still see my mother and we talk. It took time to forgive and I realise that despite being asked to leave the family, they did try and help financially where they could. It's still something that isn't really discussed, though. Deep down, I could see they both felt the blame and shame and I felt responsible. They tried in their own way to deal with the situation by asking me to leave; it was always about what the neighbours thought and how things looked to the outside. My mum's now 84 and we've discussed the Armed Forces Review, although not in great detail. My family never talked about it and her recollection of events are very sketchy, but the ban and the scars of how it was handled broke the family and myself.

I've now been seeing a therapist for the past twelve years on a week-by-week basis. I think I thought when I started that I could learn how to have a relationship and what to do, but after a few years, I realised I was actually learning about who I was. All the things in my head that I'd

257

blocked out just to survive. How I'd managed to survive such trauma, loneliness and abuse. I've now become a person; I understand Andy and Andrea and embrace and enjoy them both. I've no urge to transition now, but what happened in the Navy and in therapy left many scars and a lack of trust. I still get flashbacks but am learning and growing in confidence. I'm starting to feel pride for the service I was allowed to give in the short time I was in the Navy.

In August 2021 I suffered a major heart attack. It was hereditary, apparently, and there was nothing I could've done to prevent it, and it was actually my fitness that saved my life. I have three stents, and had I not had the heart attack, I wouldn't have been watching Remembrance Sunday on the TV for the first time. I'd always blocked it out as it was too upsetting, but there was Fighting With Pride on the TV. They did an article for the BBC and that's how this journey started. I'd no idea others suffered the way I did and I'm able to recollect the past and know it wasn't my fault. It's helped me come to terms with everything and myself. It's OK to be me. I am non-binary, I am fluid, I change on a daily basis. If I want to cross dress, I do, although as I've got older, this has become less frequent but can change. I have friends who I trust, who trust me and see me for myself. I'm sure one or two may not be convinced as everyone likes to pigeonhole, but who can blame them? I tried to pigeonhole myself. One day I can be incredibly feminine, other days I want a Viking or someone intelligent. I'm attracted to the person and not the gender and that can change just like that.

This traumatic journey has taught me so much. I've been through a lot and learnt a great deal. I've learnt to forgive, to love myself (although I'm still learning and need reminding at times), I've learnt to trust again, and even how to be physically close to someone. I don't mean sex, just proximity and who I am as a person. I've learnt how strong I am, I am a fighter. The Navy and the ban destroyed me, my family didn't want me, and I came back from the brink of suicide on several occasions. I retrained, got qualified, have been made redundant ten times in my career since the Navy, but I was strong enough to find a better job each time. Yes, there are regrets, I lost my job, my career and a dream which I still think about thirty-eight years on, as well as the disappointment of my father before he died. I'll probably never have a relationship but I can be close to people now. I didn't get a pension as I was discharged before being eligible, and I probably won't be able to buy a house as all my savings were used finding work and fighting to survive.

But for all this trauma and pain, there are still so many positives to take and to come. If none of this had happened, I wouldn't be able to write my story today. I know who Andy and Andrea are now and am starting to love myself. Many people in life never find who they are and allow themselves to be themselves. I'm still learning, which is fun, although can feel daunting. Physically, I don't have much, but to be able to learn and love who I am and know this journey is still happening is a blessing and shows the strength and courage I have in myself. To be someone I'm proud of. Ironically, isn't that what the Armed Forces are looking for? After all, it's not always the biggest and physically strongest who are the bravest and best.

My journey will continue, but there isn't a day I don't think of the time I served in the submarine service.

Chapter 25

The Shame of It All

Elaine McCrory

I was born in a small town in the backwaters of the west coast of Scotland in the early 1950s. I grew up with my mum and dad, two brothers and two sisters. My parents were of the Second World War generation, Dad having served in the Fleet Air Arm and Mum with the ATS. Nevertheless, there seemed no assumption that any of the five of us would join the Armed Forces. Our house was busy and during the school holidays, I enjoyed spending time with my aunt, with whom I was very close. She'd been an anti-aircraft ack-ack gunner and her stories of her time in the ATS seemed full of fun and excitement. Meanwhile, my uncle (her husband) was in the RAF.

After my schooling I went to work at Boots as a dispensing assistant. It was interesting at first, but over the years became more and more mundane. I lacked excitement in life. I wanted to see the world and became increasingly fed up, so after seven years with Boots, I felt an itch.

One day, on the way home with friends, we walked past the Armed Forces recruitment centre and in the window, I spied the cardboard cutouts of a sailor, soldier and airman. I was struck by the pale blue serge of the Royal Air Force uniform and on an impulse, we went in. I found a recruiter in a pale-blue uniform and arranged an interview. That day, I put in motion changes that would alter the course of my life. In the end, I was the only one of my friends who joined up.

In so many ways it was a bold move to leave Ayr, but it was time for me to find out what the world had to offer. I attested on 8 February 1976 and the next day boarded a train to Hereford, changing at Crewe. I'd been streamed to join the RAF Military Police, but everything in the

WRAF would be new to me and I'd decided to keep an open mind. On arrival at Hereford, a particularly scary sergeant met us at the station and ordered us on a bus. I didn't need telling twice and obediently scampered onboard. The training was difficult, with early mornings, late nights and long days filled with polishing, cleaning, running and all manner of physical activity, followed by more polishing and cleaning. There was never a chance of insomnia and each night, as my head hit the pillow, I breathed a long sigh of relief until the next day. In those days, I had a strong voice and wasn't short of an opinion, so the hardest lesson to learn was not to answer back! Still, I adapted, learned and found my place.

After about four weeks, I felt that the military police wasn't for me, so I asked to see my commanding officer. There were parts of my seven years at Boots that I'd enjoyed, not least the time talking to customers and working with medicine. I quite liked the idea of being a nurse, but was quickly told there was no room at the next intake for me. There were places in training for supply cooks, clerks and drivers none of which tickled my fancy, but the sergeant said that if I chose one of them, there might be a chance I could join the next intake for nursing later, so I plumped for being a driver. By the way, they lied!

After basic training, I went to St Athan for six weeks to learn driving skills and then to Shawbury for three years. However, I still had a wanderlust and was thrilled when a posting came through in 1979, sending me to Rheindalen. It was the height of the Cold War and there was tension, excitement and a hint of danger in our work. I loved it. Sometimes my trips took me to Berlin, where I drove down 'the corridor', a dual carriageway which divided East and West, complete with soldiers with machine guns on both sides of the road. If we broke down, we had special instructions to stay in the lorries until friendly forces rescued us. It was tense! At the time, there'd been IRA bombings in England, which added to the need for vigilance. We were always on our guard.

I'd had feelings about my sexuality prior to joining the WRAF. It was a time when it was just unacceptable practically anywhere, especially in my small, backward town and I had pushed my feelings into a closet. I'd had boyfriends in the RAF, but now I was in Germany, seeing other women having relationships with women meant my feelings came back to the surface.

I had a relationship (of convenience) with a woman for several months, but, just my luck, she was posted back to the UK and I was left alone again in Germany. Towards the end of 1980, I was told my new posting would be to Brize Norton and that I'd be promoted to corporal. I was incredibly happy and proud that I'd been promoted, but that happiness didn't last long.

I arrived at Brize in early February 1981 and in all honesty, my first few days there were a bit of a haze; my day-to-day existence seems out of the reach of my memory. What I do remember, however, is that when the crate with my personal effects arrived at the base, all hell broke loose.

I was interviewed, sorry, interrogated, by the SIB and told my room and personal effects would be searched and examined at great length. It was quite clear it'd come to their attention that I was a lesbian, or words to that effect. I don't remember what happened and in what order, but I was cross examined, humiliated, asked about how I had sex with a woman and told that maybe I just needed a good man. It was a shaming process done with no care or regard for me as a servicewoman or even a human being.

Of course, I denied everything, but they found some very incriminating evidence in my personal effects and eventually I confessed. They then had the audacity to tell me to give them names of other lesbians I knew about, which I declined to do and told them to do their own dirty work!

According to my discharge papers, I was discharged on 20 June 1981 on grounds of QR607(22)B (Queens Regulations). I had no idea what that meant at the time, but I later learned it meant I'd been discharged for 'other circumstances beyond his or her control'. I'm not sure whether that was a good thing or a bad thing.

Brimming with feelings of humiliation and shame, I couldn't go home to Scotland after my discharge, so for about six months I lied to my family and said I'd bought myself out and had got myself a job in England. To this day, my family still don't know I was discharged for being gay, even though I'm well and truly out of the closet. For many years now I've lived abroad with my wonderful wife, geographically apart from some difficult memories. Europe is an amazing and welcoming place to live and is where I've found some peace in life. As for the past, much of it is hidden in a box in my mind, tied up with string. Perhaps one day, when it feels safe, I might undo the knot.

Chapter 26

Guilty Until Proven Innocent

—————— An Airman's Story ——————

It was twilight, the trees were rustling in the graveyard. I was sitting in the shadow of an old oak, with a bottle of malt and a random over-the-counter packet of drugs. I remember making a point of wearing layers as there was a cold wind on that night, and I wanted to stay warm, until I eventually fell asleep.

I'd left the military only days before and was at my lowest ebb ever. I'd spent the previous twelve years serving my country and felt completely deflated; some of my feelings were no doubt attributable to the trials and tribulations of military service, such as serving in theatres of war, but the way I was feeling on that evening was because of the treatment meted out to me during my time served, because I was gay. In that moment I felt like an absolute, unadulterated freak.

Serving in the British Armed Forces before January 2000 was a great honour, unless you were homosexual, because if you were, then you were a criminal.

Although my service had been peppered with bouts of bullying, that final year had been the worst of my career and had led me to that quiet corner of a secluded, ancient graveyard, in order to go to sleep. It was a bleak mid-February and I was 30 years old.

As a young child, I always felt that I was more female. I looked, walked and spoke like a female, and it felt so natural for me to play with dolls as opposed to an action man or a football.

I very quickly fell victim to name calling from other, older children; names the likes of which I was too young to comprehend, such as poofy, sissy, tramp, freaky and pansy. My only realisation of these names being unkind was the reaction of my protective family members, who were distressed at the regularity of hearing them.

I was a late child and my siblings were a lot older than me. My parents and many other family members were ex-military and worked hard to support the family. Time was always put aside for recreation and I spent a lot of time with my dad on day trips. I have vague memories of these times, but I know they were happy. As I got older, I started to recognise the hostility more and more, but I still didn't comprehend why it was happening. The days out with my dad were an escape for me, I was just 5 years old.

It was on a dark November night that the knock came. I was sitting by the fire, probably playing with a toy, or watching TV, awaiting my dad returning from exercising my new Labrador pup. The rest of my memory of this time is very vague and hazy, although the knock on this night, wasn't my dad returning home but a policeman delivering the news to my mum that Dad had just been killed in a road accident while walking the dog. The main man and protector in my life had gone in a matter of minutes.

At this point, my father's father, my grandad, stepped into the void left by this horrific loss as my protector from the harm caused by others, but his heart was quite literally broken by the loss of his son; he succumbed to a heart attack and died just a few months later. Once again, I was without the main man and protector in my life.

I've mixed memories of my early school years, but there were some good times and good laughs with pupils in my class, who'd become used to my characteristics. Beyond this circle of safety, however, my life was plagued with bullying from other kids, and sometimes adults as well. It was around this period, when I was about 7, that I suffered the first of many physical attacks and was left bruised, bloodied and sore.

The negativity stemmed from being an extremely effeminate boy, who everyone – and I mean everyone – assumed without a shimmer of a doubt was a girl. Why would they think any different? It was exactly how I was feeling, too.

I started to take solace in food, particularly junk food. This was something that I'd always struggle with. As my weight increased, there was an additional target on my back.

When I was 8, my mother met my future stepfather. A veteran of the Second World War, he was a professional man who worked hard, but he was strict. I didn't take to his stricter ways easily back then, but looking back in hindsight, this strictness was inadvertently setting me up for my military days.

As I reached the age for attending high school, I remember my growing sense of angst and sleepless nights, knowing that I'd have to endure a new period of enhanced harassment in a new school. I clung to a glimmer of hope that this might not happen, but sadly, I wasn't to be so lucky.

There were periods during these formative years, particularly in my early teens, that the bullying became so bad that I prayed to God for help. As I reached my mid-teens, the femininity that had plagued me all my life slowly seemed to disappear. I was becoming more masculine. If you, the reader, are confused about this, you're not alone. I'm also just as confused as you. But it happened.

Seemingly, because I was less feminine, the bullying subsided for the most part, but I struggled to settle in my first four years of high school and decided that I'd remain for a fifth and sixth year to gain some proper qualifications and the chance of a decent job.

I was about 16 when I decided that I wanted to join the Armed Forces and serve my country. I also saw this as an ideal opportunity to remove myself from the theatre of my own personal war. Although by now I knew I was more attracted to men, I was still at an age where I was a little confused because I also had some feelings towards women.

During the recruitment process for the Royal Air Force, I've no memory of homosexuality even being mentioned, let alone being informed it was illegal. At my attestation I swore allegiance to the Crown and joined the RAF, I was 18 years old. I remember being very optimistic, seeing this as a new beginning and the chance to rid myself of those ominous memories and the trauma and psychological turmoil of my formative years. Basic training was in Lincolnshire and involved six weeks of 'shock to the system' basic training for us raw recruits, where we quickly learned that working as a team made the training easier to endure. There was little time for any hostilities towards each other. Not so for some of the training staff, though, who devised the name Gloria for me, which I ignored because I was too preoccupied with concentrating on the training. This was the very first indication of things to come.

It was during these weeks of training that I met my first girlfriend. She was a lovely person, but I simultaneously came to realise that I was predominantly attracted to men. I went through the motions of a courtship with her, but it didn't feel natural for me. The relationship didn't last long, and although I was saddened, I was also relieved when it was over.

The next phase of training was when I suffered my first homophobic attack. It was during the wee small hours one night, while I lay in the twilight zone between being awake and asleep. I heard the distant muffled voices of the braying mob of three drunken men: serving personnel attending a training course at the base. They burst into our multi-man room looking for an individual who apparently had upset one of them earlier in the day. The individual they sought happened to be in the bed next to mine. He was defenceless and evidently terrified. When I instinctively stood up to the men, trying to protect this lad, they must've been able to sense my femininity, and so turned their aggression on me. I was kicked and punched, while my bed space and wardrobe, which contained my carefully prepared uniform for the following morning's inspection, was ransacked. I was left in a crumpled heap on the floor as they disappeared, laughing. I couldn't cry, though; I don't think I had any tears left in me to cry by this stage of my life. As with all the previous incidents that had happened to me, I never reported this incident. In hindsight – and knowing what I know now – it would probably have just been swept under the carpet anyway.

As you can probably imagine, it's difficult for me to recount everything that happened to me during the twelve years I'd signed up to serve. There were many good times and I met and worked with amazing people that allowed me many occasions to revel in the medicine of laughter, which kept me sane.

But there were bad times, too, and despite the human mind having a natural function for deleting harmful memories in self-preservation, there are still some dark reminiscences that remain. The detail and chronology of some of these, I will recall as best I can for you.

My first posting was in London. A great first posting and the reason I was always skint. During my two years in London, I allowed myself to become intimately involved with a few lovely ladies, in part because this was what we, as men, were expected to do. I was a young man in the prime of my life, why would I not be loving life around these beautiful ladies? And besides, what was the alternative? Having intimacy with any women never, ever, felt natural for me, but I was to venture deeper and deeper into the unnerving and somber gloom of the closet. It wasn't long before the tentacles of gossip began to spread about me being disinterested in women and that I might be gay.

I was rudely awakened one afternoon by a bang on the door. Before I could get out of my bed, two policemen had acrimoniously invited themselves into my room, informing me that I was suspected of – and being investigated for – being homosexual. I was 20 years old, terrified and innocent. Had the opportunity arisen for me to have had sexual relations with another man, I would've been far too afraid to have pursued the object of my very human desires. The RAF police searched my room, which was a basic barrack room containing a bed and a wardrobe from the Jurassic period. I was then hauled into the police guardroom for questioning. Although there was nothing they could get me for, the mud was already thrown and it stuck!

Word got out and a few nights later, at the end of the night, I was ambushed in the NAAFI by a bunch of drunk guys who I'd not seen before. I fought back, but given the unfair ratio in numbers, I was overcome, beaten and stripped of my clothes. I never reported this. I just buried it away in my mind, in the growing cache of hurt.

It was in these years that I started drinking heavily. Partly as a form of self-medication, but also for Dutch courage that enabled me to get drunk and act up as the class clown; the village idiot, if you will. I thought that if I could make people laugh, then this would act as a cover and divert attention from my lack of interest in women. My theory appeared to work, but unbeknownst to me, my wayward behaviour was laying the foundations for the destruction of my career.

My next posting was an operational posting to Germany. I was now working with a lot more people, most of whom were great, although I felt under enormous pressure to hide who I was. I was becoming known for my sense of humour and drunken antics, but speculative gossip and rumours were still rife.

On the base there were a couple of separate incidents where people were caught in gay and lesbian relationships. In both cases, the British media were invited over from the UK because this was apparently worthy of headline news. These unfortunate people were sent back to the UK to face their impending doom. I've never seen anyone treated so badly. This this kind of behaviour towards humans is illegal in the civilised world, but back in the dark ages of the 1990s it was permissible, especially when aimed at military personnel who were even remotely suspected of being homosexual. As a very young gay guy in my early twenties, who was already living a life of anxiety and fear, the fate of these unfortunate people had a profound impact upon me.

At that time, the Irish Republican Army (IRA) had an active campaign against the British Forces in mainland Europe, with a few military personnel killed and maimed. This in itself caused a lot of trepidation and fear amongst everyone serving there. Leaving our bases on a daily basis made us moving targets and it scared me no end.

August 1990 saw Iraq invade Kuwait and the start of Operation Desert Shield, which was effectively the gradual buildup of British, American and Allied troops in the Persian Gulf. It was the prelude to Operation Desert Storm; the first Gulf War. I served in this war, but due to my mental health becoming increasingly worse by this time, inclusive of the constant strain that I was under in my personal life, I remember being totally indifferent as to whether I'd survive.

It's difficult to say, because some people may not understand, but I actually thrived on being in the Gulf, even with the constant dangers and risk of potential death. Women weren't allowed to serve in Saudi Arabia at the time due to the strict Islamic laws, which gave me a few months of respite. Although I had some good friends serving in the Women's Royal Air Force (WRAF), by now I'd developed a real psychological fear of women in general, seeing them as a threat and the cause of my life of misery. I hated myself for feeling this way.

During my time serving in this theatre of war, all my excess body weight had melted away and I was fighting fit. On my return from the Gulf, I should have been having the best time of my life because I was still in my prime, however, this made the nightmare even worse! I was getting extra, unwanted attention from some women, which was only adding to my angst. Consequently, I decided to make a conscious effort to put on weight, so that I could once again cocoon myself in a blanket of fat in the hope that no woman would find me attractive.

The next couple of years of service were daunting, particularly my last year in Germany. Even my outlandish facade of getting drunk and doing stupid, career-destroying things, was wearing thin. I was clutching at straws now, anticipating another dreaded knock on my door by the police at any given moment. In my desperation, I made one last feeble ditched attempt to convince people that the only reason I didn't want a girlfriend was because I had one back home. Luckily, I did have a platonic female friend at the time who would send me the odd photo. Little did she know she was actually my surrogate partner. We laugh about it now, but my actions were imperative to my survival back then, although not everyone remained convinced.

My depression was the lowest it had ever been, not least because I couldn't seek any help for it; there wasn't the empathy back then for mental health issues, particularly for people like me.

More and more sheeple were gradually turning against me. Even some friends, who'd once offered me camaraderie and comfort, were turning their backs on me. Nobody wanted to be associated with someone perceived as being gay, because for them to show any mercy or understanding would cause them to be suspected too.

I was called names and there were the unfamiliar faces who'd often point, giggle and whisper as I passed. The suffocation of me feeling ostracised to this extent caused me sheer, arduous sadness, similar to what I suffered as a child, bringing back all the same perturbation and foreboding.

On one occasion, when I was out, I forgot to lock my room door and when I returned, I found my room had been trashed and my belongings thrown outside and strewn on the muddy grass in the heavy rain. Another time, as I lay cowering in my room, pretending not to be in so that I didn't have to answer my door to the same drunken gang, I could hear them sitting in the corridor with their cargo of alcohol, laughing and sharing ideas about what they could do to me. It's important to say that these people weren't personnel from my own workplace, but from a couple of other trades. Such was the nature of how rumours would spread, however, and some of the accommodation blocks had a mixture of personnel. Although I was no push over and could handle myself, I'd learned the hard way over the years that going up against more than one or two people at a time would inevitably end in defeat for me.

269

It was around this time that I contemplated suicide for the first time. I bought a packet of some kind of tablets, along with a bottle of vodka. I ventured into the woodland that adorned our base, ate a handful of the tablets, then drank as much vodka as fast as I could. I was terrified and didn't want to die but could see no other way out. I eventually became drowsy and fell asleep.

I've no idea why, but I woke up a few hours later with nothing more than extreme nausea and a hangover from hell. I was very weak. My suicide attempt hadn't worked. I was devastated, although I kept this incident under wraps.

The next four and a half years saw me serving in the beautiful, majestic countryside of Oxfordshire, just on the edge of the Cotswolds, although the first few months there were fraught with difficulties thanks to the hype that preceded me. Eventually, I was able to win over the hearts and minds of most of my colleagues and was able to settle into having probably the best years of my whole service.

However, as I've already mentioned, it was difficult for me initially. After the harrowing previous few years, and certainly the agony of the year I'd just come through, I was at the stage where I'd had enough. It was like my mind was giving up the ghost; I couldn't take any more abuse, or being treated differently. I was starting to think of an escape plan. I wanted out! My mind was starting to think irrationally and devised a plan to fly to the USA and start a new life.

A few days later I flew to North America, where I went by Greyhound bus on a whistle-stop tour of certain states, trying to find work and accommodation. Had I been successful in my quest, my plan was to remain there indefinitely. Sure, this would've meant I was committing desertion, and I would be unable to return to the UK, but at the time, this was the lesser of two evils. It wasn't long, however, before I realised my plans were proving futile, so I reluctantly returned to the UK.

By now I was officially Absent Without Leave (AWOL). Despite this, I remained steadfast in my plans to escape and took myself up to the Scottish Highlands. I was planning on living wild for as long as I could, but the subzero temperatures quickly put paid to that and I returned to civilisation. The next couple of weeks saw me living rough and sofa surfing, before I eventually handed myself in to the authorities.

As a result of my subsequent disciplinary hearing, I was incarcerated in military prison as punishment for my time away.

If it were up to me, I would've completed the rest of my service on the base where I was currently serving. The nature of the work, and the amazing people whom I met and worked with, created some of the best memories I have in life. To this day, these tremendous memories help me to cope better with the rest of the ferment and tohubohu that I had to suffer.

Unfortunately, I had to serve out my final year at another base.

While I will reiterate that, as was always the case – at least initially – before some people succumbed to their own fears and peer pressure, most of my colleagues throughout my whole career were good, wholesome, caring people to be around, and to work with. There were unfortunately always one or two who took a distinct disliking to me, and who did everything in their power to make my life even more of a misery than it already was. This was never more evident than in my final year of service.

The hot summer of 1997 was an enjoyable one. I had become naturally hardened to whatever occasional, derogatory comments were being aimed my way. Or so I thought. After taking it upon myself to do some basic research on the psychology of bullying, I started taking a little refuge in the fact that the act of bullying was universally and generally accepted as a personal issue with the perpetrator and not the victim.

I spent all that summer training hard, physically and psychologically preparing myself for completing my service. The end date was imminent and was due to happen early the following year. If things had been different, and there was no such draconian law in place banning homosexuals from serving in the military, then I would've gladly signed on to extend my contract. This would've allowed me to have continued to serve the country I love proudly, doing a job I loved. I'm confident I'd have gone on to have had a very successful career, and I probably would still be serving to this day, albeit fast approaching retirement.

Sadly, this wasn't to be the case. After my lived experience, and even though sheer grit and determination had got me through it, enabling me to complete my contract in the face of adversity, I was now completely and psychologically drained.

The untimely and horrific death of Princes Diana in summer 1997 was the first of the final two nails in my military coffin. The second came in the form of the harassment I faced on one final, major field exercise.

Without going into the full parameters, not least because the memory of it is too much, given everything else I've had to conjure up for this memoir (as well as the limited space in this book), in a nutshell, someone I worked with, and had a falling out with, thought it'd be funny to spread more lies and rumours about me.

This particular exercise involved working with a lot of unfamiliar personnel and such was the ensuing shit that I had to put up with, including threats to attack me in my tent as I slept, I had to all but sleep with one eye open on a nightly basis. I was also told I was going to be attacked in the makeshift shower Porto cabin, causing me to refrain from using the showers full stop.

I kept thinking of ways I could get myself to safety. I pretended to be ill, which afforded me the safety of the medical tent for a couple of days and nights. I even got drunk one night and purposely swore at, and threatened, two RAF policemen out on patrol. At least I was assured the safety of a night locked in the guardroom, as well as the inevitable charge I'd have to face when back in the UK.

On the final couple of days, as we were driving in convoy back to the UK, we had to park up at the docks somewhere in Holland overnight, before we boarded the ferry in the morning. By this stage hardly anyone was speaking to me. Apart from the occasional, discrete sympathetic look from an individual, which proved paramount in giving me some hope, I literally was made to feel alone in the universe. Everyone was scared to be seen having any form of conversation with me in case they, too, were suspected of being gay.

As we all battened down the hatches in our individual wagons to catch some shuteye for the night, I was suddenly startled by a knock on the window of my cab. It was a stranger I'd never clapped eyes on before, or since. However, he had a stern warning for me, saying I had to be on my guard because he'd heard it on good authority that there was a mob planning on doing some real damage to me, before throwing me into the sea. After this, the mysterious guy just disappeared into the night as quickly as he'd arrived.

There was no way I could sleep now. Even though I was absolutely exhausted, and even if it was an idle threat, or some kind of hoax, I knew that I couldn't succumb to any slumber and wasn't prepared to take any chances. Luckily, I had some pro-plus, over-the-counter caffeine tablets in my pocket. I devoured the lot.

I sat up with eyes like a rabbit in headlights all night. Every minuscule noise from outside was amplified. It was the longest night of my life but eventually, the cold light of dawn was upon us and it was time to board the ferry. During the voyage, I found a quiet corner and managed to catch an hour's sleep. I'll never know how I managed to drive the truck the 150 miles back to base safely without falling asleep at the wheel. I'm sure there must have been some divine intervention.

Everyone involved in the exercise was granted seven days' leave for the following week. I'd made plans to go home but was physically and mentally incapable of doing anything. I couldn't eat and literally lay like a zombie on my bed in the barrack block the whole time, unable to move, segueing in and out of catnaps. I forced myself to drink water, because I knew I had to. When I explained this to my psychiatrist many years later, he informed me this was my first experience of PTSD.

I completed the last couple of months of my twelve-year contract in a very gingerly manner. I was a broken man. All I'd done was go to work everyday then back to my room; I had no interest in socialising with anyone anymore. I trusted no one and couldn't wait to leave. I never even attended my own leaving do! On my final day, I was out of those gates like a racing greyhound out of a trap, or at least as fast as my car would take me.

That was me done.

So, while I sat in the graveyard on that night I mentioned at the start of this narrative, poised and ready to go to sleep, overpowering thoughts of what the devastating effect of me killing myself would have on others overwhelmed me and thus prevented me from carrying it out. Had it not been for those sobering thoughts, I wouldn't be here now writing this, telling you what life could be like for innocent people who were persecuted for their natural love and attraction to members of the same sex.

I was one of the lucky ones: far too many of my comrades in arms who were caught and treated abhorrently were dismissed in disgrace, losing everything, including their medals they'd so gallantly earned. They're the brave men and women for whom the reparations are in place, these are the valorous veterans who deserve to be compensated for their experiences and loss.

The ironic concept of all the negativity I'd gone through during the previous twelve years was literally founded in dangerous lies, gossip and rumours spread by a very small minority, but it only ever takes one or two bad apples to ruin a barrel. Although there'd been ample opportunity for me to become involved in cloak and dagger relationships with other men, I couldn't find that courage. I was far too afraid of being caught. I was robbed of the best years of my life, all the time bearing witness to the heterosexuals who were free to enjoy the natural functions of life and love, while us homosexuals had to live a life of separation, isolation and desolation.

As a result of those years, I've undergone psychotherapy and have regular visits with my psychiatrist. I'm on a cocktail of medication, including antidepressants, anti-anxiety tablets and antipsychotics. However, as a psychiatrist once told me, all the trauma that happened to me during these first thirty years of my life would be the hardest trauma to treat, if at all, and can often only be managed.

My complex PTS depression has caused me to struggle with holding down careers. I've honed a couple of criminal convictions for aggression-related incidents. I self-medicated with alcohol and drugs for years and have serious trust issues, which has affected my ability to have proper relations with people, including friends, family and partners.

It's too late for me now; the damage to me is done.

Anyone reading this who may be in a situation wherein you're the victim of bullying or harassment, my advice to you would be to deal with it as best you can now. Seek help and remove yourself from the situation where possible. Don't make the same mistakes I did and bottle it all up inside. There's always hope.

My message to any perpetrator of bullying and harassment is to reread this story, then read it again. Think about the impact your actions are potentially having on other innocent people, then think again!

Having the power to be a bully, and choosing not to be, is to have real power.

Having the ability to respect difference is one of life's greatest accolades.

Sticks and stones will, of course, break your bones, but names will always hurt you!

Chapter 27

Last Man Out

—————— Charlie Brown ——————

It was a freezing cold mid-February morning on a British air base close to the Dutch border in Germany. I, a very experienced sergeant technician and a young mechanic were just completing a last-minute, pre-flight repair to a multi-million pound Tornado jet in one of the bombproof shelters that were a legacy of the Cold War on airfields all over Europe. I heard a Land Rover approach and enter through the open clamshell doors into the armoured lair of our swing-wing bomber and watched as a very good friend of mine climbed out. I could see by the look on his face that something was wrong.

'Charlie, you've got to go and see the squadron warrant officer. Now, mate!'

There was a feeling like a thump in the stomach and an icy shiver went down my spine that was far more piercing than the chill of the wind blowing across this bleak airfield on the North German plain, and I knew that the half-metre thick reinforced concrete walls and huge steel-plated blast doors of this Hardened Aircraft Shelter couldn't protect me from the bombshell that was about to explode.

I'd been expecting this moment, or something like it, for some time and knew the cat was very much out of the bag now. This was going to be the day of days and nothing would ever be the same again.

I was born in an East Yorkshire market town near Hull in 1963. My father was an engineer at a local aircraft factory and had worked there since leaving school in 1933, including during the war years. He'd met my mother, who was also employed there as an aircraft fitter (and later a supervisor/inspector), in the 1950s. There was clearly going to be aviation in my blood!

I had a pretty normal childhood. I wasn't really an underachiever, but nor was I going to excel in either academics or sports at school. I experienced a very mild amount of what I'd call bullying: my mates and I were pretty unappetising prey in the playground and I just blended in with the other nerds.

Those aeronautical genes of mine were, however, developing from an early age. I was mad crazy about everything connected to aircraft and flying from my preschool days. The 1960s being the era of Apollo and the first moon landing meant I was glued to our black and white television for the coverage of those early missions into space.

At the age of 13 my dad enrolled me into the Air Cadet squadron based at the factory where he still worked. The Air Training Corps (ATC) was to transform my early life because in it I found something I had a real interest in, and that I was actually pretty good at.

I was aware that the other teenagers around me were developing physically, both at school and in my Air Cadet squadron. I was also aware that I was behind most of those who were the same age as me. I was unaware of any sexual thoughts about girls or boys at this time. I had a good group of friends at school, we still played rough and tumble, and hunted rats and rabbits with our air rifles, but I could also be quite content in my own company, searching for gemstones or fossils on a lonely beach or designing and building something in my dad's garage.

I think I'd realised at the age of about 14 that I wanted to join the Royal Air Force and with just three weeks of the 1970s remaining, I attended the RAF Careers Office in Hull and swore my allegiance to queen and country. That evening, I handed in my Air Training Corps uniform and the following morning took a train to begin a whole new chapter of my life.

I got through the six weeks of basic training during the December and January of 1979/80, although the cold, dark, early morning starts and being shouted at were a bit of a shock to the system. I did have a few advantages over some of my fellow recruits from my experiences in the Air Cadets, such as some general service knowledge about the RAF and perhaps how to polish (or 'bull') boots and shoes to a high gloss.

My passing out parade was attended by both of my parents. They were very proud, but I can remember seeing my dad shivering in the bitter cold as we waited to part company after the post-parade drinks in the 'Newcomer's Club' bar. Afterwards, I was going directly to start my trade training at a large RAF Technical School near London.

RAF Halton nestles in the picturesque Chiltern Hills. We arrived on a freezing cold, late January night, to hear the scream of 'Get off this fucking bus!' We were split into groups; I was to train as an airframe mechanic (known as a 'rigger' in the RAF). Meanwhile, the 'sooties' and 'leckies' (engine fitters and electricians) went to a different part of the school. However, about thirty of us were to be employed doing menial tasks for a month until the next 'rigger mechanic' course was due to start. Why we weren't given a week or two's leave on completion of our recruit training is still a mystery, but I think we were getting our first lesson in the age-old military art of 'Hurry up and Wait'.

We were put under the control of a flight sergeant from a completely different part of the technical school. He was a kindly guy and we were treated to discreet early finishes on Friday lunchtimes, especially if we had train tickets to travel any distance. I think he even let one lad from Scotland scoot off on a Thursday afternoon after work. However, this easy life came to an abrupt halt when our airframe course started four weeks later. Now it was back to being screamed at every morning to parade and marched from the accommodation area to the training hangars and workshops. We were often kept back until the designated cease work time on a Friday, which made getting home on the train very difficult and consequently, many weekends were spent on camp. When I could, a mate from Leeds and I sometimes travelled up to Yorkshire on the train together. Some weekends we'd go to his parents in Leeds, and on others we'd go to mine in Hull. They were always short weekends, arriving late on a Friday night and departing again on the Sunday morning. I also had a friend from London and I think for the first time in my life I started to have confusing feelings about our friendship. Nothing ever happened between us, perhaps they were purely feelings from my side? There was something stirring inside me, but whatever it was, my focus was upon learning the ways of the RAF.

I finished my trade training and was next posted to a flying training base in Yorkshire. I obviously wasn't going to be doing any flying training, but these were the type of aircraft that I was going to cut my teeth on in the 'real' RAF.

I was to share this first day entering productive service with another new RAF recruit: the Panavia Tornado, a brand new high-tech, multi-role attack aircraft that was also the new kid on the block on 1 July 1980.

If recruit and mechanic training were new to me, working in an aircraft servicing hangar with about 100 other mechanics and technicians was a bit bewildering at first. I was assigned to a team with a sergeant, who came from the same place as I did. I didn't get an easy ride, but as the youngest lad in the entire hangar, I did receive an element of protection from him.

I became good friends with another mechanic I worked with, who was about six months older than me. We started to become close and I remember starting to have feelings about him. These weren't necessarily sexual feelings, but I wanted to be close to him and when I was, my heart beat differently. It was a new sensation for me and I somehow knew I had to keep it to myself.

The two of us spent many weekends at the base together, we didn't have a lot of money and a typical Saturday or Sunday lunchtime was a few pints in the NAAFI, then back to one of our rooms to listen to music (neither of us had a television). We both shared rooms with three other guys, but at weekends we very often had our rooms to ourselves. I was probably 17 and a half the first time we were physical together. It wasn't sexual to begin with, just wrestling that turned into a kind of passionate holding of each other. I can still remember the pounding of our hearts as we embraced. No words were ever said, but I remember if we heard the slightest noise of footsteps in the corridor outside, we instantly disengaged our hold.

It wasn't long before this relationship turned sexual. It went on for a year or two, and we were both very pretty careful and very discreet. There was the odd occasion when we almost got caught, although I think there was an element of thrill in the risk of this. I can honestly say that nobody knew about us, but we had to be very, very careful, especially as we were close at work, too. My friend had a girlfriend at home, but I only had one person on my mind. I knew we felt differently about each other and I think I was aware that this was going to cause me pain.

Not for one moment did I consider myself to be gay! This was just something my best buddy and I did when we were alone together, especially after a few beers. Gay was something totally different. There was apparently a pub in the local town where those people hung out; I'd certainly never been there and had no intention of doing so. But I did know that if my friend and I were caught together or even suspected of doing what we did, we'd be in deep shit, deeper than anything I could imagine and with implications reaching deep into our lives. Despite this, the feelings I had made the risk feel worthwhile.

When my friend was posted away, I missed him hugely but knew our friendship could be nothing more than a friendship.

I was now working with a group of lads who were all around the same age as I was (between 18 and 21). We worked as a pack and after work we played the same way; we were quite hard drinkers. I did have a friend among them that I felt differently about, but although we were close pals, I knew in this case, it was only me who had feelings deeper than just 'mates' and I'd begun to accept this was just how things had to be.

I was selected for further training and advanced to the rank of junior technician. As I neared the end of this course, any choice for a specific geographical area for my next posting appeared pointless because the RAF had their own ideas. The Tornado was entering squadron service in great numbers now, both in the UK and Germany, and they needed to equip these squadrons with technicians, as well as pilots and navigators. This meant I was posted to a very busy unit in East Anglia where the aircrew who'd already learnt how to 'fly' the Tornado were training to 'fight' it.

Again, I found myself as part of a hard-working and hard-drinking crew. My personality was evolving and I was becoming a bit too confident. I'd been riding motorcycles for a few years now and they were starting to get faster and more expensive. I was letting myself slip into debt and dangerous behaviour out of work. Perhaps I was trying to make up for a part of my life that was missing?

Luckily, after a few years, I found myself posted to Germany and a 'front line' Tornado squadron. This was the height of the Cold War and the squadron was the UK's contribution should the war turn hot! It was also a new start for me, so I tried to reset the faults that had started to develop.

We were based close to the Dutch border, so visits to the many sex shops in the local town were quite common when out with the lads on a Saturday afternoon. I had to be very wary where my eyes strayed to when in the magazine or video section, but sometimes I'd head into the Netherlands alone where I'd do more than just look. I just had to be careful bringing anything back onto base in Germany and equally careful where I hid my secret porn collection.

I still didn't accept that I was actually gay, but I was starting to realise that this wasn't a passing phase. By now, I'd reached the rank of corporal and had a small team of lads to supervise at work and to lead astray in the bar at night and on weekends. Ironically, my little gang became known as 'Charlie's Angels'.

I spent four fantastic years in Germany, travelling all over the world with the squadron. I had many friends among the aircrew right up to the squadron 'boss'. We were an amazing team and in 1991, were called upon to be used in anger! This wasn't to be the war we'd trained for, however, the Armageddon of a confrontation with the Warsaw Pact in Central Europe, but a far-flung conflict in the Middle East. I was initially seconded to another squadron to deploy to Bahrain shortly after Saddam Hussain's invasion of nearby Kuwait. I spent three months operating there, practising doing our tasks on the jets in full chemical protection gear and in temperatures we certainly weren't used to. I think we all knew this was going to end up as a war, and unsurprisingly, my now elderly parents were very worried for my safety.

I returned from Bahrain in late November 1990 but deployed again with my own squadron to Saudi Arabia the day after Boxing Day. We were now under no illusion that this was going to end up with 'our' aircrew mates flying offensive operations deep into Iraq once the United Nation's ultimatum for Saddam to pull his forces from Kuwait had expired.

I'm not going to go into graphic details about the war, but it was one of the most significant experiences of my life. My friends and I went through every range of emotions on the spectrum, from the highest high to the lowest low. We discovered the incredible bonds of comradeship often found by those who've experienced armed conflict. Real Band of Brothers stuff. We also felt the crushing loss of colleagues who were never to return home with us.

After the war in the Gulf, the world changed for me. I struggled to find anything else as fulfilling and after a short posting to a base near

Dundee, I needed some excitement in my service life, so I applied and was posted to a helicopter squadron in the trouble-torn province of Northern Ireland.

The life of a helicopter squadron in Northern Ireland was very different to that of a fast Jet one, but the guys were the same as ever and the shifts at work were long. Outside of work, I also discovered motorcycle road racing and started to visit the Isle of Man to watch the world-famous TT Races.

For the first time in adult my life, I found a place I could go to and not be in the RAF. My Pandora's Box was shut, but now in my early thirties, I'd worked out what it contained but wasn't yet prepared to confront it. I was starting to get used to the idea that I was probably gay and that it wasn't going to go away. In the Isle of Man, I met people who I started to feel would accept me for whoever or whatever I was and so I visited more and more, not just for the TT Races. I started to realise that I needed to live my life and that wasn't just my life in the RAF, but a private and personal life as well.

Back in Northern Ireland, the news came through that I was to be promoted to sergeant and assigned to a Tornado squadron in Scotland. However, soon after this news, I noticed some administrative indicators that made it look as if there was another and very imminent posting on the horizon. This one involved another tour in Germany and, more than that, it was to be on the same squadron I'd gone to war with back in 1991.

I settled into life back in Germany reasonably easily, although it was a very different Germany to the one that I'd known before. The was no more Cold War, no more nuclear weapons, just the now regular deployments to the Middle East with our Tornados policing the 'No Fly Zones' over Northern and Southern Iraq.

I decided to be honest and tell a good mate on the squadron that I was gay. We'd known each other for years and although he was 'straight', I knew he'd be cool with it and would keep my secret. We often went into the Netherlands at the weekend and sometimes strayed as far as Amsterdam. It was in this big city that I discovered there was such a thing as male prostitution and so my mate would cover for me for an hour or two as I went to a different part of the city to seek some intimate company. 'Charlie's just slipped off to visit an old friend on the other side of town', he'd say. 'He'll meet back up with us in the next pub.'

These simple, string-free encounters freed me of any effort to try to actually form a relationship; a skill I'd never had the opportunity to practice.

One day, I received the news that my dad had suffered a massive heart attack. The RAF pulled out all the stops to get me home as a priority compassionate case, which involved a flight from Düsseldorf to Amsterdam, Amsterdam to Humberside Airport and taxi to the hospital. I made it there in time, but knew he wasn't going to survive for long. My mother had her sister and nieces around her, while I was like a fish out of water. I decided to go to to the Isle of Man; it just seemed to be where I needed to be or, more precisely, there was someone there I needed to be with. Dad died a few days later and the RAF were very good, giving me time off for the funeral, after which I returned to my squadron in Germany. The group had just deployed again to Saudi and I was going to follow them on a later flight.

The death of my dad somehow changed things, however. He could never have accepted that his only son was, in fact gay, but he was no longer here to make that choice.

I spent Christmas 1998 in the Isle of Man. I'd found a really special friend over there, and while he wasn't gay, that didn't change my feelings for him and after all, I was well and truly used to not having my affections reciprocated. So, on New Year's Eve 1998/99, in the back room of a local pub, I told my mate that I was gay. Oh, and not only that, I was also pretty much in love with him as well!

The response to my first admission was 'I kind of guessed', and to the second, 'I pretty much guessed that, too, but you know I'm not gay, don't you?' Of course I knew this, perhaps I was hoping he'd say differently, but he didn't and so we just hugged and got seriously shit faced together. The next day I was very hungover, but my mate managed to go to the pub and faced a lot of questions from our friends: 'Is Charlie really gay?' 'If he is, are you?' My friend faced them all and answered them honestly.

I was heading back to Germany the following day, but it seemed that my friends in the Isle of Man weren't at all phased by my coming out. Surprised yes, but phased, no.

Back in Germany, my confidence grew. I'd actually come out as gay to friends and been accepted. Surely if it was okay on that little rock in the Irish Sea, the world must be changing, so, against the advice of a good friend, I started to become braver with my new-found confidence.

'Be careful, Charlie. Not everyone thinks the sun shines out of your arse! You're telling too many people!'

One evening, in the rugby club bar on base, I confided in a younger mate from the squadron about my sexuality. I was sure he'd be another one who was fine with it, but no, he took a step back from me, looked me up and down and declared, 'Charlie, I'm pretty disappointed with you!' I was taken back a bit by shock; it wasn't at all what I'd expected. I told him I was still the same old Charlie, but he now just knew something else about me. He calmly told me he had loads of gay friends from school, but they all apparently had the most wonderful dress sense, so, he exclaimed, 'What the fuck went wrong with you, Charlie?' He then hugged me and told me he didn't care if I was gay or not, I was still his mate. A couple of other mates who were standing at the far end of the bar and out of earshot saw us hug and shouted over, 'What are you two homos up to over there?" Everyone laughed; the two of us more than the others.

Yet just a day or so later, one of the lads came to me very apologetic. He told me how he'd accidentally mentioned what I'd said to him in front of an SNCO on the opposite shift to me. Apparently, this person hadn't seemed to want to drop the subject and wanted to know more. I told the lad not to worry and certainly not to blame himself for anything that might come from this, after all, it was me who'd foolishly let slip a secret I knew could be used against me in the wrong hands.

So, here I was on that freezing cold February morning in 1999. I'd been summoned to see the warrant officer (WO), who was actually a brand new arrival to the squadron – I'd not even spoken to him yet.

I could only be being called in for one reason and when I entered the building where our squadron's engineering was coordinated from, I was met by my shift flight sergeant. He was a good guy, in his fifties, and in the final weeks of his long career in the RAF, but I could already sense I was probably going to be out in 'Civvy Street' before he was!

He didn't have a clue why both he or I were being called for by the new WO. He asked if I knew, but I played dumb and said that I didn't. We both entered the WO's office, he apologised for not having met me already, and then calmly explained the situation. He'd been called into work the previous evening by a SNCO from the nightshift because he'd heard from tradesman on the squadron say that I was a homosexual. Personally, he didn't know if there was something or nothing in this allegation, but he wanted to ask me 'face to face'.

'Sergeant, are you a homosexual?' Straight and to the point. This was it, the $64,000 question and me on the spot to answer it. I felt like a man standing on the hangman's gallows, the trapdoor waiting to be unlatched for the final drop. Should I lie? Sure, I could say I'd said something stupid when drunk or I'd that I'd been joking or misunderstood?

No, lying wasn't my style. I certified multi-million pound aeroplanes fit to fly, with people's lives often depending on my honesty and integrity, so I wasn't going to abandon my morals here, even though I was well aware of the almost inevitable outcome.

'Yes, Sir, it's true.'

Wow, that was easy!

'Shit!' was my WO's reply. 'I was really hoping you were going to answer differently.'

He told me he personally didn't have any problem with gay people, however, he still believed the RAF did and asked me if I was aware of that. He also said that as this had been brought to him officially, he couldn't 'sit' on the information or my admission.

I knew this was going to be one of the hardest days of my life (so far), but I had a strange feeling, almost like a huge weight being lifted from me at this moment in time, and it was an almost calming relief.

He asked my flight sergeant to take me to his office and get me a coffee, but the poor sergeant seemed incapable of speech. He was frozen in absolute shock at what I'd just admitted!

The WO then told me he was going to call the WO from the RAF Police and the warrant officer in the main Administrative Office for the base; a kind of 'old boy's' network. They were very knowledgeable and experienced people, but I was slightly unnerved at the mention of the RAF Police. I told him that as an SNCO with twenty years' service, I didn't expect to be treated to the indignation of having my room in the sergeant's mess searched by the 'Gestapo', or any of my friends being hauled in for interrogation under the guise of 'guilt by association'. My WO explained he would put my point forward (without obviously referring to the RAFP as the Gestapo, as I had), but he was clearly not going to have any control of what was going to happen as the snowball of my admission gained momentum.

My flight sergeant was still rooted to the spot in absolute shock.

'Charlie, go and make him a coffee and take him to his office', said my WO.

Poor guy. It seemed I'd really messed up his morning and when he finally regained the power of speech, he asked me, 'How the hell are we going to explain this to the rest of the squadron?' I told him that quite a few already knew and for those that didn't, I'd jump up on the pool table in the groundcrew crew room and announce it publicly to all gathered. He seemed in utter disbelief that I could do this, whereas I was in utter disbelief that on the brink of me losing my entire RAF career after twenty years' loyal service, he was more bothered about what the lads on the squadron would think.

I was informed by the WO that he'd spoken to the two other officers, and that the RAF Police had told him this was clearly an 'administrative' situation and nothing to do with their department. This was a surprising development and certainly not an unwelcome one. The Gestapo must've been snowed under with a major crime wave somewhere else on base, perhaps one of their own was taking drugs or had committed the cardinal sin of being found with a female in a barrack block? The WO in the base Administration Office asked for me to report to OC Personnel Management Squadron as soon as possible.

I reported directly, and the officer commanding asked me to repeat my admission of homosexuality to him. He informed me that although the world was changing around us in this final year of the 1990s, he was pretty sure that the Ministry of Defence, and therefore the RAF's policy for dealing with anyone caught, suspected or admitting to being a homosexual, was to have them administratively discharged from the service with no right of appeal. For some strange reason, he then asked if I was a practising homosexual? I was very tempted to answer with 'No, I'm actually pretty fucking good at it, Sir!' but decided to bite my tongue instead.

Afterwards, I walked from the Admin HQ back to the sergeant's mess. I'd been told that I could take off my uniform and that I was now officially on 'Gardening Leave'. Walking back to the mess was a strange experience; I was passing other RAF people going about their normal business, but I was a ghost.

I changed into jeans and t-shirt and headed back to the squadron. In the engineering HQ I bumped into my junior engineering officer (JEngO), who'd clearly been briefed on the situation and was less than happy. He didn't give a toss about my sexuality and was more bothered about losing one of his most experienced technicians. However, he did recognise that I was losing something much greater, my entire RAF career and the life that came with it, and he was very sympathetic, as was the squadron boss.

There was now just one thing to do: jump onto that crew room pool table and tell the guys on the squadron my news. So, I switched off the TV, hopped up on the green baize and called for everyone's attention.

'Right, guys, I've got something to tell you all. I'm leaving the squadron, leaving Germany and leaving the Royal Air Force!'

'Whose wife have you been caught shagging?' Came one reply.

'Close, but no cigar', was my answer, before telling everyone about my recent revelation.

'So, guys, this Friday, after flying's finished, we're having a piss up to end all piss ups.' It was going to be 'Charlie's Coming Out Party' and it was going to be epic!

Two of the guys asked me, 'Would it be okay if we turn up in drag?'

'Of course. I've lost my job, not my sense of humour!' I replied.

I was totally devastated by my imminent and forced separation from the service and the life I loved, but the only way I was going to do this was with my head held high and by looking people directly in the eye. I was being treated with respect, which was far different from what I'd known had happened to other people who'd lost their military careers for the same reason in previous years. The world was changing, it was just my sense of timing that was particularly shit. Little did I know at the time how close it was to the day when being gay in the UK military would no longer be a reason to lose your career!

I was to be offered no form of resettlement and no courses to help me adjust to civilian life. In fact, the base education officer seemed totally uninterested in my predicament. I had to hand in all my uniform, not just clothing, but all the combat gear, gas mask, webbing, tropical gear, desert gear, cold weather gear, etc. There was so much stuff that I needed a mate from the squadron to bring a Land Rover and help me take it all to clothing stores. The Dutch 'civvie' working behind the counter refused to accept the return of my kit. The hours for the 'issue and return' of gear were clearly posted on a notice outside and he wasn't budging on this, despite me trying to explain my situation. I took my stuff outside and unceremoniously dumped the whole lot into a waste skip, so the Dutch guy went hunting for his boss to report me. I don't know what was said, but I spotted the same guy an hour or so later, in the skip and fishing out all my kit. I couldn't resist the temptation to give him a friendly wave.

There was one final and very important thing to do before leaving the squadron for the final time. Charlie's Coming Out Party! The lads constructed my 'closet' in the middle of our squadron bar from an old wardrobe, probably from the same store that held furniture for the married accommodation on the base. It had a sign on the door saying 'Charlie's Closet' and I was to be inside waiting for my JEngO, who was to knock on the door when everyone was in the bar and ready. This thing was only being held together with matchsticks and cigarette papers, so as soon as I opened the door, the whole thing fell apart around me.

The next couple of hours are a bit of a blur. I do remember some of the bits of my leaving speech, such as getting a bit emotional at the nice things being said about me. I also made a bit of a speech, cracked a joke or two, and even the RAF station commander turned up to share a beer with me. It was an absolute irony that nobody seemed to be bothered about my sexuality, yet here I was losing everything I'd ever known and we were throwing a party to mark it.

I left Germany with just a small rucksack on my back, not all my worldly belongings, just what I could safely carry on my Ducati 748. All my other stuff was boxed up and being shipped back to my mum's house. I'd now received confirmation of a job at the Isle of Man Airport and a start date in a few weeks' time. I was only visiting home to explain to my mother why I was leaving the RAF, having not told her the real story over the telephone. She was convinced I'd binned my RAF career because of some fleeting whim for a woman in the Isle of Man, and it probably took me two hours to convince her that I'd actually been discharged against my will and that her only son was, in fact, gay. She never really got over the shock of this, but she did agree with me that my dad could never have accepted me being gay and that keeping it from him had been the correct thing to do.

I moved over to the Isle of Man to start a new life among the other 75,000 alcoholics clinging to that little rock in the Irish Sea. I've now been here twenty-five years and still love the place. I spent a further twenty years working in the aviation industry (passenger & cargo), I still ride a motorcycle, am still friends with the lads I went to school with, as well as most of the people I served in the RAF with and especially those from the Gulf War (Class of 91). I'm also still in contact with, and occasionally meet up with, a few 40-odd-year-old friends who are now retired rent boys living in Amsterdam!

My discharge from the RAF was justified under Queen's Regulation 607 (22) (D) (I) and I was to be the last person ever to be dismissed from the British military for being gay. It stated on my paperwork 'SERVICES NOT REQUIRED, BEING UNABLE TO MEET SERVICE OBLIGATIONS THROUGH CIRCUMSTANCES BEYOND HIS CONTROL.'

Discharges for homosexuality were actually halted on 27 September 1999, less than three months after my official discharge date of 30 June, and the abhorrent ban was finally lifted the following January.

Fighting With Pride has brought me into contact with other LGBT+ veterans, many of whom were treated like I was and some much worse. I can still remember the exact moment when I first spoke to someone who'd also been discharged after twenty years' service and listening to other veterans' stories and finding a common bond has been seriously therapeutic for me.

I've always been proud of my service and although they could kick me out of the Royal Air Force, they've never been able to kick the Royal Air Force out of me!

Per Ardua ad Astra.

Chapter 28

Finding Carol Morgan

—————————— Carol Morgan ——————————

When I was 17, I flew to Germany where my father was serving in the army. I'd decided I wanted to join, but it took me some time to persuade him to allow me to fly there.

While in Germany, I met a female officer, 2nd Lieutenant Marshall in the 48 Field Regiment Royal Engineers, and told her I wanted to join the WRAC. What I didn't know back then is that this meeting would change my life. She arranged for me to take my entrance test in Germany and to go to Bedfell for two weeks so I could discover what it was I wanted to do in the army. In those two weeks I had the time of my life and particularly remember taking PE lessons with Sergeant Gascoigne and socialising in the NAAFI with the rest of the girls. Boarding the plane back home at the end of the two weeks was a wrench and my stomach was filled with butterflies, excited about what my future looked like in the forces.

After spending the weekend with my aunt and uncle, they drove me to the train station early in the morning so I could get the train to Guildford and begin basic training.

I remember seeing other young WRAC members waiting to board the coach to the Queen Elizabeth Barracks. You could almost feel the nervousness and excited energy in the air.

We were put into different companies for six weeks, but for our accommodation we shared a room known as Foreman Room. We were responsible for making sure it was 100% clean AT ALL TIMES! We banded together and learned to depend on each other; helping each other with ironing, bulling our shoes, anything we could think of to make sure it didn't get trashed when it was inspected. We learned many new things; first aid, maths, English, map reading, etc., and had to pass tests on all of them. I was filled with a realisation that this was where I was meant to be. I was having the time of my life; friendships formed and lessons were learned and at the end of my training, I stayed at Guildford for a further six months to learn about chassis vehicles and becoming a driver.

It was also during this time I learned I'm gay.

I'd met a few other girls who were gay and formed a relationship with one who'd caught my eye. Later that year I was posted to Woolwich, the Royal Artillery training depot, which was a mixed-sex camp. The new recruits were referred to as 'fresh meat', but I'd already realised I was gay and wasn't interested in any of the men there.

When a new recruit was posted there named Sue Taylor, I instantly fell in love. Because it was illegal to be gay in the military, our relationship was a secret we guarded with our lives. We could only go out together in big groups of other people, and we'd stay at my sister's overnight. We'd go to mixed discos together and avoided gay venues completely. It was sometimes funny, but when you look back on it, they were worrying days for us and it was a really difficult time. We were living a double life and were trying to look 'straight' when we were out in the world, but it's difficult to imagine that anyone was ever fooled. We couldn't be ourselves and we couldn't show our love to the world. We lived in the closet and felt like we had a dirty secret, an unspeakable truth that made us something less than others. I very quickly learned, from seeing what happened to others, that if anyone had suspected us and reported us, the Special Investigations Branch would come down on you like a ton of bricks. I witnessed other girls being thrown out or sent away to other bases; little did I know, I'd soon be investigated by them myself.

I was due to be posted to Northern Ireland, and Sue was coming to visit me for the weekend before I went. She missed her train home and had nowhere to stay for the night, so I told her to stay in my block. Unbeknownst to me, a new girl in my block didn't like the fact she'd stayed over and reported us the next morning. I was hauled in front of the SIB, my bed and drawers were ransacked, and they took personal letters, photographs, and anything else they thought 'incriminated' me as being gay. They interrogated me about my sexuality for six hours straight and lied to me to say that Sue had confessed our relationship already. They even tried to force me to name other gay recruits. They asked me about my sex life and forced me to see a psychiatrist. This lasted for two days. I couldn't take it anymore and disclosed my sexuality to them. In that moment, it felt like I'd lost everything.

They discharged me instantly. I had no home, no job, and was marched off the camp completely humiliated and utterly destroyed. I didn't know how my parents would react; it was the '80s and attitudes to LGBT+ people weren't quite what they are now but, in that respect at least, I was lucky. My parents understood and accepted my sexuality. They supported me and Sue and helped us get a place to live together.

For the next two years we lived in a secret gay relationship, but living a secret life was too much to handle; our relationship broke down and she returned home. From that moment on I went back into the closet. I lived my life as a 'straight' woman because I couldn't face living my life as a gay woman. For the next thirty years I lived my life this way; not being fully open about who I am, and to this day I still feel the impact. I struggle to form relationships, I find it hard to trust people and after thirty years hiding who I am, it sometimes feels like I just forced all those feelings below the surface and pretended they didn't exist. It's so suppressed that I really struggle to open up to people.

I hid my sexuality from the world for decades, until, that is, I met another amazing woman: Mandie Aldridge. We had a connection and although it didn't last long, we've remained friends and I can honestly say had it not been for this incredible woman, I wouldn't be the person I am today. It was through Mandie I found Carol Morgan; a woman lost for too many years. She gave me courage, she showed me I'm not worthless, and most importantly, she gave me a purpose. I used to worry about what everyone thought about me and how others would see me. Not anymore. Somewhere along the way, the mix of worrying far too much about how I looked and being wracked by worries about whether people liked me meant I'd become a pale shadow of the woman I was meant to be. Today I realise I didn't need anyone's approval or permission to be happy and comfortable in my own skin.

My journey to a better life began with doing more of the things that made me happy and leaving all the opinions, comments and judgements behind. Life didn't change in an instant. It took me a while to build a thicker skin and stronger will, but once I reached a certain point, I started feeling something I hadn't in a very long time, maybe ever. I felt free.

Free to dress the way I wanted.
Free to act how I liked.
Free to say, think and become whoever I chose to be.

And I have to say, I can't believe I waited so long. Knowing I can walk into a room and not care what anyone thinks about me? That's a level of peace and freedom I can't say I'd ever experienced before. It's more than just happiness I felt, more than calm or peace. I feel empowered.

Empowered to start living life by my own rules.
Empowered to start loving whoever I wanted.
Starting with me.

I became more comfortable in my own skin and that's transformed and lifted me from the shadows into the sunlight. I'm not going to look over my shoulder and worry about what has been. I can't change where I've been and I wouldn't if I could. All the heartache, hardship and hard feelings have made me into the person I am today: strong, resilient, confident and happy. What can I say? I'm really starting to like this gal!

I've got a lot of living, loving and laughing still do in this life, and every chance I get, I'm going to grab it and run! There have been times in my life, when alone, that I've not been comfortable in my own company. Now, Carol's worth spending time with! Being happy hasn't come easily, but I smile and laugh today because despite this wretched ban and its impact upon me and so many other wonderful members of our Armed Forces, I can say that I love myself, my life and my people. This is what I hoped for all those decades ago when I got on the bus at Guildford. Life doesn't get any better than this.

One morning when I was getting ready for work, I heard on the radio about Fighting With Pride, a punchy little Armed Forces charity who'd successfully campaigned for an LGBT+ Veterans Independent Review about what'd happened to the thousands of members of our Armed Forces who'd been discharged for being gay or had lost their careers. I contacted them and, since being a part of their group for the last two years, have encountered people I served with, and built lifelong friendships with people just like myself who've struggled through life since being dismissed for being gay. We can talk to each other and understand each other in a way nobody else can.

I'm 62 years old, I'm a veteran and I live my life as an openly gay woman; something I could never have dreamed of before. I'm finally proud of who I am and look to the future full of hope.

Chapter 29

Standing Tall

—— Jacks Connor Fox MBE ——

Reflecting on my past, I've come to realise that perhaps I was destined to wear a uniform. Little did I know as I stepped off that it wouldn't just be one, but a multitude of them that I'd wear throughout my life's journey. Each uniform, a new chapter, a new role, a new adventure.

I was born in 1971, as Britain's pounds went decimal and we adopted decimal currency, and as Margaret Thatcher became the milk snatcher and violence erupted in Northern Ireland. I was the younger of two daughters, a bundle of energy and mischief, much to my parents' occasional exasperation. My mum and dad tied the knot in 1961 and had an interesting tale of their own. My mother, a native of Portsmouth, met my father while he was stationed there as a Royal Marine bandsman. On that very day, she'd contemplated joining the police, a dream she eventually decided not to pursue.

Growing up, my sister and I led a comfortable life. We were fortunate enough to experience life in Dubai in the late '70s, thanks to my father's job with an engineering firm. My mother often reminisces about this period, considering it the golden era of our family life. Back then, Dubai was a far cry from the bustling metropolis it is today. It was a modest city nestled in the Arabian Peninsula, its future as a global hub still a distant dream. This chapter of our lives, living in a city on the brink of transformation, remains a positive memory in our family's story.

In 1980, we made our way back home and the ensuing decade was dedicated to trying to get through school. Senior school, however, was a challenging phase for me. I always felt like a square peg in a round hole, never quite fitting in. From the tender age of 4 or 5, I sensed a difference in me, but I couldn't quite put my finger on it. I was the quintessential tomboy, shunning the typical girl toys and yearning instead for the rough and tumble of play with the boys. My faithful blue skateboard was my constant companion. My parents often urged me to be more 'ladylike', a concept that was alien to me. I simply shrugged it off and focused on navigating the labyrinth that was senior school. Academics was a constant struggle, and I was far from being a standout student. It wasn't until I was 38 that I was diagnosed with dyslexia, finally providing an explanation for my academic difficulties.

As I neared the end of my school years at 16, I found myself grappling with questions about my sexuality. The '80s were a time when the concept of homosexuality was shrouded in negativity, largely due to the AIDS crisis that was making headlines. The media, particularly the right-wing press, painted a grim picture, offering no positive lesbian role models, only a barrage of negative press. This was the era of Margaret Thatcher's Section 28, a law that cast a long shadow over my formative years. It was a challenging time for many, me included. The law fostered an environment where teachers felt powerless to intervene in cases of bullying or provide support for students who identified as gay.

Amidst this turmoil, I could no longer deny my attraction to women, but kept this revelation to myself, fearing judgment and the shame that society seemed all too ready to impose. It was a secret I carried, a part of my identity I was yet to fully understand and accept. A journey of self-discovery and coming to terms lay ahead. At the age of 16, I found myself drawn to the idea of joining the police. However, my father's words of caution led me down a different path. He suggested that policing wasn't a 'proper' career and encouraged me to attend secretarial college. Thankfully, I spent less than a year at college before a relative persuaded me to join them in the Civil Service. This marked the first time I found myself bending the truth on a security clearance form, denying any 'questionable' behaviour and getting on with my first job. I think my hidden sexuality must've shone out of me, however, as everywhere I worked there were rumours and whisperings about me.

Two years later, an advertisement in the local paper caught my eye. It was a call to join the Royal Navy Reserve, a part-time commitment. The idea of joining the Armed Forces had always intrigued me, but again my father had dissuaded me, although this time he agreed that joining as a reservist was a good compromise. Back then, I was acutely aware that being gay in the services wasn't permitted, however, I believed I'd successfully concealed my sexuality. I was so deeply closeted I thought I could hide it indefinitely. Looking back, I realise I was quite naive, not fully understanding the potential consequences of my situation. So, in 1990, aged 18, a new chapter of my life began. With a mixture of excitement and trepidation, I signed on the dotted line, marking my initiation into the world of uniformed service. My new home became HMS Sussex in Brighton, a part of the MCM10 Minesweeping fleet. Every Monday evening, I found myself immersed in new entry class learning about the rich history and intricate operations of the Royal Navy. As a woman, I was a part of the Women's Royal Naval Service, as integration was still a concept of the future.

My initiation into the Royal Navy was marked by a two-week basic training course at HMS Raleigh. Looking back, I remember the whispers and rumours that circulated about me. Standing at 6 feet, clad in an ill-fitting tunic and skirt, with shoes that were a size too small, I was hard to miss. The rumours of me being a 'lezza' started, perhaps because of my larger build which came to the rescue during survival training, pulling my smaller female classmates into the lifeboats. My parents came to see me pass out at HMS Raleigh, even though earlier in the same year, my father had been diagnosed with Motor Neurone Disease. His health deteriorated rapidly, and by April 1991, he was no longer with us. It was only years later that my mother revealed to me that he'd questioned her about my sexuality before his passing, but she'd denied it.

In the aftermath of his death, I attempted to open up to my mother about my feelings and my attraction to women, but she shut down the conversation, insisting it was not a topic for discussion. By then, I'd started reading books by queer authors and exploring queer narratives. I even had a Pink Triangle pin badge pinned on the inside of my favourite jacket at the time. My mother's discomfort with the subject forced me to hide such books whenever family or her friends visited. She suggested I see a doctor about my 'feelings', but I never did. I remember feeling profoundly unhappy during this time: the fear of rejection from my mother was overwhelming, and I chose to shut down instead. This marked the beginning of my struggles with mental health.

The following years were filled with training to become a communicator, short sea voyages over the weekends, and a constant internal debate about whether the Royal Navy was the right fit for me, especially given my struggle with severe sea sickness. But I loved every minute of it as it felt like an escape from home and every bad thought that went with it.

In 1994, HMS Sussex was decommissioned, coinciding perfectly with my decision to leave home and move to London. I joined the Foreign and Commonwealth Office (FCO) through an internal transfer within the Civil Service. Spring 1994 saw me joining HMS President in London, a new unit with new faces, and a new city to explore. Moving to London also presented an opportunity to try to hide my sexuality even better at work and in the military, but to explore it more outside of this. Before moving to London, my interactions with women had been limited to a few 'dalliances' and pen pals, as the internet was not yet a part of our lives. Joining the FCO required a higher level of security clearance, and when faced with the dreaded question about my sexuality, I hesitated. By then, I knew I was a lesbian, but the fear of admitting it to myself and others was overwhelming. So, I chose to remain in the closet, doing my utmost to hide my true self. Deep down, however, I knew that my true self was shining through, no matter how hard I tried to hide it. My time at HMS President was a period of my life I truly cherished. I formed friendships that have stood the test of time and remain strong to this day. The opportunity to travel was an incredible experience, and I had the privilege of serving in diverse locations such as Norway, the USA, and the South China Sea region during the historic Hong Kong handover in 1997.

Living away from home for the first time, I was finally experiencing freedom. Yet, beneath the surface of these exciting experiences, there was a deep-seated unhappiness. I was still grappling with my identity, trying to hide and deny my sexuality. Despite the outward appearance, I was engaged in a silent battle with myself.

In 1998, a significant shift occurred in my life. I was promoted within the FCO, which required me to apply for a high level of security clearance. This process involved an in-depth review of my life, including my relationships and moral compass. My managers and friends were interviewed as part of this process, and by this time, my closest friend in the Royal Naval Reserve (RNR) knew about my sexuality. She'd asked me directly and I'd confirmed it. Her support was unwavering, but she warned me that people were starting to talk. The potential consequences of being discharged from the Royal Navy were becoming increasingly real to me. At 27, I was taking these risks very seriously, and the fear was palpable. The worst-case scenarios were daunting: being found out, losing my Civil Service job or even facing imprisonment for being gay from the military.

As the date for my security clearance interview approached, the fear became too overwhelming. I couldn't lie in my security interview as I risked losing my job and knew that the security team would speak with my unit as part of the process. I was terrified of the potential repercussions of remaining in the RNR and being found out. So, one night in May 1998, I made a difficult decision. I went to HMS President, handed in my ID card, all my kit, and resigned. My divisional officer asked me why I was leaving and tried to persuade me to stay, but I likely gave some vague excuse and left that night. The memory of crying uncontrollably on the tube ride home still lingers in my mind. It was a moment of profound sadness and fear that I don't think I've felt since.

The security team at the FCO advocated for transparency among LGBT staff regarding their sexuality, emphasising it as a precautionary measure. At the time, I took this advice at face value, without skepticism. The following day, I approached the security team and shared a vague narrative, expressing uncertainty about my sexuality, while omitting the reasons why I'd recently resigned from the RNR.

After undergoing a candid security clearance interview, I was relieved to receive clearance, allowing me to proceed with my career in the Civil Service. However, I couldn't shake off a sense of indignation. Until 1991, the Diplomatic Service had a policy that excluded gay men and lesbians from representing Britain abroad, fearing that societal attitudes towards same-sex relationships heightened the risk of blackmail. This policy, a relic of the era following the Sexual Offences Act of 1967, reflected the pervasive anxiety among diplomats that gay individuals might be coerced into secrecy to avoid exposure.

Within the FCO, I was aware of other gay and lesbian colleagues, yet my own reticence had barred the way to forming deep connections. It wasn't until I began to openly acknowledge my lesbian identity that I discovered a sense of community. A fortuitous introduction by a member of the diversity and inclusion team led me to a supportive colleague, Jonathan, an advocate for starting an LGBT network. His recollection of our first encounter always brings a smile to my face, as he remembers me asking, 'I hear you're a friend of Dorothy?'

He shared his vision for establishing an LGBT network, expressing his discontent with the historical ban that lasted until 1991. Despite the formal allowance for LGBT individuals to serve within the FCO, lingering prejudice and outdated attitudes meant many still lived in apprehension. The conversation I had with Jonathan that day ignited a passion for activism within me, a flame that burns just as brightly now as it did then. In the unassuming setting of a timeworn corridor in Whitehall, back in June 1998, we laid the foundation for the FCO's inaugural LGBT network group, FLAGG.

Through people Jonathan and I knew and the grapevine, word spread about the setting up of a group. We got together in the downstairs room of some bar in Soho and the committee of five came together and the name FLAGG (Foreign Office Lesbian and Gay Group) was chosen.

Looking back, it's hard to believe the FCO wasn't always the champion of LGBT+ rights it's known as today. Despite public claims by some ex-colleagues, the environment was far from progressive. When the FCO approved the creation of an LGBT+ staff group, some of those tasked with distributing diplomatic telegrams attempted to prevent the announcement of the group's formation. The founders of FLAGG faced opposition, sustained harassment from colleagues, and even direct confrontations.

Yet, in the face of such adversity and the FCO's institutionalised homophobia – evident in the lack of recognition for same-sex partners, the marking of LGBT+ officers' security files, and the exclusion of same-sex partners from already established family networks – a foundation was laid for future progress.

Over the span of a dozen years, FLAGG emerged as a pivotal force within the FCO, driving a transformative shift in both perception and policy. This group championed the cause of LGBT+ staff, advocating for their safety and equality, particularly for those stationed in nations where homosexuality remained criminalised. Their efforts extended beyond the confines of the office, reaching out to embassies and consulates worldwide, providing support and fostering a global dialogue on LGBT+ rights. FLAGG's activism played a crucial role in enlightening senior officials and government ministers, contributing to a broader change in the diplomatic landscape. Their persistent engagement was instrumental in revising personnel security policies and enhancing the inclusivity of LGBT+ staff serving abroad.

The impact of FLAGG's dedication was recognised on many fronts: the FCO was honoured as a top twenty employer by Stonewall, a testament to its commitment to LGBT+ inclusivity, for five consecutive years. In a crowning achievement, FLAGG was bestowed with the 'Star Network' accolade in 2010, a symbol of the group's exceptional contribution to the cause of equality and diversity within the diplomatic service. This recognition served as a beacon of progress, illuminating the path toward a more inclusive future for all.

In 2009, an unexpected letter arrived from the FCO, its contents elegantly presented on exquisite stationery. It conveyed the astonishing news that I was to be honoured with an MBE in the Queen's Birthday Honour's List. The revelation was so overwhelming I had to sit down, my hands trembling as I processed the magnitude of the recognition. This journey was never about accolades; it was driven by a desire to create a better, more accepting world – a stark contrast to the years I spent grappling with shame for simply being myself.

The ceremony at Buckingham Palace that December, presided over by Prince Charles, then the Prince of Wales, marked the pinnacle of my life's achievements. My family, including my mum, travelled with me to the palace and amidst the opulence and the gathering of extraordinary individuals, I was consumed by nervous excitement and a sense of unworthiness. Yet, as Prince Charles bestowed the award upon me, affirming, 'I think you're marvellous', any doubts were eclipsed by a profound sense of pride. That moment, etched in memory, will be cherished for a lifetime.

In 2009, I finally realised my dream of joining the police in the role of a special constable with Sussex Police. Over the course of eleven years, I supported the local community alongside the neighbourhood policing team, a role I really loved. My career path took a new direction in 2011 when I bid farewell to the FCO and ventured into the realms of the NHS and private sector, eventually joining the private sector in 2016. Throughout these transitions, I remained actively involved in various network groups, continuing to advocate for LGBT+, women, and gender issues, and served as a volunteer representative for the British Association of Women in Policing.

As the Covid epidemic loomed, I relocated to the southwest of England and once again aligned with the NHS supporting a local vaccination centre. Departing from my volunteer role with Sussex Police was a difficult decision; I'd ascended to the position of chief officer, guiding 150 volunteer officers through a rigorous change programme. The absence of volunteering left a void, but a friend from my Sussex Police days presented a new avenue for service, volunteering with the RAF Air Cadets.

After concluding my tenure with the NHS, I returned to the Civil Service and embarked on a new journey in my volunteer experience by submitting an online expression of interest to my local Air Cadet Squadron and was subsequently appointed as a civilian instructor in December 2021. I pursued an officer's commission in 2022, a decision that led me through an exceptionally challenging interview process comprising four distinct stages.

In the midst of my commission recruitment, I reached out to the Royal Navy to obtain a copy of my service records. Anticipating a straightforward process, I was met with unexpected delays that extended over two years. A year into my inquiry, I received correspondence from the Royal Navy confirming only my military number and service dates, with no further details. This revelation left me perplexed and concerned, prompting me to wonder if others who'd served alongside me had encountered similar issues.

My quest for answers led me to discover Fighting With Pride, where I learned about others in the forces whose records had been inexplicably destroyed. Finally, in March 2024, two years after my initial request, the Royal Navy issued a letter confirming my service and extending an apology for the loss of my records. The reasons behind their destruction remain a mystery, and I can only speculate whether the LGBT ban might have been a factor before my resignation.

The timing of the Royal Navy's apology was serendipitous, coinciding with the week I officially passed the officer's board for my RAF Air Cadets commission and was confirmed in the rank of pilot officer. Volunteering with the air cadets has been a passion of mine, enriching my understanding of military history, a subject I've always held dear, and allowing me to engage with the cadets. Their curriculum has introduced me to the realm of cyber and space, and I've had the privilege of accompanying them on flights, gliding sessions, and visits to various establishments that would otherwise have been beyond my reach.

My life's voyage has been one of profound self-discovery and wanderlust, blessed with the fortune to traverse the globe extensively. For forty-eight long years, I grappled with a sense of alienation, battling the twin shadows of depression and anxiety. Then, destiny introduced me to Samantha, the beacon of my life, who awakened my true essence. With her unwavering support, I embraced my authentic self and found joy in the person I've become. Today, I stand stronger and more fulfilled, with Samantha by my side, my heart's true companion.

The quest for equality marches on, and I harbour a deep-seated fear that our opportunities to live authentically are gradually being erased. We must stand firm against regressing to the oppressive era of Section 28 and its ilk. My dedication to Fighting With Pride remains unwavering, as I champion the incredible strides it makes in supporting proud veterans like me. Many have endured harrowing trials during their service, and their courage and resilience must always be remembered and honoured. Indeed, the battle for equality persists.

Chapter 30

Anchored in Silence

— Christopher Voce —

It was a warm Sunday afternoon in August 1981, as the echoes of a vicious football match ended, we, a motley crew of military personnel, gathered in a musty hut to watch a documentary about sexually transmitted diseases. As I was about to enter, a tall, stern RAF sergeant pulled me to one side and whispered, 'People like you should not be in here'.

There were twelve individuals with various charges, from absent without leave (AWOL) to violent criminals, that I shared this lifeless Nissen hut with, its glossy tiled floor good enough to see your face in. There was a lone, black metal fire stove sat in the middle of the room, rows of rusted metal bars on every window; there was no privacy even in the toilet. Outside, soldierly officers patrolled the secure gravel grounds day and night, now and then peering through the thin, clear glass.

Wherever we went, always at mealtimes, we double marched in rows of two throughout D wing, the glasshouse/Colchester's Military Corrective Training Centre (MCTC). Some would say this is not a prison, but for me, it was a prison in 1981.

The sergeant's shrill command sliced through the morning's silence. 'Pick up the pace! Those leaves aren't going to collect themselves!' he barked into the mist.

Hunched over, I felt the ground's chill seep into my bones. My bare hands replaced the broom that should've been there, and the sergeant's orders reverberated in my ears.

With their drab grey concrete, the Nissen huts framed the only colour we knew; the vibrant flowers we nurtured, defiant splashes against a dreary canvas.

Inside the cookhouse, the rich aroma of stewing meat hung heavy. I dished out the rations, my voice firm but fair, 'Just one spoonful of peas,' as the queue of hollow-eyed inmates shuffled past.

Then he appeared, towering and ominous. His eyes were slits of malice. 'We get out on the same day, and you're dead. But not before I rape you, then cut your throat,' he whispered, venom dripping from every syllable.

I met his stare, feeling my heart race. 'We'll see,' I said.

The glasshouse had gained a reputation for its brutality and there I became a target of relentless torment from a towering Scottish army lad. His whispered threats were loaded with rape, murder, and how he would cut my throat. Trapped in the confinement of the glasshouse, I was stripped of my humanity and a target for their cruelty.

As my days dwindled within the glasshouse, I had a chilling encounter with an Irish Army officer.

The door's hinges groaned as it swung open, revealing the Chief Petty Officer from HMS *Nelson*, his gaze as icy as the ocean depths. 'Voce, the Commander wants to see you,' he stated, his tone devoid of warmth.

I trailed behind him, each footfall a drumbeat of dread. The Commander's office loomed ahead, his formidable presence barely contained by the confines of his seat. His piercing eyes sought to unravel me, demanding answers I refused to give.

'Do you remember the duty officer from HMS *Excellent*?' he demanded. 'Is he ... one of your kind?'

My response was the silence of the tomb.

'We have it on good authority he's a homosexual? Speak!'

Yet my lips sealed the secrets tight, and my will was an unyielding citadel.

The Chief stepped forward. 'Sir, Voce's service concludes shortly. He's under no obligation to respond.'

A sneer twisted the Commander's mouth. 'Understand this, your kind are a disease. And do you know what we do with diseases?' he snarled.

'No, Sir,' I answered.

'We cut them out,' he declared with a growl. 'And should you ever speak to the media, we'll bring you back to Winchester prison. Now, get out of my sight!'

Dismissed, I felt the weight of his threat like the shadow of the executioner's blade.

The day of release, morning, arrived with the sun taunting us in its fierce glare. Chris Ellis, a mate from HMS *Bullwark* and two slim shadows on the truck exchanged a vacant snicker.

At Colchester station, the group dispersed, each to their sought-after delights, while I found solace in the train's last carriage, a haven I came to share with two nuns and an elderly gentleman. Their smiles were kind as I settled by the window.

The door slammed open with violent force in the hush of our shared space. Chris staggered inside, his face marred by agony, his blood a crimson mask of conflict.

A shriek tore through the silence, its source lost in the erupting chaos. 'They're coming for you,' Chris gasped, his words a chilling omen.

I clutched my bag tight, my past life bundled within.

'Come with me,' I implored.

But he shook his head; a sailor succumbed to his fate. 'My things … I can't leave them.'

Heavy-hearted, I fled alone, the spectre of vengeance nipping at my heels.

12 September 1981, a Saturday, was the day I leapt from a train as it slowed past an empty train station. As it picked up speed, I saw the angry Army lads, their heads and clenched fists hanging out the windows, mouthing obscenities; the same lads who wanted to rape and murder me.

Hot tears rolled from the corners of my eyes and down my cheeks. I had escaped my oppressors.

I sat for hours on the empty platform, plucking up the courage to get home; I never saw those men again.

I found my human spirit strong in adversity. Those eight words from the RAF sergeant, 'People like you should not be in here' resonate with me today; no place should be rife with hate and prejudice.

Though the Navy may have disowned me in 1981, I proudly wear the badge of service. In telling my story the hope of a brighter future lies where love knows no bounds and bigotry is just a distant memory.